The strategic impoı

the Political land

MW00877988

Waiss Djaffar Guedi

Published on 24 January 2017

Content

Preface

This book is covering many issues about the ongoing political situation of the Horn of Africa, the Geostrategic importance of Djibouti and finally the Ethiopian government agression to the region and how it's undermining the U.S. strategic interest in the region as well as other World powers that are currently stationed in Djibouti.

Introduction

The East of Africa was placed as one of the most conflicted regions of the entire world. The countries within the region have all been affected by the internal crisis, political uncertainty and border conflicts. 150 years ago, the Horn of Africa was politically affected by a series of political events including; the settlement of the European colonial powers to seek dominance in the Red Sea as the region maintains a strategic geopolitical importance, the Egyptian domination of the Nile river water, and the impacts of the Cold War in which the main countries in the region to switch sides at an important juncture, like the most recent U.S. government's 'War on Terror'.

The East of Africa was initially a major regional commercial trade hub. For centuries, the region had served as a trade route between the Arabs and the rest of Africa. The river Nile rose in the region and travelled to Egypt, connected all the states in a mortal association for survival. The eastern coast of the region hosts the Red Sea, the Gulf of Aden and the Indian Ocean. The people of the region at that time were engaged in trade for centuries and as a result linked themselves to the Gulf countries and beyond.

The truth about this region is that the region maintains a strategic geopolitical location which has attracted world powers, currently some of the world's great powers e.g. U.S. Japan, Spain, China France have established military and Naval bases in the tiny nation of the Horn of Africa, Djibouti. In recent years, the region has significantly suffered from the increasing terrorism as a result of the presence of world powers. The conflict in Yemen has had a major negative impact on the security trade through the Red Sea, making the trade between the East and West less secure than ever before. Another problem that the region is facing is the contradictory interpretation of Islam that some scholars are conducting which has disturbed the cohabitation among the different ethnic communities throughout East Africa.

Geographically, the Horn is a fragile neighbourhood to Europe and has caused major problems to Europe such as increasing migrant going from the Horn to Europe, and the fact that many of these migrants from the Horn are exploiting terrorism to Europe. Also, the Horn situates next to the Arab World, which often themselves face greater conflict and political instability. The Western powers including China have settled the region to counter terrorism and maintain its influence in the Red Sea and the Indian Ocean and to sustain a momentum towards stability and coherence.

There are two main challenges that lie in front of the region. The first is the concerns over regional integration. For long this region was relatively inhabited by marginalised communities that straddle borders and later became envoy in the politics among the states in the region. Secondly, the region has been a centre park for foreign players, particularly former colonial powers and few other players from the Gulf states. The increasing destabilisations, foreign military interventions and the fact Westerns are turning blind eye to dictatorship and horrific human rights condition by regional dictators have instigated even further the political instability and conflict that the region is currently experiencing. This is the challenges that are blocking the Horn to shift towards political and economic integration and forming a regional economic market to achieve strong, powerful economic region.

Ethiopia is currently the regional economic and political power, despite the internal crisis. The country has managed to increase its political influence often by military force, especially with Eritrea and Somalia. In 2006, Ethiopia invaded Somalia, as part of their mission to counter the Islamic Courts Union and to assist the Transitional Federal Government of Somalia to relocate itself from Kenya to Mogadishu. Ethiopia was the only country in Africa that was briefly colonised by one of the Europeans (Italy) from 1936 to 1941.

In June 1977, Ethiopia and neighbouring Somalia engaged in a territorial war after the Ethiopian armed forces along with several Somali ethnic militia groups invaded Somalia and conquered several cities within the country. The war was impetus for U.S. military assistance in Somalia, which later halted the conflict. As the relationship with the two neighbouring states was worsening time after time, both regimes were on the path towards destructions as opposition groups from both states shifted towards insurgency. By early 1991, both regimes were toppled by armed opposition groups. Ethiopia was immediately taken over by EPRDF (Ethiopia People's Revolutionary Democratic Front) and built a democratic federal system that drove the country towards regional economic power and made Ethiopia a country that works not just for a privilege few but for everyone.

While Somalia was immediately taken over by opportunistic tribal militia, and plunged the country into further chaos. There was major violence across the country, ordinary people were subjected to human rights abuses, thousands were forced to flee, while other hundreds of thousands of Somalis were displaced from their houses. Today after almost twenty-six years of longstanding conflict, the country is still in the recovering process and taking the path towards good governance.

The United States strategic interests in the Horn increased significantly following the 9/11 attack and more importantly after the rise of ICU in Somalia to prevent Somalia from becoming a safe haven for al-Qaeda and other international jihadist movements. In maintaining its strategic counterterrorism strategy, the United States has decided to ally itself with Ethiopia as they both maintained common interest towards Somalia, which was to destabilise the country even further and plunge it into more chaos by funding rebel militias and disintegrating the state and society of Somali, so Ethiopia could realise its dream of dominating politically the region.

The successive Ethiopia regimes had long feared the Somali irredentist claims on the eastern region of Ethiopia (Ogaden), or if a powerful Islamist movement creates major unrest among the large Muslim population in the country. The regime feels besieged by strong indigenous separatist group (ONLF) in its Somali Ogaden region and its unprecedented border dispute with neighbouring Eritrea.

However, the Ethiopian regime's outrageous behaviour in recent years, both in Ethiopian and its neighbouring countries have posed major difficulties for the US and its strategic interest in the region. The United States has to force its ally (Ethiopia) to change its aggressive approach to political oppositions, and counterterrorism or the US will have no other option but to end its relationship with Ethiopia.

Since the collapse of Mengistu Hailemariam, the country has struggled with internal political reforms. Ethiopia's economy has grown and emerged significantly, but efforts to institutionalise a framework a system of multiparty democracy have staggered. In 2005, Ethiopia held a so-called free and fair elections. During the election campaign, there was the major opening of political space. Opposition parties were able to hold meetings and rallies, the media was able to publish political analysis, and the local and international observers were allowed to monitor and observe the election.

But the regime's provisional efforts to increment political space was not remunerated. After the results announcement, various political parties have contested the results. The government responded with brutally; arresting thousands of peaceful demonstrators and opposition leaders, and later declared a state of emergency. Ethiopia was plunged into a period violence and turmoil, during which the regime had arrested all forms of dissidents, including civil society and journalists. Several among these state of emergency measures has been institutionalised and as a result criminalised all the civil society and organisation who received foreign charitable funds, and introduced severe punishments on so-called terrorist acts, including public demonstrations

Impact on U.S. Policy Objectives

For the U.S., cooperating with such autocratic regime presents major difficulties to the United States policy goals. First, the Ethiopian regime's effort to decrease political competition in the 2010 elections have instigated ethnic tensions in Ethiopia. Many Ethiopians feel strongly that the ruling party (EPRDF) is largely dominated by a single minority ethnic group, the Tigre and its grip on power may be an assault on the majority ethnic Oromo and Amhara populations. Since 2005, the public dissatisfaction with the regime is in a record high, and the recent Oromo and Amharic uprising against the EPRDF signals that regime's days in power is counted.

Also, Ethiopia's war with neighbouring Somalia and Eritrea, and with the most powerful separatist group ONLF, have a jihadist impact. Therefore, while the Ethiopia-U.S. affiliation has had short-term advantages, it's on the brink of undermining the United States counterterrorism objectives.

The U.S. reliance on Ethiopian armed and intelligence force on the Somali soil has widely instigated the instability in Somalia and plunged the country into further chaos. The 2006 Ethiopian invasion of Somalia and the occupation of the Ethiopian troops in Mogadishu has led to the rise of the Islamic Courts Union. The international jihadist groups have motivated the local Somali insurgency, and on U.S. support of the Ethiopian invasion, as a chance to globalise Somalia's conflict.

The strategic importance of Djibouti

Djibouti is a tiny country located in the Horn of Africa with a total area of 23,200 km2. The country is bordered by Gulf of Aden southern entrance to the Red Sea, south-east to Somalia, Ethiopia to the west and Eritrea to the north. Djibouti is a country that is globally considered to be one of the most strategic locations on the planet and for this reason; the country has attracted foreign powers, and investors to invest in the country's economic and energy infrastructure.

The country has largely benefited from its strategic location on the Red Sea, making the service sector the most predominant economic asset, but with little development agricultural and industrial sector.

In 1843, Djibouti was acquired by France as a result of French interest in the area. Between 1883-1887, France has officially signed numerous agreements with the ruling Issa and Afar Sultans at the time, which allowed it to expand the protectorate to include the Gulf of Tadjoura. Leonce Lagarde was appointed by the French colonial as the protectorate's governor. Lagarde founded the port city of Djibouti in 1888 and moved the whole administration from the city of Obock. He then expanded the French territory outwards around the Gulf of Tadjourah. In doing so, he created the protectorate known as the French Somali coast and later changed to the French territory of the Afars and the Issas till independence in 1977.

During 1958, two years before the neighbouring Somali independence in 1960, a referendum was held in the French Somaliland to decide for independence or to stay with France. The referendum outcome forecasted that indeed all voters were in favour of a continued association with colonial power (France). However many seen this referendum as controversial and massive fraud as France had taken harsh measures against thousands of Somalis before the referendum reached the polls. The vast majority of Somalis ethnic, who voted no in the referendum, was largely in favour of joining the Republic of Somalia. Mahamoud Harbi, who was in favour of enjoying Somalia, was the vice president of the government council. Harbi was later killed by the French administration under mysterious circumstance.

In 1960, Ali Ref Bourhan, a French puppet politician, assumed the post of vice president of the government council of French Somaliland and held the position until 1976, just one year before Djibouti's independent. Also that same year, the government in France rejected the UN recommendation to grant French Somaliland independence. In August the French president at the time, General Charles de Gaulle made his first official visit to the territory and was welcomed with huge demonstrations and rioting. Therefore in response to the mass protest, General de Gaulle promised another referendum.

In March 1967, a second referendum was held with an outcome of 60% of the voters opted to retain the association with France, but Issa ethnic again argued that the electoral lists had been unfairly restricted in a way that favoured the Afars. After the election outcome, the French Somaliland was officially converted to as the 'territory of the Afars and the Issas.

The territory's independence movement was largely motivated by the Issa ethnic, but their movement was opposed by neighbouring Ethiopia and the Afars, who extremely feared Issa domination of power structure. Finally, in 1975, France was increasingly pressured to grant the territory independence. The territory's citizenship law, which had been favoured the Afar minority, was revised by the French administration to concede more Issas. In a referendum in May 1977, the Issa majority had massively voted for independence, which was officially established on 27 June 1977, as the country officially became the Republic of Djibouti.

Three days before the official date of the independence (27 June 1977) the chamber of deputies has elected Hassan Gouled, the territory's premier as the nation's new head of state. Gouled, from the Issa clan, has immediately appointed an afar as the country's first Prime Minister and a cabinet consisted of the two largest ethnic Issa and Afar, making Issa the dominance which later led to a political dispute, including cabinet crisis. Gouled was re-elected as the head of state without the opposition by universal suffrage in June 1981 and April 1987. After the independence Hassan Gouled, has put in place one-party rule political system similar to the one in china and the soviet socialist republic, without opposition. The national assembly at the time consisted of 26 Issas, 23 Afars and 16 Arabs. The newcomers won only 12 seats in the April 1987 election of a one-party list.

Hassan Gouled was born in a small village called Garissa in the Lughaya district of northern Somalia. He hails from the most political powerful Mamasan subclan of Issa. Gouled has taken a predominant role in Djibouti independence from France. During the period of colonial in Djibouti, Gouled has launched a powerful campaign against the late hero of Djibouti Mahamoud Harbi Farah, who sought to join the neighbouring Republic of Somali.

Hassan Gouled during the period of the pre-independence has served in several positions. He first served as Vice-President of the Government Council from 1958 to April 1959, he then moved to France and served in the French national assembly from 1959-1962 and the French Senate 1952-1958. He was then appointed as Minister of Education in Ali Aref Bourhan's government. Later he served as Prime Minster between May to July 1977.

In 1981, the government of Djibouti led by Hassan Gouled had established authoritarian system making the country as one single party state. The Peoples Rally Progress (RPP), which had been replaced LPAI in 1979, was declared as the only legal, political party in the country for a long period of time, as a result of this president Gouled won the presidential election in 1982 with 84% of the vote and 89% in 1987 comfortably.

A decade later under the reign of Gouled and a strong stability of the Republic of Djibouti, a civil broke out in 1991, following a political discrimination on Afar ethnic and the rejection of genuine democratic power-sharing. The Afar political elites formed Front for the Restoration of Unity and Democracy (FRUD) in November in 1991, with the intention of ensuring the right of Afar ethnic and a genuine of power sharing. Few weeks after the establishment of the rebel group (FRUD), they have launched their first offensive armed rebellion in the northern part of the Republic of Djibouti due to the political alienation and the massive inequality that politically mobilised Afars felt they were experiencing constant political repression from the government dominated by Issa.

During the Djiboutian civil war from 1991 to 1994, the war had a devastating effect on Djibouti economy and foreign investment. Since then, the country has enjoyed a political stability. In recent years, Djibouti has widely experienced major improvement in macroeconomic stability, with its annual

GDP improving at an average rate of over 3% since 2003. This came after a long decade of low growth. This ascribed to fiscal adjustment measures to improve public finance, as well as reforms in port management.

Djibouti, the tiny state in the Horn of Africa has small geographic size and population, with an economy that relies on port services for goods in transit to and from Ethiopia. Since the border dispute and the subsequent war between the two nations (Ethiopia and Eritrea) that took place from1998 to 2000, Ethiopia was prohibited to use the Eritrean routes, therefore came towards Djibouti and used the port facility.

Djibouti's economic structure hasn't changed much since the country's independent from former colonial France in 1977. The economy is mostly based on services, but little on the primary and secondary sector and the service sector accounted for over 75% of the gross domestic product.

In 1998, the importance of the service sector was linked to the country's strategic location and the free trade in the northeast of Africa. The primary parts of the sector are the port and railway service, the civil service and the French military base stationed in Djibouti. The public administration is the largest sector in the economy. The country has no significance mineral resources, and farming is constrained by the poor quality of the land. Uncertainty over the size of the population makes an estimate for per capita gross national product rather dependant, but when using conversion the figure is estimated US$750. The UN gave a figure using purchasing power parity conversion of $1,300 in per capita GDP in 2000. Both of these estimates puts Djibouti in the low-income category of countries.

After a moderate economic growth during the country's first ten years of independence, but reduced foreign assistance and poor planning led to GDP growth that averaged only 1% per year from 1989 to 1991. Growth became negative following the eruption of the civil war of 1991-1994, which encourage the minority Afar community to take the arms following political discrimination by the Issa dominance government. Informal sector activities, which evade both tax and customs, flourished in the mid-1990s, resulting in the apparent 5.5% per year decrease in the GDP from 1991 to 1994 as reported by the UN development program.

From 1992, the port has recorded a fall in the number of imports for domestic use, leading to the closure of any many outlets. The reduced number of the French military since 1999 have also reduced the country's economic growth. However, the increased provision of services for the transit trade with Ethiopia due to its border conflict is expected to provide compensation.

During the years of 1980's, the government has attempted to improve the state of the infrastructure and decrease structural issues within the economy to generate wealth and employment, but the end result resulted in little impact on the economic growth. The government has launched a program for the decentralisation of the economy, the development of the free trade zones and agricultural, but these major program's depended financially on foreign aid, which came to an end in 1991 following the outbreak of the civil war. In 1992, an economic crisis led to the suspension of government investment which halted the development programmes on infrastructure and most importantly the electric power.

Djibouti for many years enjoyed political stability since independence under President Hassan Gouled and his successor Ismael Omar (IOG). Nonetheless, the government policies since 1991 had a series of short-term responses to both external contributor pressure (mainly France) and internal demands. The government had total control in all the main economic sectors, such as port facilities, railway, and utilities. However, there are currently plans for privatisation of these enterprises.

During the period from 1991 to 1994, the civil war has disturbed an already limited tax base, and budget controls disappeared as income declined. The government caused major deficits and built up debts in salary arrears with private lenders, although irregular accounting hid the extent.

In 1996, the government proposed budget cuts resulted in a general strike and huge civil unrest which later led to a policy reversal. The foreign contributors drafted a more comprehensive financial package to solve to facilitate the economic issues. This culminated in an IMF US$6.2 million assistant credit, which began in April 1996. A creditor conference in 1997 ensured limited funds for reforms, in particular for the reduction of the army after the civil war, and this has been the biggest cause of the budget deficit in the recent years.

During the first year of President Guelleh in 1999-2000, the government started plans for the privatisation of all the major utilities such as water, electricity, railway, telecommunication and many several others. The government also hoped to attract private capital in free trade zone programs.

In July 1993, the government armed force also known as 'Djiboutian National Army' had launched a heavy offensive in response to the insurgency, leaving almost thousands of people dead. The government has received considerable support from the neighbouring countries such as Ethiopia and Eritrea; although both countries have large Afar ethnic within the borders. The governments of Ethiopia and Eritrea was surprised by the success of the FRUD and weakened the prospect of a reversal in the balance of power in Djibouti. After few years of internal conflict, it has come to the conclusion that the government to adopt a peace deal with the FRUD and initially signed a peace agreement with the FRUD in both 1994 and 2001. These two agreements were made within the context of political reforms.

According to the 1981 and 1992 constitutions, Djibouti is a semi-presidential republic, with executive, legislative and judicial power remaining in the hands of the President of the Republic, currently Ismael Omar. The president, who is the head of the state according to the constitution, is elected by universal suffrage; the President appoints the prime minister who is the head of government according to the constitution. The legislature who are the law-making body whose 65 members are elected for five-year terms. Before 1992, candidates came from a single list submitted by the ruling party, the Popular Rally for Progress (RPP).

In January 1992, the government at the time led by President Hassan Gouled appointed a committee to draft a new constitution that would allow the functioning of the multi-party system, limit the powers of the president, and the establishment of an independent judiciary system. On 4 September 1992, 75% of the voters approved the constitution in a referendum.

However, despite the commitment of the government for democratic reforms, the government has created a system that is called 'winner-takes-all electoral rules', which the party is obtaining a majority shall be awarded all the seats within the national assembly. On 2003 at the legislative elections, the former rebel group converted to a political party after the peace deal agreement FRUD has won almost 40% of the vote but received not even one seat in parliament.

Despite constitutional changes in 1992 that have allowed the creation of more political parties in Djibouti, Djibouti has remained strongly in the hands of the ruling party. On 18 December, the legislative election was held, with the ruling party RPP gaining 74% of the vote and the democratic renewal party 25.4%. Other parties have boycotted the elections as they accused the government of fraud.

Following the adaptation of the multi-party system in 1992, several government key ministers have resigned due to the crisis within the government and disputes over the government policies on social issues, within the intention of those who left the government to create their own political party and participate in the presidential elections in 1993.

On May the 7th 1993, a presidential election was held in Djibouti. Following the constitutional changes approved in a referendum the previous year. This election was the first presidential elections to feature more than one candidate. The key pre-eminent contenders were; Hassan Gouled the incumbent president, who was also the candidate for the ruling party, Mohamed Djama Elabe, a long-term minister, who held several ministerial posts and from the Democratic Renewal Party (PRD). Aden Robleh Awaleh former minister of commerce and tourism, who was a key political figure in the history of Djibouti and was the candidate for the National Democratic Party (PND).

Mohamed Moussa Ali (Tour Tour), an independent candidate who was one of the first economists in Djibouti and formerly severed as the economic advisor to President Hassan Gouled, and finally Mohamed Ibrahim Abdi, a businessman who stood as an independent candidate for the presidential election. The election result came favoured the incumbent and made him the successful candidate who won the majority in the presidential election.

In 1993 after the presidential elections, the rebel group FRUD has suffered significant following a heavy offensive led by the national army, which has resulted in severe casualties in the northern part of the country. In 1994, an internal dispute occurred within the FRUD over the issue of negotiating with the government to find a valuable necessity to the long-term conflict. A more moderate wing branch of the FRUD has entered negotiations with the government and called for a ceasefire.

In March 1995 as required by the peace agreement signed in December 1994, FRUD began to disarm most of their armed force, and a segment of FRUD members joined the national armed force and was given high ranks. The two main leaders of FRUD were also promoted to ministerial posts. In March 1996, FRUD was given legal recognition as a political party. A radical wing of the FRUD, led by Ahmed Dini, opposed widely to the truce. Djibouti and neighbouring Ethiopia have jointly attacked a wing of the FRUD, led by Ahmed Dini in October 1997, and skirmishes continued in 1998. The human rights record of the authoritarian Gouled regime came increasingly under attack in the late 1980's and 1990's.

Gouled in 1995 began to experience severe medical conditions and suffered from an illness that was later put him in a position to be hospitalised in a hospital in France. During this period, a struggled has occurred between Ismael Omar and Ismael Guedi Hared as to who will be the successor of the current President Gouled, both was severed as key advisors to the president and were both loyal to the president. In part to cut down on inter-party disputes, Gouled was elected by his party to remain as the head of the party after his convalescence. After two decades as the head of state, Gouled suddenly decided to step down and retire. In February 1999, he officially announced his intentions to step from the office and would not participate the scheduled April 1999 elections.

After the announcement of the president, the party quickly took an immediate decision as to elect a candidate that would represent the party in the upcoming elections. The ruling party (RPP) named Ismael Omar Guelleh (IOG) as the party's candidate, Guelleh a key advisor to the president and the chief of staff for 20years was close to the president and even hails from the same clan (Mamasan) to the president.

Following Ismael Omar nomination for president by his political party, the FRUD in alliance with the RPP, also accepted Ismael Omar as their candidate. The opposition coalition alliance, which consist of PRD (Democratic Renewal

Party) led by Daher Ahmed Farah DAF, the PND (National Democratic Party) by Aden Robleh Awaleh, and unofficially FRUD Renaissance, together with the key political opposition figures such as; Moumin Bahdon Farah, former minister of foreign affairs, Mohamed Moussa TourTour, former presidential candidate and several others have designated Moussa Ahmed Idriss as their candidate for the presidential election of 1999.

The election results showed that only 60% of the electorate participated, making Guelleh successful candidate with 74% of the votes cast to 26% for Moussa Ahmed. There was no official boycott of the election, for the first time since Djibouti's independence from France in 1977.

After a decisive victory in the presidential election of 1999, Guelleh quickly appointed members of his Issa clan in key government positions and positioned himself strategically to oversee political operations. The challenges that he faced after taking office was enduring ethnic hostilities between his own people, the Issa and the minority ethnic group Afar. The internal crisis between both ethnic groups that have led to political strife which eventually resulted in the boycott of the two largest opposition groups in 2005 presidential elections. Guelleh was then re-elected as the head of state in 2005 to another six-year term, making him the sole candidate in the election and promised that he would step down by the end of his second term.

Guelleh was born in 1947 in Dire-Dawa, Ethiopia and hails from the political powerful Mamasan clan of Issa. In his youth time, Guelleh attended an Islamic school and later entered in civil service in 1968, under the French colonial administration. Few years later, he became a police inspector but left the position in 1975 to join the independence movement. Two years later, when Djibouti gained independence, guelleh was appointed into a pre-eminent position which was the chief of the security forces for the next twenty-two years by his uncle Gouled, the president of the republic. Guelleh also had special duties for overseeing the domestic security forces.

By 1979, the independence movement LPAI has converted into a political party, the Rassemblement Populaire pour le Progres (RPP), after the establishment of the party, Guelleh held key positions within the party as well as his other position in the government.

Djibouti has experienced some hostilities during its early years of independence with the majority Issa taking most government positions, which dominated the country. Though President Gouled appointed some Afar in his cabinet, the longstanding rivalries between the Issa and Afar escalated, and civil war broke out in early 1990's. FRUD (Front for the Restoration of Unity and Democracy) was the engine of the strife, and the majority of the organisation were Afar. President Gouled outlawed all political parties, but international pressure forced multiparty elections in 1993, and Gouled was re-elected as president with 75 percent of the vote.

The economy is based upon free-enterprise economy; the economy extremely depends on the country's strategic position at the narrow straits at the southern entrance to the Red Sea. During the years of 1990's, the French military base in Djibouti was the country's largest single source of finance and commercial activity. The rest came from the service sector such as the free port of Djibouti, the railway terminus, the airport and government administration. The free port had a deep-water container terminal. Therefore former colonial (France) has invested enormously to modernised the port. There is also an active construction industry.

Djibouti due to its horrific climate, the country lacks hugely from the agricultural sector, and as a result, the country produces only 3% of its food. Over half of the population receives its income from livestock: goats, sheep and camels. As the country is located in the Red Sea, the fishing industry is the primary commodity that vast population consume. As a result, the Islamic Development Bank helped finance a canning factory.

Since 1990, a combination of recession, civil war and a high population growth rate took place to reduce per capita consumption by 35%. The unemployment rate rose to its highest by 50% (some other places in the country reached 70%).

The border conflict between two neighbouring states (Ethiopia and Eritrea) had an impact on commerce in which Djibouti allowed Ethiopia to use its port and conducted regular trade relations. As a result, average annual growth of GDP between 1988 and 1998 was -3.1%, and the economy was at zero growth at the beginning of 2001.

In 1997, due to the weakening health conditions of the President Gouled, Guelleh increasingly took several lists of duties for his uncle with the intention to become the successor of his uncle. Gouled at the time 81 years of age was re-elected in 1997, but with the declining of his health, he chose to step down in 1999. As the party then (RPP) elected Guelleh to become the candidate of the party, he faced Moussa Ahmed Idriss, a longstanding deputy of the national assembly in the election.

After the announcement of the election result, the opposition began to reject the results and accused the government of rigging the election. The government then responded to the opposition with heavy bombardment resulting a mass imprisonment and economic sanctions to the opposition key figures such as the rival candidate Moussa Ahmed Idriss, Aden Robleh Awaleh, Daher Ahmed Farah, Ismail Guedi Hared former entourage to the former president and once believed to be the potential successor of President Gouled.

A year later, President Guelleh fired the head of Djibouti national police force, Yacin Yabeh, who later carried out an attempted coup to overthrow Guelleh and his regime. Yacin Yabeh, a close ally of the president Guelleh served the country's chief of police from 1977 to 2000, when he was appointed to the advisor of the interior minister. Shortly afterwards the polices that were loyal to him carried attempted a coup d'etat. The coup then became unsuccessful as the military managed to stop the coup. After the national army intervention, Yacin Yabeh then fled to the French embassy but was turned over to Djibouti authorities on December 9. On 13 December, Yacin Yabeh was charged with breaching state security and was sentenced to fifteen years in prison. Yacin Yableh was a very close friend to President Ismail Omar Guelleh, but the relations between the two had worsened prior to the attempted coup.

After the September 11, attacks on the World Trade Centre, the U.S. has decided to carry out anti-terrorism operations. The US interest in Djibouti arose and eventually resulted that US Special Forces to be deployed in Djibouti, under the pretext of combating the terrorism and piracy. Djibouti lies about 13 miles distance from Yemen, the hub and the headquarters of the so-called Al Qaeda terrorist group, the militant group that assumed the responsibility for the 9/11. At first, the US operation in Djibouti in the fight against the terrorism was limited, but in 2002 the US government led by President Bush has realised that to reduce extremism and to end the existence of Al Qaeda it would require long-term engagement with the local government. Therefore, it established the Combined Joint Task Force-Horn of Africa to conduct stability operations in the region. In November 2002, the Combined Joint Task Force-HOA staff, a Marine-based organisation, arrived off the coast of Djibouti aboard USS Mount Whitney, a naval command ship.

The US military base in Djibouti, Camp Lemonnier is situated at Djibouti capital city next to the main international airport and is home to the Combined Joint Task Force – Horn of Africa of the US Africa Command. It's the only permanent military base in the entire Africa. The camp is operated by the Combined Joint Task Force-Horn of Africa. The camp became the most important tenant command located at the facility as of 2008. The prime objective of the establishment was for the support of Operation Enduring Freedom – Horn of Africa. After negotiations between the governments of Djibouti and US from March to May 2001, the Djiboutian government allowed for the base to be used by the US, in return, the US has provided humanitarian aid and launched counter-terrorism efforts. This base is now the location of which U.S. and Coalition forces are operating in the Horn of Africa.

This agreement was made by officials from the Djibouti government and the U.S. Embassy in Djibouti to allow for the use of the camp, as well as a nearby airport and port facilities. According to a former senior U.S. military commander, "Camp Lemonnier is the centrepiece of a network of around six U.S. drone and surveillance bases stretching across the continent. The latter air bases are smaller and operate from remote hangars situated within local military bases or civilian airports. Due to its strategic location, Camp Lemonnier also serves as a hub for aerial operations in the Gulf region".

The 2001 US-led campaign in Afghanistan, establish a haven in the Horn of Africa and continued to carry out any future attacks from there. It is a multi-service formation operating under the protection of the US African Command (AFRICOM), which since March 2010 has been led by Rear Admiral Brian Losey. Since 2003, the task force has been housed in Camp Lemonier, a former French Foreign Legion camp adjacent to the Djibouti-Ambouli International Airport, which is managed by Dubai Ports World and has suitable runways and lighting conditions. The US government pays Djibouti an estimated sum of US$30 million annually for Camp Lemonier, which is currently United State's only official military base located in Africa.

During 2003, despite the strong relation between both US and Djibouti, Guelleh publicly criticised and opposed the US-led invasion of Iraq in early 2003. Djibouti depends on large aid packages from the United States and other countries. Djibouti maintains strong relation with France (former colonial), which has the largest deployment of the French army on the African continent. The foreign aid is widely needed in the country. Djibouti has an average per-capita income of $1, 200; an infant mortality rate higher than Rwanda, one of Africa's poorest nations; and a life expectancy rate of just 51 years for men and 53 years for women. The unemployment rate hovers near 50 percent, and many of the country's 721, 000 citizens live in desperately poor conditions.

US relation with Djibouti

The United States created a diplomatic relation with the newly Republic of Djibouti in 1977, following the country's independence from former colonial (France), and the US had a consular before the independence since 1929. After the independence, Djibouti was ruled by two President Hassan Gouled and Ismael Omar Guelleh, both from the mamasan subclan of Issa, this made Mamasan subclan the powerful subclan in the country similar to the Marehan in Somalia during the leadership of the late president of Somalia Mohamed said barreh. The current president was first elected in 1999 by universal suffrage.

Djibouti, for one decade, had one legal party from 1981-1992. In 1992, the government alongside the lawmakers amended the constitution to introduce multi-party system due to the great need for democratic reforms. The country's longstanding internal civil war between the government and Afar rebel militia officially terminated in 2001 following a final peace accord was established between both sides.

Djibouti's location was always the backbone of the country's economy and long-term prosperity, as the country is situated in a strategic location within the Horn of Africa and is a key US ally in security, regional stability and humanitarian efforts in the greater horn. Since the 2001 chaotic terrorist attack in New York that resulted in the destruction of the world trade centre, the government of Djibouti led by Guelleh has been supportive of US interests and takes an active position against terrorism. Djibouti hosts a US military presence at Camp Lemonier. The US military also has access to the port facility and the airport by a bilateral agreement.

The U.S. Organization for International Development's (USAID), Food for Peace program, maintains a distribution centre for pre-situated food assistance items in Djibouti, serving as a centre point for fast reaction in parts of Africa and Asia. Global Broadcasting Bureau offices in Djibouti transmit Arabic-dialect programming, and Voice of America Somali Service telecasts to the Horn and the Arabian Peninsula.

Djibouti's national economic growth is delayed by a fast expansion workforce that is poorly equivalent to the economic needs of the country, resulting in high unemployment and insufficient qualified candidates for employment in certain sectors. Other issues that have direct negative impact to the economy consist of; expensive cost of electricity, extreme water shortages, poor health system and major food insecurity, the US relief intent to improve significantly the health, education and to consolidate stability, which is extremely important in improving the government's ability to provide basic services to its people.

The US Agency for International Development supports the Ministry of Education of the Republic of Djibouti; to train the teachers, build the education systems for managing information, improve the quality of primary level reading standards, to increase access to education. USAID is taking important steps to improve the state's education system and boosting the quality and efficiency of the learning environment.

Likewise the Department of Health, USAID concentrates on the wellbeing dangers connected with Djibouti's position as a periodical path and critical cross-border commerce route. Programs that focuses specifically on HIV/AIDS prevention and other assistance to the Ministry's effort to treat HIV, malaria, TB and polio, the US became the largest contributor to the global fund for HIV/AIDS, TB and malaria for Djibouti, assisting 30% of the total fund. In 2011, 1338 individuals were getting ARV treatment for HIV, which speaks to 30% scope on a national level. Shockingly, 80% of HIV contaminations in Djibouti are analysed in the last stages of AIDS. Djibouti additionally challenges the third highest TB prevalence rate around the world. A huge number of cases, around 100 every year, are analysed as multi-medication safe TB, which is significantly much harder to treat.

When considering the bilateral economic relations between Djibouti and other countries, Djibouti is qualified for advantageous trade benefits under the African Growth and Opportunity Act. During 2009 a collective venture between the government of Djibouti and Dubai Ports World agreed to the construction of a modern container terminal, which enhanced the growth of their logistics and service sector. The US exported plenty of commodities to Djibouti such as vegetable oil, machinery, wheat and machinery due to the great demand for this sort of commodities in Djibouti. This port also served Ethiopia that was similarly received significant US food aid. The government of the United States has signed a trade and investment agreement with the common market for Eastern and Southern parts of Africa, which Djibouti is part of it.

China (a US rival) has understood the greater importance of Djibouti's geostrategic location and now intending to have military presence in the Horn of Africa and increase their stake in Africa by investing enormously investing in the African economy, energy, infrastructure and job creation and return collect all the natural resources and shift it to China.

Washington and Beijing both paid significantly for their presence in the tiny state in the Horn of Africa, but strategically important in terms of location and both countries (China and the US) it seems that their interest coincides calmly.

For many decades both countries contended over many geostrategic significant countries, but perhaps nowhere as important as the Republic of Djibouti. Djibouti, a former French colonial and member of the Arab League and the African Union, has managed to attract the attention of foreign world powers due to its strategic location. Djibouti is already a permanent home for US Base Camp Lemonier, the largest military base in the continent of Africa. This camp host 4000 US personnel and is launching a drone operation to permanently eliminate terrorist militant group affiliated with Al Qaeda in Yemen and Somalia.

The US pays a total amount of $63million annually to Djibouti for the base facility; the base is used to ensure the US interest in the region and counter-terrorism. In addition to this, several other countries maintain a military base in Djibouti and France is among the countries that have a base in Djibouti. Also, some US allies countries including Spain, Germany and Japan have carried out military activities to fight against piracy and counter-terrorism.

The US also uses this military base to wage support to its Saudi ally led operation decisive storm in Yemen against the Houthi by providing significant intelligence. The Houthi rebel led by Abdul-Malik al-Houthi has managed to overthrow the legitimate government of Yemen led by President Mansur Hadi. The international community alongside the UN Security Council has backed the Saudi government to lead a military offensive operation against the Houthi to bring back stability and security in Yemen. Another connection Djibouti has to the conflict raging across the Strait of Bab al-Mandeb is that it has become one of the key hosts for Yemeni refugees, who sail across the Red Sea in small boats to escape the fighting.

The reasons in which foreign powers are attracted to Djibouti, it's not because of Djibouti's strategic location but the country's permanently stability compare to other neighbouring countries e.g. Somalia, Eritrea and Yemen. There are concerns that foreign presence could ultimately attract terrorist to Djibouti soil. To prevent the possibility of terrorist attacks inside Djibouti, the government has reinforced the security and the stability from the revenue that it receives from the foreign powers.

The government has invested these revenues in building the state of the economy, creating employment and invest in small and medium businesses to generate more wealth. However, not all Djiboutians have benefited from this economic advantages that foreign powers are indeed bringing to the country, as the unemployment is very high and the poverty line has reached its highest of 40%. This is because the Corruption is widely spread in the country, and state revenues do not necessarily trickle down to the population past the ruling classes.

China interest in Djibouti is very different to the one of the West. The western interest it's to protect its interest and counter the terrorism and piracy;

however China interest in Djibouti could be interpreted to as commercial interest since China intends to invest in Africa and return take all the necessary natural resources to China.

In May 2015, President Guelleh indicated that Chinese authority is negotiating with him for the establishment of its first official naval base overseas. China intends to install a permanent military base in Obock, an Afar region in the north of Djibouti which is the northern port city of Djibouti. China is willing to pay to pay $100 million annually for the base. Also, China is also investing several infrastructure projects including developing the countries ports, airports and railway.

In recently, President Guelleh increased his efforts to establish a strategic partnership with China, a move which angered Washington. China is keen to expand its military presence in Africa. China, which already agreed to build a railway linking Djibouti to Ethiopia, has negotiated a $400 million deal to develop Djibouti's port facilities, a deal which Pentagon officials believe will lead to China establishing its own military presence just a few miles from the highly sensitive Camp Lemonnier complex.

Beijing's presence in the country, furthermore, has raised fears in Washington that Mr Guelleh is turning away from his longstanding ally in the US, with all the connections that could have for the future operational security of Camp Lemonier. Therefore, U.S. policymakers are now hoping to prevent Guelleh from running for a fourth term in office when the next presidential elections are due to held in April 2016. Surely, if China continues with its plans to establish a military presence in the Horn of Africa, the Pentagon will have to give serious consideration to relocating some of Camp Lemonnier's more sensitive operations elsewhere.

This trade deal between Djibouti and China has raised serious concerns concerning Camp Lemonnier, and there are genuine concerns that if President Guelleh gets too close to China, then he may be tempted to impose restrictions on US access to the base. If Mr Guelleh continues with his confrontational approach towards Washington, then President Obama is likely to come under pressure to press for political reform in Djibouti, thereby ending the president's long-running dictatorship.

China, a gigantic investor in Africa, has turned their focus to Djibouti and seeking to make Djibouti their first Indian Ocean outpost. Following the understanding of the Djibouti's geostrategic importance, China began to diplomatic and legal foundations to ensure their share in Djibouti by creating a long-term naval presence in Djibouti. Since then Beijing began to negotiate with the Djibouti government for naval access in the country to fulfil their objectives in the Horn of Africa. The facility in which China intends to get as their naval base is located in Obock, an Afar region located on the northern coast of the country. However, China will not call the facilities a 'base' in.

The reliable access to the facilities in Djibouti can regularly be maintenance by the Chinese firms and return China could have the chance to maintain and permanent maritime and possibly an aerial springboard deep into the North-western Indian Ocean. The increasing presence of the Chinese military in Djibouti is far beyond the realm of speculation and its now in a stage where both Chinese and Djiboutian government is agreeing on the Chinese installation process in Djibouti, moving assets and potentially soon pouring concrete.

During the process of the negotiations, President Guelleh has made it clearly to the western media that his government is negotiating with China to establish a Chinese military facility, a move that angered the western powers and could result in a direct termination of the Guelleh's regime.

Djibouti has played a key role with its western allies to fight against the piracy in the Horn of Africa and mostly the fight against the radical extremist that operates some part of the horn of Africa e.g. Somalia and predominantly in the Middle East. The Chinese naval ships have reportedly visited the port of Djibouti several times since the mission began in December 2008. China has constructed the ideas for constructing a base in Djibouti on February 2014 during a meeting between the Djibouti President and General Chang Wanquan following an agreement of defence and security treaty signed by the countries.

Since then, Guelleh has conducted strong diplomatic ties with the Chinese government for the interest of the two sides and the continuous Chinese invest in improving Djibouti's infrastructure. On July 2015, the Djiboutian press told that the Chinese President Xi Jinping has sent his best wishes to Djibouti for its National Day and praised the ongoing economic and diplomatic relation between China-Djibouti. Beyond the growing economic cooperation that led to the huge investment of the infrastructure in Djibouti funded by the Chinese firms, the tiny state in the Horn of Africa is beginning to receive technological blandishments from Beijing. On June 2014, the Djiboutian Air Force received from China MA-60 aircraft. During the Djibouti's Independent Day parade, the Djiboutian armed force showed a Norinco WMA301 Assaulter tank destroyer.

For many months, Beijing denied that its intending to build a permanent military base in the East African country of Djibouti and this could that China is up to something. Evidence increasingly shows that China intends to maintain a naval presence even if the risk of piracy declines. Having advanced deployed naval assets in an important and strategically vital region like the horn of Africa is simply too useful a capability to relinquish, as fully shown by non-combatant evacuation operations from Libya during the uprising in 2011 and Yemen after the fall of the legitimate government by the Houthi Shia backed by Iran.

So the question is why Djibouti? Djibouti extremely offers exceptional access to the Gulf of Aden and sits on one side of the strategic Bab al-Mandeb, a major international maritime energy transport channel that shifts 3.8 million barrels per day of crude oil in 2013, making it the world's 4th busiest maritime energy station. Also, Djibouti is the entrance into the Arabian Peninsula, the North-western Indian Ocean and small entry section of the Eastern and North-Central of the African continent.

Secondly, Djibouti is the most secure and stable politically country close to the biggest number of key maritime and the interest that China in the region. China has balanced the great opportunities that Singapore and Djibouti are offering in terms of their military operation in the Northwest Indian Ocean because Singapore is politically stabled and secure but is located too far from the location that China is seeking make a permanent military presence. Djibouti became the ideal location for China to operate due to Djibouti being very close to the Bab al-Mandeb and the Northwest Indian Ocean. The primary contenders among current ports that are hosting the Chinese presence are Djibouti (Obock), Aden, Salalah, Karachi, and Gwadar. Down the road, Bagamoyo (Tanzania) and Mombasa could enter the mix.

Yemen is a dangerous port area due to its complex violence divided the country following the uprising that led to the fall of Ali Abdallah Salih. But even before the contemporary upheaval, Yemen had a bad history. The USS Cole attack in 2001 and the October 2002 attack on the super tanker almost certainly cooled Chinese naval planners' willingness to risk using Aden as a resupply port. Another place that poses security threat challenges is Pakistan.

If China intends to use heavily the Gwadar Port, which is located near the area of a decades-long Balochi chaotic that has even claimed the deadly attack on the location that ended the lives of the Chinese workers' lives in the past 15 years. Furthermore, as for Karachi, the port is too crowded to manage, and an overflowing as well as the continuous violent city that the plan likely doesn't need its sailors' attempt into. Lastly, Karachi is extremely far from major Indian Ocean transit routes as to impose extra sailing distance with its use.

Therefore, Djibouti is the most appealing location, which fulfils the interest of China. The tiny state in the Horn of Africa has hosted a decade long of thousands of French, the US and Japanese personnel who are actively operating military combat against the piracy and the terrorism through the use of different military equipments such as drones, etc. Since the military presence of the West and its allies, there have not been any disclosed security incidents. Many democrats and opposition activists would embrace the fall the President Guelleh due to his corruption on public finance and his authoritarian attitude that dismantled the fundamental principle of democracy, but the country's population has been Pacific for years, and nothing appears poised to destabilise things in the foreseeable future. In the region, this is about the best political set up once can ask for. It is made all the better by the fact that the bases are largely self-contained, thus avoiding problems triggered by soldier misbehaviour off base, but the bases inject enough money into the local economy that local officials (and probably a decent number of residents) are happy to host them.

The third reason in which China is extremely thirsty for a military base in Djibouti is that Djibouti offers the facilities to accommodate any PLAN vessel in service now or in the foreseeable future. China's biggest deploying warship at present is 071 LPD and draws seven meters of water. The existing port in Djibouti have the capacity to accommodate vessel drawings of up to 18 meters; this is incredibly deep enough that the port could host the entry of an aircraft carrier into the port of Djibouti. China wouldn't need all of this to carry out an operation, but the fact is that because Djibouti is capable of accommodating such facility that China can deploy any warship vessel necessary regardless of their size.

The port of Obock stood out amongst the candidates ports in Djibouti, this is because Obock offered China the best potential for the seclusion and expansion that China doubtless seeks and also Obock would give the Chinese military a relatively exclusive operating area, while at the same time offering Djibouti the chance to develop its economic infrastructure and the public sector. Obock is a tiny village in the north of Djibouti with little development on infrastructure, health and education, but the significant Chinese infrastructure investment could become an excellent military support facility.

China has a great interest in Djibouti due to its useful strategic location on the outskirts of Bab Al Mandeb and currently refugee point for non-combatant evacuation operations, and China could use this as an opportunity to evacuate Chinese citizens from the different conflict zones in Northern and Eastern Africa, as well as the Middle East. In 2015 during the ongoing civil war in Yemen, China evacuated their citizens to Djibouti to secure their citizens (Chinese). On 30 March 2015, the Foreign Ministry spokesperson the People's Republic of China has acknowledged the country's reliability and clearly stated that relevant parties in Djibouti had provided great assistance, to which the Chinese side expresses sincere appreciation.

If China has ever needed to conduct an operation, Obock would be the best location for the Chinese military forces to settle and this base could include an airfield accommodation of IL-76/Y-20 class aircraft that could move huge quantities of military equipment and personnel. It is located within the un-refuelled flight range of an IL-76 taking off from airbases in southern Xinjiang carrying a 40-tonne payload. Chinese rivals e.g. US are increasingly concerned about the permanent plan Chinese presence in Djibouti, but China and Djibouti are committed to consolidating their powerful relationship to include a more permanent Chinese military presence in the country.

The government of Djibouti has become an essential landlord to foreign powers. Djibouti's economy is small; the total Gross Domestic Product of the country in 2014 was approximate US$1.6 billion. Also, the total economic output generated by the western ally forces (French, US and Japan) military facilities offered an extreme economic boost to the economic structure of the country which generate wealth and employment opportunities that have decreased the unemployment. Under these conditions, a Chinese naval facility, particularly one that comes with major construction investment, facility improvements, and financial sweeteners, is almost irresistible because it would be another large shot in the arm for the local economy.

A greater and permanent Chinese military presence could give a useful political and diplomatic protection to the longstanding Djiboutian leader in the event of political disagreement between President Guelleh and the US and its western allies. Also, Guelleh will be less beholden to the US and French political and military influence if he has the option of siding the Chinese during difficult situations. It could also increase Guelleh's prestige by allowing him to claim that he hosts bases by the two largest economies on earth, as well as two other G7 countries.

Furthermore, different military presence could ultimate secure the peace and stability of the tiny state in the Horn of Africa and perhaps offer a excellent insurance policy to Djibouti, which inhabits a less secure neighbouring states whose security can easily fall into the trap, as we've recently seen in Yemen, where an ongoing war has undermined the state sovereignty and the functioning of the economy.

Moreover, the diverse foreign military presence offers a superb insurance policy to Djibouti, which inhabits a tough neighbourhood whose security tectonics can rapidly shift, as we have seen in the past year with Saudi Arabia and Iran fighting a proxy war in Yemen. The Chinese military has filled the last decade with hardware and posture developments that surprised many external analysts and materially improved the country's military capability. The emergence of the Yuan-class submarine, the J-20 fighter, the J-31 fighter, the anti-ship ballistic missile, and the decision to engage in South China Sea land reclamation operations offer illuminating examples. Given the size of the previous developments, the ideas of China gaining more permanent military facility in Djibouti capable of supporting forward-operating military forces would not be a surprise at all.

As for now, the biggest matter to China is to achieve a permanent military access that China could use it to help them its strategic goals. The Chinese intention of seeking a permanent military presence represents historic achievement for the Chinese policy on military and diplomacy. China for many decades inspiring to obtain a military facility in a foreign and strategic country, so seeking long-term military access in Djibouti will be seen as a great strategic achievement. With China's long-term plan access to Obock likely coming soon, China is poised to cross the rubicon. Djibouti is thereby helping to catalyse a potentially significant symbolic and substantive shift in China's foreign security policy.

China is not seeking to build a foreign base network capable of supporting high-end naval combat the way the US has. But, for now, at least, it need not take that path to achieve its strategic goals. More permanently deploying warships, and potentially aircraft, in the Indian Ocean region furthers Chinese diplomacy and geo-strategy without firing a shot. Presence and perception matter greatly in this regard. By signing and operationalizing a forces access deal in Djibouti, the PLAN will be laying roots in a vital region that is likely to see sustained, significant growth in Chinese naval activity.

Regional disputes and instability

The conflict between Eritrea and Ethiopia of 1998-2000 constituted an extreme threat to the stability of the region and opened an enormous opportunity for Djibouti. Due to the war between Eritrea and Ethiopia, Ethiopia has shifted all their trade of import and export to the Djibouti port, where it has previously sent to Eritrean port. Following the Ethiopian shift to their trade in Djibouti, both states reinforce economic, political and security ties since the trade protocol was signed in 1996.

During the year of 1999, Djibouti and Ethiopia also concluded a military cooperation protocol. The emergence, in April 1999, of Ismael Omar Guelleh as president strengthened these ties. President Guelleh came from the Somali ethnic and was born in the second capital city of Ethiopia 'Dire Dawa', many sees him as a close ally of the Ethiopian government due to his commitment to working alongside the Ethiopian government to maintain their interest in the region and the Ethiopian continuous direct involvement in destabilising Somalia. Guelleh since his arrival to the presidency in Djibouti has shown his strong commitment in converting Djibouti into an Ethiopian province, following the economic, political and social integration he did with the neighbouring Ethiopia.

In 1998, Eritrea had under suspiciously accused the government of Djibouti of granting Ethiopia to use its port for importing weapons for use in the war against Eritrea. In June 1998, Djibouti stationed their troops to the north to protect its borders with Eritrea and prevent any further aggression. In addition to this, the French troops went alongside the Djiboutian army to participate in a de-mining programme. During 1999, France made two warships available to control the coast and prevent military aggression from either Ethiopia or Eritrea.

Djibouti's president at that time Hassan Gouled tried in June 1998 to mediate in the conflict between Ethiopia and Eritrea, but during the course of the Organisation for African Unity summit in November 1998, in the capital city of Burkina Faso, President Hassan Gouled was refused as mediator by Eritrea as the president wasn't sufficiently independent. Djibouti at this time cut apart its relations with Eritrea and therefore recalled their ambassador. Afterwards, the former executive secretary of the intergovernmental authority on development (IGAD), Tekest Ghebrai, who was Eritrean national, was refused to enter Djibouti as Djibouti was the host of the IGAD headquarters.

A framework agreement that was signed between Djibouti and Eritrea in 1997 to increase cooperation has not been fully engaged and respected by both parties. In 1999, Eritrea again accused Djibouti of siding Ethiopia. Meanwhile, Djibouti alleged Eritrea on supporting the Afar rebels that were fighting with the government.

The economic dimension of Djibouti doesn't allow the country to endanger its overall relationship with the much greater and expanding the economy of Ethiopia, which is an important aspect for both politically and economically. The war between Eritrea and Ethiopia has given economic benefits and a significant amount of growth annually to Djibouti. Its income has expanded significantly as a result of the five-fold rise in Ethiopia freight movement since 1998. Cargo traffic had expanded from 1.3 million tonnes in 1994 and 1.7 million tonnes in 1997, 3.1 million tonnes in 1998 and 4,2 million tonnes in 2002. This increase in products and services transmitting to and from Ethiopia has become the backbone of Djibouti's economy. Indeed, with few natural resources, 60% unemployment and domestic consumption falling 35% from 1999 up to 2006, Djibouti now depends firmly on its significantly economic ties with Ethiopia.

In the challenge for Ethiopia's business, Djibouti is much better position than any other country in East of Africa and is currently investing hugely to extend and enhance the port of Djibouti. This may permit Djibouti to serve as a regional commercial hub, and the expanding of the port capacity could ultimately speed up the regional trade. With Ethiopia transporting all their imports and exports to Djibouti, neighbouring Eritrea has lost millions of dollar in annual revenue. If both Ethiopia and Eritrea reconcile and compromise to end the longstanding conflict, and Ethiopia starts to use the port of Eritrea (Assab and Massawa), which Ethiopia used before 1998, the competition between Djibouti and Eritrea is going to be very difficult and could easily deteriorate provocative and never-ending war.

Djibouti and Eritrea, following the severe attack on US soil of world trade in September 2001. Both countries were enormously competing to host a US military to combat terrorism in the Middle East. Eritrea was deeply disappointed following the US military base establishment in Djibouti. This means a great privilege for Djibouti to host the US military base, despite the latter small size and hostile climate. The developments that US base brings to Djibouti was a major blow to Eritrea in terms of investment opportunities lost and most importantly the guaranteed security that US base would provide to chosen country.

Eritrea has dramatically lobbied to host a US base military. In October 2012, the Eritrean authorities circulated a paper in the US entitled 'why not Eritrea?' To ensure a greater relation and with the US. The US government was more determined to base in Djibouti, a smaller state with a western patron protector, was more attractive as a site of a military base, considering that the country's internal politics was predictable and manageable and that its reliability is more easily guaranteed than Eritrea.

The US was cautious of the hostile and aggressive tendencies of President Issayas Afeworki and his character as a regional troublemaker. The doubt was over the strategic location of Eritrea, Eritrea has a longer coastline and its relatively stronger military and secure operational environment with more than one area to base troops and conduct operations, and its two ports and airfield facilities. It also had to take into account the sensitivity and interests of Ethiopia, with which it had to build more important relationships. Ethiopia was arguably the most important state in the Horn of Africa, endowed with a very large geographic size, a sizeable and growing population, an enormous of economic assets and an enduringly superior diplomatic standing.

In Eritrea, the three powers of the nation (executive, legislative and judiciary) are concentrated in the hands of a single person, President Afeworki. He was born in Asmara on 2 February 1946. He hails from the Highland Tigrinya clan. He attended secondary school in Asmara; he later joined Haile Selassie I University in 1966, studying there for a period. He then dropped out and joined the Eritrean Liberation Front, which was established in 1961. Afeworki received military formation in the late 1960's and served as a political commissar within the liberation front military.

Afeworki was the co-founder of the Eritrean People's Liberation Front, during the years of 1977-1987, President Afeworki was the deputy secretary-general of the EPLF. In 1987, he officially took the position of secretary-general of the EPLF organisation. On January 1993, Afeworki began to experience unprecedented illness. Due to inefficient medical health care system in Eritrea, the president was airlifted to a hospital in Israel which has established a military base on the Eritrean island of Dahlak. In May 1993, he was elected president of Eritrea by the National Assembly. President Afeworki used his inaugural speech in 1993 during the OAU summit in Cairo, Egypt, to denigrate the OAU for failing to live up to its lofty ideals.

He was particularly upset by the OAU's silence throughout Eritrea's thirty-year struggle for independence. In the collective Eritrean memory, President Issayas used to be the unquestioned embodiment of the 1961–1991 struggle against

Ethiopia. Austere and unpretentious, he used to drive himself to work and moved around with few bodyguards in Asmara. Recently, however, he has moved to a palace in Massawa, about 110 kilometres north-west of Asmara. He does not tolerate criticism of his political orientations to the extent of criminalising it, and non-conforming advice differing from his predispositions. He has consolidated his power through raw repression and displays a strong contempt for Western-style democracy and a near-paranoiac suspicion towards foreigners.

He is regarded as a remarkably stubborn and diffident man who does not respond to threats and diplomatic influence and, in fact, has a distaste for compromise and diplomacy, both of which he considers weaknesses. President Issayas has shown a relish for intrigues and displayed an extraordinary taste for undercover manoeuvers with wide regional repercussions in relations with neighbouring states. His militaristic or trigger-happy pattern of behaviour in foreign relations has transpired over an extended period (Sudan in 1994, Yemen in 1995, Djibouti in 1996 and 2008, and Ethiopia in 1998). The misguided policy that he loves to call 'forward policy' has not been conducive to the building of a stable regional security in the Horn of Africa.

President Issayas has thus established a reputation and record for toughness and ruthlessness, trying to alter borders by force, willing to go to war for what he perceives to be Eritrea's interests, regardless of the outcome of past confrontations. He has tried to sustain war-time discipline and instil a spirit of national pride and sacrifice to the younger generation which did not fight during the struggle against Ethiopia.

Djibouti's relation with Eritrea was re-established in March 2000, following a direct mediation from Libya's longstanding leader Muammar Gaddafi. In 2001, President Afeworki paid a visited to Djibouti, and then later President Guelleh made the similar visit to Eritrea. This resulted in an agreement to establish a joint commission which would meet annually to review cooperation between the two states, and in 2004 Eritrea and Djibouti signed cooperation agreements in the political, economic and social sectors. Following the agreements that were signed by both parties, Guelleh sought to establish a friendly relationship with neighbouring Eritrea, recognising the power of imbalance and especially the military imbalance that existed between the two countries.

In colonial perspective, the border between both Djibouti and Eritrea was the former border of Italian colony of Eritrea, and the former French Somaliland was delimited in a framework agreement signed in Rome by the Italian government and its counterpart of France during 1900 as result of a dispute in 1898. The northeast part of the border was composed of the north tip of Ras Doumeirah on the Red Sea coast, through the Gulf along the Peninsula for roughly 15 kilometres and afterwards along a straight line towards the south-west to bisidro on the banks of the We'ima stream.

According to Article 1 of the framework agreement signed on 1900 Italian and French possessions on the coast of the Red Sea are separated by a line having its starting point at the end of Ras Doumeirah, following the watershed line of the promontory name, and then extending in the direction of the southwest, reaching, after a journey of about 60 kilometers from Ras Doumeirah, a point set according to the following: having taken as a benchmark on a next line, about 60 kilometers apart, the Directorate General Red Sea, the point equidistant from the Italian coast of Assab and French coast Tadjoura, we will fix as extreme point of the line which has been discussed above, the northwest point of the landmark at a distance 15 to 20 km.

Also, Article 3 of the 1900 agreement suggest that until both parties (France and Italy) is resolving the issue of the dispute, the two colonial powers would avoid claiming to occupy the island of Doumeirah. The alignment of the border was set in another protocol marked in 1901 after the conclusion of the boundary by a special joint commission. The second protocol of 1901 that was also signed in Rome recognised the border as running from Ras Doumeirah for 15 kilometres, after which it takes after a straight line towards Bisidiro on the banks of the We'ima River.

Several decades after independence for both states, the Eritrean thug who is considered to be the regional troublemaker (Afeworki) due to his catastrophic and appalling behaviour in the region and his abusive campaign against opposition leaders in Eritrea in breach of human right, has commanded his army to launch military position in the Ras Doumeirah area of Eritrea-Djibouti border. The escalation involved the preparation of reinforced position and battlements on Djibouti's side of the Ras Doumeirah area. However, large military equipment wasn't accelerating to the area at that decisive moment, as confirmed by the French forces.

On 22 April 2008, Djibouti's long-term president Guelleh launched a joint political and military tour of the area, and Djibouti's foreign ministry afterwards claimed that the position of Eritrea was being built few hundred meters within Djiboutian territory. Then later the Eritrean government led by the wild Afeworki has denied the accusation that Eritrean soldiers had breached the territorial integrity and seized the border land of Djibouti. On 24 April 2008, both countries military leaders met to compare border maps.

Following the Eritrean offensive operation on Djibouti's territory. Djibouti had no choice but to send troops to the border against the enemy to signal their military presences and defend their territorial integrity. On May 2008 President, Guelleh stated that the two armies are facing one another and the situation could ultimate go out of hands, he also asserted that there is a hostile action which poses a real threat because it is a blatant violation of our territorial integrity. Qatar subsequently began a diplomatic activity to mediate in the border conflict between the two neighbouring states. Also, President Guelleh has called his counterpart President afeworki, during the telephone conversation they've agreed to resolve the border dispute through peaceful negotiations.

Ethiopia, which borders with Eritrea and Djibouti, depends totally on Djibouti's port for its imports and exports, declared on 12th May 2008 that it has the means to secure its important trade corridor in the event of a wider conflict between Eritrea and Djibouti. The Ethiopian prime minister has revealed the clear threat posed by Eritrea to the peace and security of the region and that it's necessary to press sanctions on Eritrea as a result of their cruel actions that drive to instability.

On the 2nd of May 2008, the African Union Peace and Security Council encouraged Djibouti and Eritrea to hold instant dialogue to resolve any bilateral dispute. On 4th may 2008, the Arab League decided to send a fact-finding mission to the disputed border area between Djibouti and Eritrea to assess the current situation and to prepare a report to the league. The Arab League Peace and Security Council accepted the request of Djibouti's government to send the mission to deal with the border dispute between the two states. The council met and discussed the border dispute between Eritrea and Djibouti in an emergency session held at Djibouti's request, its first ever meeting at delegates' level. The council also requested that the secretary-general of the Arab-league to personally contact the concerned countries, the chief of the African Union Commission and the African Union Peace and Security Council in a bid to secure Arab-African joint press conference to address the issue and the impacts that it has on the region and to finally come up with a resolution to end the border conflict.

On 10th June 2008, aggressive hostilities have erupted between the military forces of Djibouti and Eritrea, resulting in the death of nine Djiboutian soldiers and more than thirty wounded soldiers following the casualties, and on the other side 100 Eritrean soldiers were killed, 100 captured, and 21 defected. Clashes between the two armed forces reportedly continued for several days before Djibouti's military announced on June 13 that fighting had was coming to an end. However, President Guelleh has indicated that his country's war with Eritrea was still undergoing.

On 16th of June 2008, France has provided logistical, medical and intelligence support to Djibouti but did not participate in direct combat. The foreign ministry of France told reporters that it was deeply worried about the ongoing conflict between Djibouti and Eritrea. Also, the French defence ministry revealed their increase military presence in Djibouti and growing their assistance for Djibouti's national army as a result of the border conflict. The announcement also indicated that France was preparing to establish a forward logistics base and an area force close to the zone where the conflicts occurred.

A few days later, the French defence minister at the time Herve Morin and his Djiboutian counterpart Ougoureh Kifleh Ahmed held bilateral talks, promising to reinforce the French military presence in the country in case further border casualties occurs.

This conflict of the border was motivated following the Ethiopian shift to their trade of import and export to Djibouti, making Eritrea lost hundreds of millions of dollars in annual revenue, revenue which is clearly non-recoverable, and the future does not seem promising either. Even if the relationship between Eritrea and Ethiopia improves, and Ethiopia starts using the ports of Assab and Massawa which it had exclusively used before 1998 (around 3 million tonnes per year of cargo traffic), the competition between the ports of Eritrea and Djibouti is going to be intense and could easily deteriorate into a never-ending conflict.

At this moment, despite diplomatic efforts from both African Union Peace and Security Council and the Arab League to resolute the border dispute between Djibouti and Eritrea. The horn of Africa is still facing an unprecedented threat to security and continuous war, on the north, there was long-term internal conflict Republic of Sudan between the central Sudanese government and the Sudan People's Liberation Army, the conflict lasted for 22 years and is one of the longest civil wars on record. The war resulted in the independence of South Sudan six years after the war ended. There was also the continuous tension between Ethiopia and Eritrea and on the south; the rise of the extremist militant Al Shabab affiliated with Al Qaeda to destabilise the Somali transitional government after 22 years of civil war.

The relationship between Eritrea and Ethiopia worsen after the failed meeting of the Ethiopia-Eritrean boundary commission in September 2007, after which the military expansion along the border reached alarming proportions. The forecast suggests that both states Eritrea and Ethiopia have deployed into their borders 100,000 and 124,000 troops in case of the rise of tension and insurgency. The borderland has been relatively stable since 2008, despite the exchange of gunfire occurred between both states armed force in the border on December 2007. Amid international effort to solve the border conflict, tensions along Eritrea-Ethiopia have continued to escalate, especially after Eritrea precipitously halts to provide fuel for the United Nation Mission in Ethiopia and Eritrea (UNMEE).

The United Nation Mission in Ethiopia and Eritrea successive removal from Eritrea in February 2008 has created tight tensions between the two states; Eritrea has excessively accused the Ethiopian government led by Meles Zenawi of launching attacks on the Tsorena front. There is huge evidence that, beside their persistent war, both countries required new weapons, upgrading supply bases, moving large amounts of military weapons and reading troops along their common border. Thus, there still is a high probability of another war between them, especially as a result of an upward spiral of either premeditated or unintentional hostile actions. On 30 July 2008, the UN Security Council unanimously adopted Resolution 1827 terminating, without any follow-on mission, the mandate of UNMEE.

On the Somali situation and their future perspective as nation part of the international community, there were many factors that were fuelling the longstanding civil war and this was partly because of the significant support from the Eritrean government to the militia terrorist group that opposed to the peace and stability of Somalia and the formation of the federal transitional government. Afeworki, the regional trouble-maker had assisted huge support to the terrorist to destabilise the situation in Somalia and opposing anything that Ethiopia supports.

Ethiopia has significantly increased its involvement in the Somali political landscape and increased their military presence in Somalia to drive out the rivalry organisation the Islamic court of union opposed to the federal transitional government. The Islamic Court of Union led by Sheikh Sharif Sheikh Ahmed, who will later become the president of the transitional government of Somalia, was supported by Eritrea; assisting financially the Islamic court of union and supplying them with weapons. Also, Eritrea has also been supplying weapons and giving training to armed Ethiopian opposition groups operating from Somalia to put more pressure to Ethiopia. These include Ogaden National Liberation Front (ONLF) and the Oromo Liberation Front (OLF), both which were allegedly aligned with the ICU against the TFG and Ethiopia.

Although Ethiopia has managed to oust the Islamic Courts of Union, Eritrea benefited from this by supporting armed opposition group to Ethiopia, to destroy Ethiopia during its operations in the conflict. However, despite the continuation of Eritrea in support to anti-TFG forces to tie up Ethiopian troops in Somalia.

So, it's obvious that unless the tension between Ethiopia and Eritrea is solved, it would very tough to even find a clear resolution into the catastrophic crisis in Somalia and to built prosperous and sustainable Somalia that leads greater for its people. But since the prospect to end this conflict peacefully in the near future is becoming less likely, the resolution of Somalia's problems in the future has correspondingly become more difficult.

In 2008, the United States launched an air strike to target the perpetrators of the terrorist group and killed Hashi Ayro, a man who widely believed to be the chief of Al Shabab, in the central Somali city of Dusamareeb. He was accused of taking an active part of the outrageous terrorist attacks in Somalia including the murder of four international aid workers, a British journalist and a famous Somali peace activist named Abdulqadir Yahya Ali.

On 16th May 2008, the UN has organised a conference agreement between the Federal Transitional Government and the Eritrea-based Alliance for the Re-liberation of Somalia. The Alliance for the Re-liberation of Somalia is a broad-based group consist of both moderate Islamists and extreme group affiliate to Al Qaeda, wouldn't agree to sit with the TFG and maintain peace negotiations until the federal government is withdrawing the Ethiopian troops out of the Somali soil. However, despite effort from the UN, the two sides have eventually met and agreed upon signing a peace agreement on 9 June 2008, by withdrawing the Ethiopian forces after the deployment of UN forces.

Ethiopia itself is facing serious security threat in the Ogaden Somali region, as opposition armed forces are greatly benefiting from the long-standing conflict of the neighbouring Somalia by escalating in the Somalia border with Ethiopia and causing huge damage to the security of the Ethiopia-Somalia region in the west of Ethiopia. The Ethiopian military forces extended their operations deeply in Somalia, to the extent where this has raised a huge concern of the Ethiopia political involvement in the conflict in Somalia and their future ambitions of breaking Somalia into pieces.

On 24 April 2007, the Ogaden National Liberation Front has managed to attack a Zhongyuan Petroleum Exploration Bureau oil facility operating in the west of Ethiopia near the Somali region of Ethiopia, killing 74 people and abducting 7 Chinese nationals, who were later released. On May 2007, following the ONLF attack, the Ethiopian forces launched a series of counter-insurgency operations accompanied by the denial of access to commercial goods and humanitarian aid in the areas which were considered to be ONLF strongholds. These counterinsurgency operations have displaced thousands of people and placed the Ogaden issue under substantial international scrutiny.

Coming back to the political situation in Djibouti, for many years the country was facing internal dispute within the two largest ethnic groups over the power-sharing, and the structure of the government formation and the significant discrimination against the Afar ethnic in the context of power. In 1991, an armed rebellion group known as FRUD, established and began a military operation in the north of the country to demand regional autonomy under the pretext of self-determination. Their desire for autonomy has come to an end following the government crackdown on the Afar stronghold in the north that has resulted in severe casualties and the deaths of hundreds of people.

On 1994, after a peace agreement between the FRUD and the government, the insurgents transformed themselves into a political opposition, the Front for the Restoration of Unity and Democracy (FRUD). The FRUD signed a peace agreement with the government in May 2001, laying down arms in return for the implementation of decentralisation and the allocation of government seats. Djibouti since independence was one party state until the revision of the constitution on 1992, allowing the creation of additional political parties. President Guelleh succeeded Djibouti's first president Hassan Gouled. Guelleh decisively defeated his rival Moussa Ahmed Idriss, despite critics said that massive fraud was involved in the election result. The FRUD (former rebellion group) quickly joined the ruling RPP to form a ruling coalition, the Union for Presidential Majority (UMP). In September 2002, the government amended the constitution to fully adapt multiparty system which has resulted in the creation of four additional political parties on that same year.

President Guelleh, a former head of the security services, has an intimate knowledge of Djibouti's political forces and has used it to practise a policy of divide and rule. To maintain his dominance, President Guelleh has kept a delicate balance between keeping the favour of France and lambasting it with nationalist rhetoric. He has been able to get France to pay more rent for its base, at the same time that he has continued to irritate it by refusing to cooperate in a longstanding investigation of the 1995 suspicious death of French judge Bernard Borrel in Djibouti.

President Guelleh has reduced significantly the dependence of France and allowed the establishment of the US military base to increase the financial strength of Djibouti and to raise investment to improve the country's infrastructure and eliminate the public debts and fiscal deficit. This move also strengthened the diplomatic ties with the Arab States of the Persian Gulf, in particularly Dubai. This diplomatic effort that President Guelleh is aiming to approach the foreign forces have forced the opposition leaders into a situation in which it cannot expect any support from the US and France to push the government to open political space and will make the US and France turn blind eye to the horrific conditions of human right status in Djibouti and the violence of the president in breach of civil liberties.

President Guelleh has dramatically increased his presidential powers to secure his dominant political position by fully controlling all government institutions, have a huge stake in all private organisation and allowing one state media to formulate propaganda and directly attack his political opponents through the only one media controlled by the state. He also refused to establish an independent commission electoral commission so that he could assure his position as the head of the state. This made the oppositions to boycott almost every election due to the huge absence of free and fair elections.

Discontent has erupted among the general population due to persistent poverty, and unemployment constitutes compelling threats to Djibouti's stability in the medium term. In the long term, if the economy has failed grow due to lack of competitiveness and limited free market in Djibouti's economic landscape.

Thanks to the geo-strategic location of the Republic of Djibouti, on July 2008, a company owned by Osama bin-Laden's bother has launched a project to build a bridge of 29 Kilometres bridge at a cost of estimated sum of $200 billion across the Bab-el-Mandeb straits on the Red Sea in order to connect Djibouti and Yemen, as well as Africa and the Middle East, Recognising the greater importance that it will have on the regional economy. The bridge will have a six-lane highway, four light-rail lines as well as water and oil pipelines.

The political economy of geostrategic location and the development of infrastructure in Djibouti has largely contributed to the various developments that Djibouti has reached during the past decade. From the year of 1999 to the present moment, the country has experienced the flexible economic environment, the constant annual growth of the economy of 6.5% and the implementation of a competitive market to boost the economy, generate wealth through the collection of taxes to create employment and the improvement of the public services.

The country has largely benefited from the international aid and funds to secure the stability of the economy and to introduce more projects e.g. the railway, the expansion of the ports, the creating of two airports, etc. Djibouti's economy is dominated by the public and service sector due to the harsh climate of the country. Djibouti's primary sector has always remained insignificant to the input of the GDP as a result of the dry climate and the lack of water. Therefore, Djibouti is considered to be economically dependent, a politically victim of influence from France (former coloniser).

The geostrategic and the large development of infrastructure that Djibouti maintains gave the country to generate enormous income from its geo-strategic location and the expansion of the infrastructure. Djibouti, since independence has received heavy investment and other benefits from their position as a gateway to the Red Sea between the Indian Ocean and the Mediterranean Sea and as a trade route for Ethiopia's import and export. Approximately 86% of Djibouti's national revenue comes from the service sector and its international Port serving of the Ethiopia trade. Also, Djibouti holds strategic military initiative as a result of its proximity to Bab Al Mandeb and the Arabian Peninsula.

Djibouti charge the US and the French garrison US$ 31-37 million annually, Djibouti economic growth has been boosted by several factors which are; the conflict that rose in 1998-2000 between Eritrea and Ethiopia, this conflict between the two States has led the way to the economic development that Djibouti has experienced for the last 15 years. The conflict event gave Djibouti the chance to enhance its strategic importance for the neighbouring Ethiopia as Ethiopia has now shifted all its commercial import and export goods to Djibouti. Ethiopia uses Djibouti as their primary sea outlet for its international trade, and this has taken an active part in boosting Djibouti's economy and development on infrastructure.

Sheikh Alamoudi (a leading foreign investor) in Ethiopia has also invested and gave facilities in the old port. Since 1998, the level of the Ethiopian cargo and petroleum products has increased. These developments between (Djibouti and Ethiopia) has accelerated to cooperation in economic, social and security landscape and made a strong relationship between the two states. Djibouti as a result has become the only port for Ethiopia on import and export. During the past decade, Djibouti has launched exceptional measures to expand and upgrade its port facilities and similar infrastructure to increase cargo capacity. Since 1998, Djibouti has generated more than US$3 million per day from Ethiopia.

Another factor that boosted the Djibouti economy is the revenue generated from the external military presence due to Djibouti's geo-strategic importance. The unprecedented terrorist attack of September 2011 in New York, United States and the Somali piracy on the coast of Somalia led the presence and the permanent shift of the US in the region.

In 2002, the government of Djibouti had approved the establishment of a US military base on its territory. By doing so, Djibouti has managed to acquire US$38 million on an annual basis and additional financial and development assistance. In addition to this, the US invested over US$70 million per year including economic aid. Djibouti's strategic importance to global political and economic security has considerably attracted foreign investment and capital from countries such as China, Spain, Dubai and Japan. During 2004 and 2009, Djibouti has gained a huge amount of inflows. Djibouti's economy has grown significantly due to the political and economic security interest of external powers in particularly the US, China, Japan and France.

Japan assisted over $30 million for its base facilities to the government of Djibouti not including to other assistance. In the same way, China has continuously assisted financial support and took an active part in improving Djibouti's infrastructure, many of the Djibouti's infrastructure projects located in Djibouti are funded by the Chinese government. Currently, both China and India are increasing their presence in Djibouti simply because of security and maritime purposes. This clearly states that foreign powers are competing economically and politically over Djibouti for economic and security reasons. During 2012 and 2013, Djibouti's foreign investment grew. The construction of

Doraleh container terminal and geothermal plants are typical examples. In 2012, the China-Africa development fund approved financial assistance to Djibouti of US$6.4 million.

Djibouti for many years was working to produce geothermal energy to self-dependent on energy and electricity; this project was heavily invested by China at the cost of US$240million, and this project is expected to produce approximately 60MW by the end of 2018. Also, the US has shown commitment to support in this massive project.

China has also funded the port facility at Khor Ambado and lately accepted to construct a new international airport. China's reconstruction of the railway from the capital city of Djibouti to Addis Ababa is the final process of accomplishment. This is clear evidence that both US and China are taking an active part in Djibouti's economic transformation just to secure their permanent presence to achieve their objectives and interests. As a result, the Chinese and the American involvement in Djibouti's economic transformation could be a serious threat to the existence and independence of the glorious Djibouti in pursuing its regional cooperation and their plans to integrate with the neighbouring countries with many aspects.

Also, Djibouti has expanded their trade partnership and flow of revenue from the Middle East. The trade has increased exceptionally following heavy investment has been launched by DPW to plant a container terminal at Doraleh Port, and since then it was under the supervision by the authorities of DPW. Consequently, the Horizon Oil Terminal owned by Emirates National Oil Company was built at Doraleh port in 2004-2005 to meet the fuel import demands in Djibouti, Ethiopia and the French and American garrisons stationed in Djibouti. The port of Doraleh has become the only deep-port port in the region since 2009 with a capacity of holding 15,000 tonnes. This incredible development that is taking in Djibouti illustrates the country's importance on bilateral cooperation plans regardless of geographic proximity to harness economic benefits. These efforts have consolidated the country's infrastructure targeting its geo-strategic location making it a hub of port services to other countries in Africa as well.

The regional cooperation on infrastructure development was another factor that boosted Djibouti's economy. Following the leadership of the current president Guelleh, Djibouti has shown growing interest in regional integration. Especially Djibouti and Ethiopia are committed to integrating and working together on main issues like infrastructure expansion, energy, water and transport. Both nations are increasingly integrating their economies by constructing a powerful cross-border economic zone hoping to appreciate common advantage and grow foreign direct investment. By doing so, they are engaging in to establish economic growth and to reduce the poverty that undermined many citizens from both nations with their respective policies.

As Djibouti is the only sea outlet for Ethiopia, Djibouti has launched new projects to build additional ports to expand their capacity of assisting Ethiopia and neighbouring states to import and export their goods and with the financial assistance by China a new railway has been built to facilitate the shifting of the Ethiopian goods from the port of Djibouti to Addis Ababa.

Djibouti also began to establish trade agreements with other nations that share diplomatic relation with Djibouti such as Kenya and Saudi Arabia to achieve common goals on trade and strengthen the diplomatic relation between them. For the past decade, Djibouti sought to wider their market to link itself to the Great Lakes region countries. But more essentially, the newly independent state 'South Sudan' oil exporter have led the way for stronger cooperation between Djibouti and other countries in the region as Djibouti will become a sea outlet for South Sudan to export oil to other parts of the world. This project was a tripartite agreement between South Sudan, Ethiopia and Djibouti on a logistical corridor port service, the estimated budget for this project will be a sum of US$3 billion oil pipeline crossing through Ethiopia.

As part of Djibouti-Ethiopia trade relation, Ethiopia has exported 50 megawatts to Djibouti on an annual basis since the beginning of 2011. The 50 megawatt covers 60% of their consumers at a lower cost than the diesel-electric supply.

In 2013, both countries (Ethiopia and Djibouti) had agreed upon the supply of additional power connection that will allow importing additional 70MW. The energy interconnection is the least costly option for addressing the energy constraint in both countries. When the energy connection from Ethiopia reached Djibouti, retail and industrial domestic tariffs were cut to ease pressure on businesses and household budgets. This has improved the economic relation between Djibouti and Ethiopia, not to mention reducing the country's trade deficit by lowering oil imports. This clearly signals the commitment for developing the infrastructure cooperation between the two states that could ultimately be a win-win situation for both countries.

Also, the idea of expanding the rail and road, the construction of the new port in Djibouti and the water projects are expected to provide enormous economic benefits to both countries and consolidating their economic ties. The projects include the Ethiopia-Djibouti railway and to boost the capacity of the old port of Djibouti. Recently, Djibouti has spent approximately $9.8 billion to develop its port to facilitate the Ethiopian import and export. Also, Ethiopia signed a bilateral agreement with Djibouti in 2013 to supply almost 103,000 cubic meters of water per day. Also, both states have agreed upon another project which is a gas pipeline project and to cooperate in the mining sector.

During 2011, Djibouti's economy was hit by three negative aspects that weighted on its economic growth. Djibouti continued to maintain a slow economic growth as a result of the global financial crisis, and financial crisis had a negative impact on Djibouti's two main economic drivers which is the port activities and the foreign direct investment.

In 2012 and 2013, port activities and the foreign direct investment has recorded growth linked to the implementation of investment delayed after the beginning of the financial and economic crisis, the development of expanding the terminal container at Doraleh and the exploitation of Djibouti's geothermal resources. In February 2012, the government of Djibouti had signed a historic trilateral agreement with South Soudan and Ethiopia. The agreement is based on infrastructure development for telecommunication, railways and oil transport in the three countries, to connect South Sudan along Ethiopia to Djibouti, which has access to the sea. This will enhance Djibouti's economy by bringing new investment opportunities to improve the infrastructure and to increase business enterprise to reduce unemployment.

Despite the economic hardship that has encountered during the past few years, the government has fully ensured to meet the conditions set by the

International Monetary Fund Extended Credit Facility. The Djiboutian authorities are continuing their efforts to develop the country with the goal of making Djibouti a regional hub for trade, logistical and financial services. The entry into service of the electric power supply interconnection between Djibouti and neighbouring Ethiopia represents a significant development for Djibouti that could lead to greater development in the business environment as a result of the convenient energy and huge reduction in Djibouti's balance of trade deficit resulting from oil imports.

The tertiary sector continues to dominate Djibouti's economy through port activities and relevant logistic services, the financial and telecommunication sector. This sector has experienced a significant growth for the past decade. However, the government finds extremely challenging to tackle poverty and improve the living standard.

The country's economy was forecasted to remain stable in 2011 at 3.5%, during this year Djibouti has extremely suffered from three factors that affected the economy poorly. First, the state of the economy has continued to struggle and failed to maintain a steady pace in the growth as a result of the global financial crises. Secondly, the harsh drought in the east of Africa during 2011 was the worse in 60 years, the country by worsening already structural food insecurity. The third factor is the presidential election in April 2011 that led to a period of wait-and-see in the private sector that reduced the performance of the economy. As predicted, the economic growth rate was set to improve in 2012 and 2013 through the port activities and the restoration of foreign direct investment.

The service sector represents approximately 77% of the country's GDP in 2011. The port activities are the main drivers of the service sector; it primarily concentrates on the transit business with Ethiopia due to the marginalisation of transhipment business in 2010. The capacity level of business with Ethiopia 2011 remained slow due to the effects that the financial crises have left. The financial and telecommunication service are playing a predominant role within the tertiary sector although they are not yet on a sufficient scale to compensate for the fall in port activities and its logistics services and the drop in FDI.

The secondary sector growth in Djibouti is around 19.5% of the Gross Domestic Product and has continued to decline for the past decade as a result of the pressure imposed by the availability and the costs of manufacturing in Djibouti. Besides the two government agencies for electricity and water, there are several companies that come under this sector mainly focused in the agri-food sector, producing mineral water, together with building and public works companies. During the past several years, the secondary sector has experience development due to the electricity supply connection between the two neighbouring states Djibouti and Ethiopia. The electricity network connection has helped Djibouti to reduce its energy pressure because of low-cost imports of hydroelectric from Ethiopia. The energy cost to ordinary households was reduced by 30% in 2012. Imposing low-cost in energy across the private sector could encourage economic and social development.

The primary sector in Djibouti has remained totally insignificant and contributed approximately 3.5% of GDP, the main causes of the inefficiency in this sector is because of the dry climate conditions, low availability of water, the lack of development in fishery activities and poor irrigation management. The food insecurity was deteriorated in 2011 by the severe drought across the region that eventually affected Djibouti. The most affected regions of the food insecurity were the north-west near Ethiopia and the south-east near Somalia along with urban areas. The nomadic populations of these areas, whose livestock provides their only source of revenue through the sale of animals and milk, were badly hit. People living in urban areas faced food price rises.

The number of people that has been affected the food insecurity crises has been estimated around 120 000, which is 15% of the population. The United Nation has played a significant role by launching an appeal for US$30 million to provide an immediate food aid to the 120 000 vulnerable people. However, Djibouti has managed to maintain a long-term policy to reduce food dependence from outside countries, by contracting farms in Ethiopia and Sudan. Supplies from these farms have allowed the government to limit the impact by drawing on farms in Ethiopia and Sudan. Supplies from these farms enabled the authorities to limit the impact of the shortage on food prices in the country.

On the demand side, the growing investment has continued to support Djibouti's economic growth; the growth rate in 2011 was almost 24% of the national GDP, coming in a practically equal measure from the public and the private sectors. Djibouti's balance of trade remains in deficit. Future development of the country needs the transformation of the country into a trade and logistics hub and financial services

The authorities are working on the exploitation of the country's geothermal energy to completely lift energy constraints. The country has significant opportunities to expand its port activities with the recently independent South Sudan a big potential new market. The country is also targeting trade with the landlocked countries in the Great Lakes Region. The risks that could jeopardise the country's development opportunities are related to competition from other ports in the region, notably Salalah in Oman and Aden in Yemen, to the continuing slowdown in Foreign Direct Investment, mainly from Dubai, and to adverse fluctuations in Ethiopian trade.

The government's initiative on accelerating the economy began in 2012; the economic growth rose from 4.5% to 5.5%, the two main factors that have driven this significant growth is the foreign direct investment and port activity. The foreign direct investment was $277 million, topping the figures between 2006 and 2008 during the construction of the Doraleh container port, and estimated around 18.6% of the GDP. The government are expecting this trend to continue over the several years to come and create enormous investment programme to improve the economy, infrastructure and other areas.

The programme begins a new chapter for Djibouti since the leaders are intending to make Djibouti into a regional hub for trade and leading financial hub. Significant investment is scheduled to strengthen the country's comparative advantage in goods trading. The Djiboutian government has launched an agenda in reducing the structural difficulties to adequate electricity and water supply that created obstacles for the growth of the private sector.

A budget of US$ 6 billion was adopted for the transformation of the infrastructure such as the construction of new ports, railways and roads, an aqueduct and desalination plant and housing that is heavily funded by the

Chinese investors and the aid from the international community. The programme's success depends on close monitoring of the government's budget and the national debt.

The budget deficits for the past years were around 2% of the GDP although projections of a balanced budget or even a surplus. Djibouti has a greater risk of over debt, and the infrastructure projects will increase the government's plan on spending as well as debt, through agreed guarantees. Djibouti has long been suffering from growing unemployment, and significant poverty has undermined the living conditions and heightened social tensions since 2011. The proclaimed victory of the ruling coalition in 2013 legislative election actively challenged by the opposition parties, who won their first ever seats but eventually refused to attend parliamentary sessions and called for protest and demonstrations against the massive fraud in the election results.

Djibouti since 2009 has witnessed huge developments and prospects in the economy in effect the huge infrastructural investment programme is a great chance for Djibouti as it aims to take advantages of its geostrategic location in the Horn of Africa and lower any structural difficulties to sufficient energy and water supplies.

Djibouti is situated at the heart of major sea path for trading oil and other goods. Therefore the regime is significantly increasing their trade profile respective to neighbouring states and also make the country a convenient regional trade hub and financial services. The investment programme will be used to expand the capacity of the electricity and water supplies enable economic transformation. As reported by the government, nearly 30% of the $6 billion programme started in 2012 was funded by the Chinese investors and the international aid community. Between 2013 and 2014, the investment programme aims to build the Port of Tadjourah to make the northern area of the country to make Djibouti the centre of the regional traffic and the connection with countries of COMESA.

The economic spillover from the development and implementation of these projects will ensure economic growth over the next several years, which ought to achieve new record rates of 6% in 2014 and 6.5% in 2015. The service sector remained the driver of the economy in 2013, primarily through transport, particularly port action, and employs most of the workforce. Other sub-sectors within the service sector e.g. commerce, communication and banking have expanded significantly. The secondary sector was around 19% of the GDP, mostly non-manufacturing industries were 15% of the GDP, constructions 12% and electricity and water 3% of the GDP. The manufacturing is remaining undeveloped due to the high cost of factors of production e.g. water, electricity and labour. The primary sector has been undermined due to the dry climate and lack of arable land.

The achievement of the current investment programme relies on the audit of public finance and the national debt. The projects for the infrastructure will increase the government's spending significantly and could eventually lead to fiscal indiscipline. The excessive borrowings by the government to invest in the new railway of Djibouti-Addis Ababa raised the public debt in 2012. The Djiboutian government have negotiated with the International Money Fund for additional loan agreement to restore the management of public finances and debt, and this loan agreement was signed in 2014.

Also the Djiboutian government were on the brink of finalising their long-term development strategy, to give formal preparation tool for political and economic development that is based on stability and national unity, good governance and regional integration to fulfil its desired to be a regional hub for trade and financial services. It will serve as the basis for five-year development strategies and aims to triple per capita income by 2035.

The government has adopted several key macroeconomic policies to strength the economy, during the past several years, the public finances have shown an estimated overall deficit in 2013 of 3.1% of GDP, but this improvement came from the tax collection. The government is intending to proceed of privatising the port of Djibouti which demonstrate a long-term surplus of 1.2% and reflecting greater tax revenue in the course of the year. The tax collection could be improved by reinforcing the VAT that was introduced by the lawmakers in 2009 which is to apply set penalties, improving the exemption system and increasing the number of collectors.

The privatisation of the port of Djibouti has raised approximately US$185 million, 40% of this sum funded in the railway construction between Djibouti-

Addis Ababa, and the remaining was partly used to clear national debt and restore the government's central bank deposits. In 2013, the International Monetary Fund urged full disclosure of the use of this money and pushed talks with the government on how to increase domestic funding especially by lowering hidden oil product subsidies, reforming tax and taking into account the likely of privatising sectors dominated by state monopolies. The main purpose of reducing invisible oil product subsidies is to limit the loss of the government revenue to lessen the impact of inflation and ensure a decent living standard for the middle and working class. The talks between the International Monetary Fund and the government of Djibouti likewise include privatising government telecommunication services and even sell another licence to a private operator to raise money to invest in public services. The discussions have not yet produced specific reform proposals.

Monetary policy

Since 1973, Djibouti has witnessed a stable exchange policy with fixed and floating exchange rate regime. No change in the exchange rate was expected in the short and medium term. The government has secured parity in 2013 through maintaining a coverage rate in foreign exchange of almost 105% of the money in circulation. The regime didn't allow the implementation and the adaptation of the monetary or exchange policies by the government, despite the government intending to introduce a bank reserve requirement under the IMF programme as a way to manage the liquidity. However, nothing much has been done, and reserve ratios haven't been set.

Although the presence of limitations, the currency board regime has given monetary stability and the chance of converting the currency of Djibouti DJF into all other currencies will boost the country to become a regional financial centre. Over the past few years, there was a significant reduction in the inflation despite the high price of food and oil prices. The annual adjusted inflation was 2.5% in 2013; the inflation was higher in the previous year's 3.7% in 2012 and 5.1% in 2011. This significant reduction of the inflation came from the reduced oil import and the agricultural imports from Djiboutian farms in Ethiopian and Sudan at a fixed price.

The new electricity supply to neighbouring Ethiopia will give low-cost imports of electricity and allow Djibouti to lower import of oil required to produce it domestically. There was a huge increase in the foreign exchange service in 2013 as a result of part-privatisation of the PDSA and rose to US$365 million From USD 234 million at the end of 2012, the equivalent of 4.9 months of goods and services imports.

Since independence, Djibouti always had a substantial dual economy, with an absolute modern segment that operates on the back of leasing military bases to foreign powers and the port activities. The presences of the foreign garrisons in Djibouti have increased significantly the domestic demand for consumer goods and real estates, and this drove the cost of living in Djibouti. As a result of the high cost of living, the salaries of government employees have risen relatively to keep up bills with wages in comparison to labour productivity. This has destroyed Djibouti's competitiveness, which persists to deter the establishment of the industrial process.

For the past several years, the employment has declined as a result of economic failure and the lack of invest in the job market. Currently, the unemployment is at 60%. Government's weak performance on creating employment reflects on Djibouti's growth model, which is hugely capital intensive.

The service sector in Djibouti plays a crucial role in boosting the national economy. Thanks to Djibouti's strategic position in the Red Sea and Bab Al Mandeb, the government has built the economy on port activities, while increasing its role as transit and regional port to serve the entire region and beyond the region. During 2011, the service has contributed almost three-quarters of the GDP, and 2.6% from manufacturing industries and 3.7% by agriculture; 14% from construction and public works.

Considering the regulations of the International Monetary Fund, Djibouti maintains an exchange regime without limitations on payments and transfers in that matter of international transactions. Since 1974 Four years before independents, Djibouti has used a currency board regime in which the country's currency is pegged to US dollars at a fixed parity of 177,722 Djibouti francs per dollar. Following the report of Djibouti's trade policy, the dynamics of Djibouti's GDP growth have kept on relying on port activities, driven by the increase in foreign direct investment. The huge inflow of investment from the Gulf States has helped Djibouti to boost significantly the economic growth of the service sector.

From 2008 to 2010, the port of Djibouti has declined following the financial crisis that created a chaos in the global economy and the slowdown in the Ethiopian economy. The strength of the foreign direct investment also faltered owing to the deferral of investments that had been expected.

For this reason, the GDP growth rate declined from 5.5% in 2009 to 4.5% in 2010 and 2011. However, since 2012, economic activities have regained pressure, and GDP growth headed upwards. Inward Foreign Direct Investment has also intensified in areas other than ports. Apart from the boom in public works and port activities, Djibouti's recent economic growth performance has also been boosted by interconnection with the Ethiopian electricity grid. This has resulted in lower rates for consumers and reduced the country's dependence on fuel imports for power generation.

Inflation was a greater concern for the government due to significant rise in food and oil price. As a result, the trade relation with neighbouring Ethiopia has helped Djibouti restraint the rise of the price by reducing imports of petroleum products. Also, the effects of higher food prices have been eased by price subsidies on consumer goods. The rate of inflation was under 5% during the review period, except when the intensive drought rose in 2008 and the surge in world food prices combined to raise it to 12%.

The price in Djibouti reflects the foreign exchange based on the currency board deal in which the Djibouti currency FDJ, is pegged to US dollar at a fixed parity. The Djiboutian currency circulation was supported by foreign assets to the extent of 300% during 2013; this ratio has subsequently stabilised at over 250% as a monthly average. The finance ministry has introduced a policy to handle liquidity in the economy. Djibouti's budget is mainly aimed at increasing the base of public income. The government spending peaked at 5.7% of GDP in 2009 fuelled by a weak revenue collection and significant exemptions, specifically for the military bases.

This has been mostly financed by collecting domestic payment arrears. In 2010 the government of Djibouti had taken initiatives to fix budgetary discipline as part of a financing program with the IMF that made it conceivable to lessen the deficit. The periods in which income reduce have been offset by controlling current expenditure and the reduction in investment expenses. Djibouti remained indebted during the review period from 64% of GDP in 2007, the public debt and GDP ratio has been stabilised 54%. Nevertheless, Djibouti risks of becoming over-indebted, considering the global economic, the external debt consists essentially of multilateral borrowing and the share of this is clearly rising.

The authorities have indicated that 66% of the debt was owed to multilateral lenders in 2013, while the Paris Club, Kuwait and Saudi Arabia share the bilateral debt. In 2008, an agreement to reschedule the bilateral debt was reached with the country's Paris Club creditors. The authorities have cited challenges posed by the high-interest rates applicable to Djibouti following its classification as a middle-income country. The current account deficit, which had grown to 22.9% of GDP during the 2008 crisis, has since narrowed thanks to a reduction in the country's reliance on oil imports. Nonetheless, the surge in international prices in 2011, which raised those of the main imported food products while total exports remained at a low level, widened the current deficit to 13.9% of GDP in that year. The country's large trade balance deficit has not been offset by the positive balance in services, transfers and factor income. Nonetheless, gross external assets covered between three and six months of imports during the review period.

The economic co-operation, regional integration and trade of Djibouti

The foreign trade is one of the factors that drove the economy of Djibouti to economic growth and has mainly focused for the past several years on the Ethiopian import and export. Djibouti has significantly increased the development in infrastructure and port activities due to its geo-strategic location in the Gulf of Aden, at the turning point of key maritime trade path. Other than the Ethiopian export goods in Djibouti, Djibouti itself exports few products, primarily livestock to neighbouring Somalia and the Khaleej countries. Also, large imports of goods to supply the domestic market will give Djibouti a very skewed trade balance with a large deficit.

Djibouti is a member of several regional economic organisation but however remains to serve neighbouring Ethiopia for its import and export and maintains few ties with the rest of the African countries. South Sudan are increasingly seen as the new economic partner of Djibouti which could boost the position of Djibouti as a regional hub. Djibouti has its membership in World Trade Organisation in 1995. Djibouti reduced its domestic consumption tax and introduced VAT in January 2009 in anticipation of member-states of the Common Market for Eastern and Southern Africa (COMESA) adopting a common external tariff in 2015.

Port of Djibouti

The strategic country positioned in the East of Africa is at the entrance to the Red Sea, one of the world's shipping lanes. The port of Djibouti has a free-trade zone and serves its primary client Ethiopia for its import and export, the service sector affiliated with the port of Djibouti worth approximately 80% of Djibouti's economy in 2012. Since 1998, the port handled 100% of Ethiopia's maritime traffic, which moves to and from Addis Ababa by truck and rail. The Ethiopian import and export account for 70% of traffic through the port. The reconstruction of the railway between Djibouti and Addis Ababa will increase Djibouti's role in serving the landlocked Ethiopia.

Since the development of the Port of Djibouti and the construction of Doraleh container terminal, there is a real opportunity that Djibouti to be a regional shipping hub for East and Southern Africa, the port of Djibouti is ideally located to serve the COMESA market, linking 19 countries and 380 million people.

A large section of the port of Djibouti is the transhipment point and receives huge container ships and relocates the goods to small ships to deliver it on the smaller port, especially along the coat of East Africa, and merging containerised goods from these small ports for forward shipment. The port of Djibouti has managed to function at a full capacity for a long period of time. The country's strategic location at the entrance to the Red Sea has allowed the port authorities to designate a clear roadmap to turn the port into a regional shipping hub for the Red Sea and the Indian Ocean and to maintain the capacity of reaching Europe, Africa and Asia. The term containerisation was the characterising idea driving period of development and Djibouti's first modern container terminal began operations in February 1985. Almost 70% of the port activity compose of import and export from Ethiopia, which depends on Djibouti's maritime outlet. The port of Djibouti is also an international transhipment hub and refuelling centre.

In 2012, the government of Djibouti in partnership with DP World began the construction on the Doraleh Container Terminal, which makes it a major seaport facility to develop the national transit capacity; the budget of this project was $396 million. The port container can host 1.5 million container units per year.

DP World is the leading company of maritime terminals; it operates almost 60 terminals across the globe. In 2007, DP World Djibouti, a subsidiary of Dubai-based has entered build operate transfer concession accord with the Djiboutian government to develop and maintain the new container terminal at Doraleh. DP world has begun to operate in Djibouti at the old port since 2000 and therefore has comprehensive experience of the challenges of operating in the country.

The main purpose of developing the new terminal at Doraleh was based on market and technical analysis that highlighted the demand for container services, in particularly for transhipment and the suitability of the site for deep water. The first development involved the construction of a 1,050-meter long quay with a water depth of 18 metres alongside. This construction will allow the port to maintain the capacity to host two giant container ships of up to 12,500 twenty-foot equivalent unit (TEU) at one time or three smaller container ships of 8,000 TEU. Likewise, the development plan involves reclamation of an island next to the new quay to provide 41 hectares for container storage.

The cost of this project was predicted at US$396 million. The Islamic development bank has participated in financing the project. In October 2007, the Islamic development bank invested almost US$65 million, while a consortium of other international investors gave the balance of the debt finance. The investors considered the risks of the port project without recourse to the government of Djibouti, due to the strategic importance of the port. The construction of the new port began in December 2006 and was completed in

2009, five months after the completion date. The final investment was under budget as a result of the effectiveness of information technology systems.

The new port has created many advantages for the people of Djibouti. The construction work generated employment for 500 local workers, and the new port has employed about 600 people full-time and over 200 part-time. The company is also providing internships for 12–18 graduates each year, allowing them to gain experience in port operations. About 50 staff from the Doraleh Container Terminal has received training at other DP World ports in Algeria, Brazil, Mozambique and Senegal. The port has generated much more employment in support sectors, including engineering, warehousing, information technology and services and contributing to the wider development of the local economy. Among its social contributions, Doraleh container terminal has also provided buses for the local community and contributed to the construction of clinics and schools in cooperation with DP World

Doraleh container terminal has brought many advantages for Djibouti in terms of creating employment opportunity for the Djiboutians, support exports, imports and transhipment to neighbouring countries. The old port of Djibouti had the capacity of hosting 400,000 twenty-foot equivalent unit on an annual basis, which was extremely sufficient enough to meet the demands of traffic to and from Ethiopia and Djibouti's domestic needs. The new port of Doraleh has the capacity of handling approximately 1,000,000 TEU's and can also accommodate the most recent container ships, opening up new opportunities. Not only will it be able to meet Ethiopia's expanding needs for the foreseeable future, it now has the capacity and capability to become a regional transhipment hub serving eastern and southern Africa – a gateway for goods coming into the region and for trade from the region to North Africa, Europe and the Americas.

This will help reduce shipping costs to and from the region, reducing local consumer costs and boosting the region's competitiveness on international markets. In 2012, the new container terminal handled over 743,000 TEUs, up from the 360,000 dealt with by the old port in 2008. The number of container ships using the port is increasing steadily, averaging close to 60 vessels per month, and berth occupancy is approaching 40%.

The political scene of Djibouti

Guelleh has long been in command of the Republic of Djibouti since 1999 after he was in favour by his uncle the former president Gouled, to succeed him after 22 years in power. Guelleh after his arrival in the presidency, he quickly appointed key ministerial departments to members of his Mamasan clan positioned himself strategically to oversee political operations. Under the leadership of Guelleh, Djibouti has witnessed an extreme economic growth that led to the social development and created an enormous amount of employment to get of the poverty. Despite the establishment of economic development in Djibouti, the unemployment and the gap between rich and the poor is very high.

Djibouti has benefited from its geostrategic positioning on the east of Africa and plays a predominant part to tackle the counterproductive issues that the region is facing by hosting several foreign garrisons. The foreign military presence has contributed significantly to Djibouti's economy and worked with the government on improving key areas like education, health and infrastructure. The government of Djibouti is hoping to increase their capacity of turning Djibouti into a commercial hub to serve the entire region for shipping route. Djibouti is already generating a huge amount of revenues from its port and is looking to become a key East African hub.

The government's ambition has slightly declined over the years due to various international companies abandoning the country as a result of the appalling record of the human right in Djibouti. For instance, many multinational such as Total, Mobil and Shell have all rejected their oil interest in Djibouti in recent years as well as other multinationals. However, a lot of Chinese companies have increased their presence in Djibouti to fulfil their interest and reach beyond their horizon. There are approximately 14 infrastructure projects that are undergoing currently in Djibouti mostly financed by the Chinese fund.

However, despite the significant efforts to boost the economy, not every problem is solved, and the economic boom under the watch of Guelleh has been led by the humanitarian bust. Although Djibouti's GDP has increased considerably over the past decade and is still expected to grow at more than 5% annually going forwards, established corruption and misuse of public funds by officials have prevented the average Djiboutian from seeing the better living standard.

In recent years a report conducted by the UN has labelled Djibouti as shadow state; as a result of less than half of the population have the privilege to access to electricity, hunger has spread widely, the number of malnourished children in Djibouti has grown significantly since 2006; meanwhile, access to improved hygiene facilities slightly shrunk from 61.5% to 61.3% between 2005 and 2011.

In Djibouti, being able to express your political views has become an act of crime as the current leader has tried to maintain his grip on power. Guelleh's regime has been accused by the international community of abusing the human right, enforcing excessive force against opposition leaders, carrying out the illegal, arbitrary arrest and mistreating the right of the opposition. A typical example of the regime's conduct in breach of the human right is the excessive force against Maydaneh Abdallah Okieh, a British-Djiboutian citizen who is an independent journalist and editor, who has been jailed three times consecutive in the last 2 years, including a six-month imprisonment for posting photos on Facebook that showed police breaking up a protest.

Guelleh went beyond his limit to extend his terms in office. It took a controversial constitutional modification to allow Guelleh to seek not only the third term in 2011 but to remain him in power until his last breath. In 2011 presidential election, Guelleh won the election in a landslide following the opposition boycott in the presidential race. In that same year, almost 70,000 people have gathered together to express their anger and to demand the departure of the President Guelleh in the wake of the Arab Spring that ousted many ruthless dictators. The police quickly responded to demonstrators with excessive force to disperse protestors, this has resulted the death of five civilians and two police officers, dozens were wounded and the arrests of hundreds of people. In 2011 following the clear majority win of the president, he clearly emphasised that he wouldn't seek a fourth term in 2016 elections.

The government of Djibouti has established a framework agreement with the opposition party coalition, the Union of National Salvation (USN) to put to an end the long disputed political crisis after the legislative election result of 2013.

The framework agreement was signed by both parties in December 2014 to ease the tension and establish a peaceful political transition. The agreed document outlined a roadmap to the 2016 elections and included an amnesty for opposition members, a rapid reform of the Electoral Commission, and an immediate halt to all acts that could lead to tense situations between public authorities and opposition activists. Unfortunately, the framework agreement was never finalised, and the situation went of hands since then. In 21st December 2015, mass killings erupted in Djibouti following a clash between an ethnic clan and the security forces as the ethnic clan held gathering to commemorate the birth of the prophet Mohammed.

The community leaders had agreed with the authorities to gather at a designated site. However, hundreds of people subsequently assembled at an unauthorised site. When fifty police officers arrived to move the worshippers peacefully to the agreed location, clashes erupted, and gunshots were fired from the crowd. It was later discovered that a small number of people at the gathering were armed with Kalashnikov rifles, machetes and knives. As the police officers did not expect armed violence, they called for additional police and army forces. In all, fifty policemen were injured.

This resulted in the death of almost twenty people, 39 people severely wounded. The government accused the opposition coalition the Union of National Salvation of perpetrating these unlawful killings and later launched an attack during a meeting of the opposition, where the security forces opened gun shots to opposition members that resulted the severe injuries of the former minister of religious affairs Dr. Hamud Abdi Sultan, Ahmed Youssouf the leader of the opposition coalition and the youngest MP in the House of Representative Said Houssein Robleh, likewise the kidnap of the secretary-general of the Union of National Salvation (Abdourahman Mohamed Guelleh) a former Mayor of the capital city of Djibouti.

In the presidential election of 2016 in Djibouti, Guelleh will use his country's strategic position as a potential concession to build international support to grip on power. Guelleh offered China to establish a permanent military presence as a backup plan to use their support, in case the western powers disapprove his intentions of seeking a fourth term. Djibouti can still rely on Beijing's financial and political support.

In Djibouti, there is a little hope of political transition, the possibility of an uprising and strong resistance against the longstanding President Guelleh in the election of April 2016 is growing significantly. After all, barring a point-for-point implementation of the December accord, the opposition figures couldn't hope to break through in the elections and bring about Djibouti's first democratic transition in 40 years. Also, with the rumours escalating that Eritrea is financing the fight in the north of Djibouti and the post-election violence could turn the situation out of control.

The implementation of the accord could ease the situation, prevent further escalation of chaos in Djibouti and could establish the stable governance to fulfil the country's desire in becoming Africa's Dubai, but only if they measure the comparison in terms of a dismal human rights record and lack of democratic credentials.

Boreh's process

First time in the history of Africa, an African president has been requested by a judge to attend in person before the British high court to provide evidence. The long-standing President Guelleh in the tiny strategic state in the Horn of Africa has been asked of him to travel to London to testify a case corruption trial involving the Djibouti millionaire Abdourahman Boreh, a former ally of the president.

Boreh, a long-term ally of the president Guelleh, was accused by the Djiboutian government of committing an act of terrorisms; as a result his worldwide assets were frozen and was sentenced to 15 years in prison in 2009 by a Djiboutian court during his absence in exile to London. However, that decision, made in absentia, was later overturned after the British court considered the trial politically motivated.

The court hearing is the final stage in the ongoing legal battle between the president and his former ally, Abdourahman Boreh, which the Djibouti authority has accused of corruption and terrorism in the UK court. The adjustment rights to the once ailing Doraleh container terminal, which is the biggest on the continent of Africa. As former chairman of Djibouti Ports and Free Zone Authority, Boreh has helped revive the terminal. However, the government is now trying to wipe his legacy and discredit him through foreign courts.

There is rumour that lawyers representing the Djiboutian government have been forced to admit that all evidence against the defendant is indeed false. The law firm Gibson Dunn & Crutcher has apologised to the court after it was published phone script supposedly associating Boreh in the terrorist attack in March 2009 in Djibouti city were falsely dated, casting severe ambiguity on his role in the attack.

This evidence had convinced Justice Flaux to order the freezing asset of Mr Boreh of $100m in September 2013; this order has been partially reversed by Justice Flaux at the court hearing, claiming that the lawyers had intentionally misled the court. The justice Flaux has also accused the government of providing false information. According to Abdourahman boreh, "the prosecutor chose not to bring the incorrect dates to the court's attention and the false conviction has been used to further the Djiboutian government's objective to destroy me internationally."

Accusations of corruption and misuse of public funds have been persistent since Guelleh took office in 1999, but his leadership has endured for almost 16 years. Guelleh and his sub-clan Mamasan has led the country since independence from France in 1977. Despite the current weakness of Guelleh-Boreh friendship, implanted in historical family connection, has not been so resentful. Abdourahman Boreh, a successful businessman, supported President Guelleh in his second constitutional mandate as president in 2005. The relationship between both men was dissolved in 2008 after Boreh has revealed his intention of running for the presidency in 2011 and criticised heavily the president of amending the constitution to remain in power for life. Since 2008, Boreh has been living in exile in London.

A second round is set to start following the decision of Justice Flaux ordering Guelleh to give personal evidence in court and to clarify the situation that the case against boreh is based almost entirely on oral evidence. President Guelleh 16 years into his leadership, the president is facing unprecedented pressure from Justice Flaux to attend the hearing court, and this could ultimately destroy his legacy as president of one of the most important and strategic nations on earth. While the legal combat between the two opponents seems to heat up in the upcoming months, the exceptional London case isn't the only international pressure that Djiboutian strongmen is dealing with. Guelleh for many years had the flexibility that he desired from the western powers and will require the deftest of political touches for him to remain on his path.

The dispute arose when Boreh opposed against the president for modifying the constitution for his personal interest; he was accused of abusing his position as the chairman of Djibouti Ports and Free Zone Authority to steal money from the government. Boreh is being pursued by the government for almost $150 million. Boreh has rejected the accusations and claimed that all charges against him were politically motivated and that the Djiboutian government spent tens of millions of dollars to launch a personal attack against him in the eyes of the world.

Since the last two decades, conflicts has occurred in the African continent over the extension of the presidential terms. However, domestic tolerance for such plan appears to be diminished. The president of Democratic Republic of Congo Joseph Kabila has attempted to similar modify the constitution to extend his terms, but this dream was relinquished by protestors. In October 2014, the longstanding dictator Blaise Compaore was ousted by force after a similar attempt to amend the constitution. In a global context, the Republic of Djibouti is considered as a semi-autocratic system. The country has been ranked by the international community 107 out of 174 on transparencies.

Djibouti 2035

An image of a more successful future, more attractive and more desirable

To establish the basis for a controlled development, the Government is committed to developing a long-term vision on the horizon of 2035 called. The development of the Vision comes in the wake of the Economic Orientation that helped guide the Strategic Framework for Growth and the Fight against Poverty, and the national initiative for social development. This aims to provide the country with an instrument of development planning on the horizon of a generation, which now enrols in strategic planning and sustainable development policies and strategies.

The vision of 2025 was developed on a participatory approach and mostly reflects a national consensus. Indeed, it is based on an articulation between the aspirations of the people, past trends, major issues and challenges, and the desired scenario for long-term development. It, therefore, reflects on the set of goals to be achieved and is, therefore, an image destination. In this regard, the vision must be understood as a coherent picture of the destination towards which efforts must converge, a realistic and credible image of the future of Djibouti and a picture of a more successful future, more attractive and desirable than ever before.

Djibouti 2035 is a structural road map to convert Djibouti into a powerful economic nation that will ensure an effective prosperity that will increase dramatically the living standard of Djibouti citizens and that will establish a strong economic environment that will strength the competitiveness in the market. The vision should be ambitious so that it remains challenging to mobilise the skills, energy and resources for its implementation.

The population in Djibouti is very young; indeed, 35% of the population are under 15 years. Particular attention is required to prepare this segment of the population for the future. As this population is unevenly distributed throughout the territory, an imbalance between Djibouti City and other regions and are likely to increase.

The Government has undertaken major reforms in the political, economic and social fields. Sectoral studies were carried out and action plans were adopted. Some of these plans are being implemented including reducing poverty. Djibouti with the support of development partners is making progress in achieving the international commitments, including the implementation of the strategy for Objectives Millennium Development and the rules of the Common Market for East Africa and Southern Africa.

This has led some momentum, thereby promoting the achievement of positive results, but still below expectations. Thus, Djibouti needs a higher and sustainable growth, which requires a sustained effort to solve the problems and create a structural transformation of the economy to make it more diversified and competitive with a greater role for the private sector. These transformations and associated objectives can not be realised in a long-term horizon, for about 25 years, integrated as part of a coherent and comprehensive strategy. The vision of Djibouti 2035 is not limited to economic and financial aspects, but it also covers social aspects, cultural, political and governance. The proposed vision was formulated as a response to the identified challenges, aspirations and needs of the population. It takes account of the driving forces of Djibouti system, opportunities and seeds of change.

It turns out that weaknesses can be overcome and that it is possible to move from the current state to the desired future. But this transition will not happen spontaneously because the vision is not located in a logical trend. Djibouti must indeed evolve from an economy in recovery or stabilisation in an emerging country, having joined the ranks of middle-income countries.

Levers of shares must be mobilised to break with the past and realise high advanced. For this, the vision assumes that all the energies of creativity and innovation be released and what a transformation in the social composition, distribution of power and wealth, in the system of dominant values and the level of science and technology.

After Djibouti's accession to national sovereignty June 27, 1977, the country experienced three distinct politically Periods. The sovereignty was acquired after long years of struggle for self-determination. The first period 1977-1989 can be characterised as Construction of the National institutional establishment of an Independent State and will be fundamental in the coming years in terms of representativeness of various trends of political and community opinions and exercise of power.

The day after the attainment of independence, the political system that came into effect was that of a single party, with the first President Hassan Gouled aptidon. The exercise of choice of the President by the people has put in place until 1981 with the organisation of the first parliamentary elections and presidential elections. The political system established following the principle of separation of powers: legislative, executive and judicial. Over this period, political stability was ensured with a relative continuity of management of state power by the same political party and the President elected in the wake of Independence.

The second period 1990-1999 was characterised by a continuation of the political system of governance at the top of the state. But history will remember a political opening due to two major factors; the armed conflict of 1991 and the wind of democracy breathed by the speech of La Baule on the introduction of Democracy in Africa.

Obviously, these events reconfigure the political landscape to prepare a stable political future, and adequate economic development. Indeed, two constitutional laws established by the Constituent Assembly in force since Independence in the country have been replaced by a new constitution adopted by referendum and promulgated on September 4, 1992. This represents an important step taken by Djibouti in its progress towards a pluralist democracy by, including an end to one-party rule in a continental context dominated by the call of the Baule and the opening for democratic reform. The new constitution provides for a multiparty limited to four parties for a transitional period of ten years. The organic electoral law 01 / AN / 92 of 29 October 1992 has realised multi-party elections and the limited multiparty four parties for ten years.

The third period 2000-2010, described a period of democratic governance and the political opening is marked on the political map, the first alternation at the top of the state after twenty-two reign of the First President of the country. After this transitional period of ten years, limited to four political parties, the integral multiparty system was introduced in 2002 by constitutional provisions. Successively, several elections were held; the January 2003 legislative which was held under the multiparty system, the 2005 presidential and local elections in 2006 that truly launched the decentralisation process.

This new political landscape will be enhanced by the creation of a new governing body of the electoral process, namely the National Independent Electoral Commission (CENI); strengthening the role of the mediator; consolidation of the rule of law with the abolition of the death penalty; strengthening individual and collective freedom as the foundation of a modern and advanced democracy, etc.

During the period 1977-1989, the economy experienced a hit evolution, marked by a succession of political crises and economic shocks leading to a continuous deterioration the competitiveness of the country, its financial situation and its economic infrastructure and social. Repetitive wars in the sub-region since the mid-70s and the conflict Inside the late 80s have resulted in the devastation of affected areas wars, the destabilisation of the state, disruption of economic networks in rural areas and the influx of refugees into under-equipped and cities unprepared to receive them. The excessive aridity climate leads to a very irregular rainfall, by limited water. Recurrent droughts have reduced rural resources and weakened the nomadic lifestyle, causing a massive rural exodus.

The combination of these exogenous shocks and weak economic growth explain the rapid development of urban pauperization some vulnerable populations are the most victims visible. Between 1990 and 1999, the start of the committed economic development has been hampered by two essential contingency, namely the internal conflict and the structural adjustment program ensued. The Djiboutian authorities have been working to restore macroeconomic balances. Indeed, the armed internal conflict in 1991 has negatively affected the functioning of the administration and the economy national, and spawned the mobilisation of resources for reconstruction and demobilising involved in the conflict. It took also curb the negative effects of conflicts in the region, especially in Somalia and Ethiopia.

All these factors have had a negative impact on all socio-economic sectors of the country, resulting in the increased impoverishment of the population, the loss of bases social and cultural destruction of several socio-economic infrastructures as well the weakening of the administration and the country's system of governance. Financial resource and important techniques have been granted by development partners but were only allowed to respond only enormous humanitarian needs to the detriment investment.

Economic growth remained at a relatively low level 2.2% annually and failed to reduce social deficits during this decade. The financial balance is not favourable, Djibouti has implemented with the support of IMF and the World Bank, the economic and institutional reform program whose objective is to reduce the budget deficit or balance the budget and reduce the debt. This will go through additional efforts at the level of the allowance Sectoral budget. The competitiveness is low, and the investment climate suffers from many weaknesses that including the availability of infrastructure, the cost and quality of production factors. The period 2000-2010 was characterised by a recovery in economic activity with the acceleration of growth (4.8% annually), due to a major effort of public investment, a massive influx of foreign direct investments (FDI) and development of the domestic private sector.

The growing sectors are transport, telecommunications and buildings and public works. The financial sector has not been left out, as it rose sharply in a decade. Indeed, the number of banks and financial institutions in Djibouti has tremendously increased from two in the early 2000s to twelve at the end of 2010. And this momentum, credit the economy and the money supply are in a continuous expansionary dynamics. Indeed, the relatively low level in early 1990, credit to the economy stood at a level of 34.5% of GDP in 2010.

In terms of public finance reform, the effort has helped to improve the situation of structural financial imbalances of the 1990s through a greater mobilisation of budget revenue and more sustained support from donors. Thus, a level of less than FDJ 30 billion in the late 1990s, budgetary revenue and respectively expenditures increased from a level of 28.751 billion to 71.07 billion FDJ and 29.829 billion to 72.141 billion FDJ. Overall, revenue increased by 147.2% and 141.8% of the expenses.

Regarding inflation, the general price level is well controlled, but the national economy remains permanently faced with external shocks related to exchange rates, fluctuations prices for raw materials and consumer goods (food) fully imported. In doing so, the external accounts are structurally loss since Independence. Regarding the sustainability of external accounts, it should also be said that public intervention although private bear responsibility in the external imbalance (deficit of current account), the main cause of excess aggregate demand causing a deficit current account, which is still not filled by substantial capital movements durable as FDI and increasing exports of Djibouti.

Despite the acceleration of growth in recent years, the latter has not created enough jobs because it comes mainly from service activities and more especially maritime transport services which investment is capital intensive. The poverty rate has unfortunately not known to decline and is at an even higher level. The government of Djibouti are intending to boost the economy to the extent of turning Djibouti into a regional trade and financial hub and improving the living conditions of the population significantly by a tripling of per capita income by 2035.

According to macroeconomic projections, to achieve this goal, the growth of GDP will be accelerated to a high and sustainable level. The selected target is to increase the growth rate to an annual average of 7.5% to 10% in real terms during the period 2013-2035 against an average rate of 3.5% during 2001-2005 and 4.8% during the five last years. The growth pattern drawn will create more than 200,000 jobs during the period 2013-2035.

The unemployment rate will drop from 48.4% in 2012 to about 10% in 2035. Growth prospects are based on two factors; firstly the diversification of the economy, a new growth model will be introduced. This is to exploit many opportunities that exist in the different sectors and in particular the fishing, tourism, logistics, Information Technology sector and new communication, the financial sector and also in the industrial sector Manufacturing whose development is favoured by the investments needed to the mobilization of water and renewable energy.

Export Development is a determinant of future growth in Djibouti, with the diversification of the economy, new sectors will contribute to growth sustained export including fish products, tourism, and offshoring. The average annual growth rate exports will be 14%, and the open rate will reach about 132% of GDP by 2035. The contribution of productivity to growth will be. The productivity of capital and work will improve gradually progresses in the implementation of reforms structural and for strengthening the infrastructure particularly in the field of telecommunications.

The pattern of growth proposed in the vision pays particular attention to the preservation of internal and external financial balances. In this context, national savings will grow, and the current account deficit of the balance of payments will decline to $ 3.1% in 2035 after reaching an average of 13.5% during the period 2013-2022. The evolution of the external debt will be well mastered, and rate debt will drop to $ 33% of GDP against 51% in 2012. Fiscal policy will be marked by further strengthening own mobilisation resources of the state and the control of current expenditure on the one hand, and the increase of the investment effort required for the overall upgrading of economic infrastructure on the other side. The budget deficit will increase slightly during the first decade down afterwards and will be limited to 3.2% in 2035.

This deficit will be financed increasingly on the domestic market in relation to the dynamics know that the financial system of Djibouti. External resource needs will be increase to finance the required investments. And a dynamic policy mobilisation of external funding resources will be continued, either as part of the international cooperation, to mobilise financing on concessional terms, or by mobilising resources in the form of Foreign Direct Investment or on the international financial market, when conditions are met.

The second factor that contributes to the growth target is an investment and the comprehensive upgrade of the economy. Ten years will be marked by deepening reforms in all areas to improve the efficiency of the economy, modernization and strengthening of infrastructure and the development of human resources.

A large volume of investment will be made by the public sector and state enterprises with the support of development partners. The challenge during this phase is to balance between the constraints of stabilisation and the need to achieve a volume increasing investment; the growth rate during this period will amount to 35.1%. Given the constraints of funding for the public sector, the Public-Private partnerships could develop during this phase, if the conditions are met.

The pillars of the 2035 vision are the peace and national unity. The government will implement all actions to maintain and strengthen executive's institutional or traditional conciliation, strengthening social cohesion and promotion of national solidarity. The state and the people are committed to using all prevention and conflict management through the promotion of dialogue, research consensus and building a culture of peace. Equal before the law and Djiboutians will feel more solidarity, more secure and more willing to build their country in peace.

The Joint initiatives including member countries of IGAD and the African Union pacify by then the space in the sub-region. Also, the presence of several foreign militaries, particularly French military bases, American and Japanese, and installation of another foreign military base will increased military campaign against terrorism and piracy and enhanced security from the entrance to the Red Sea, but also in the region. The border conflict between Eritrea and Djibouti has been finally resolved.

On the horizon of a generation, the democratic process towards a peaceful transition to put an end to 40 years of authoritarian administration will soon be a reality; this will be strengthened by effective institutions that respect the law and enforce, and legitimate leadership, that faces the challenges. The exercise of power will be marked by trust between rulers and the people, as the government manages the state affairs, including the use of the transparent public resource, and remains open to any criticism from citizens. The civil society formed with moral, civic, and citizenship, aware of its obligations to fully participates in policy formulation and decision making. The media helped to improve good governance and the management public affairs.

Djibouti 2035 aims to increase significantly the average of standard living at a rate of GDP growth per capita by 10% per year. The need for a strong, stable and sustainable economy is a very significant. This requires the construction of a model based on the deepening of economic liberalism, a larger creating capacity sectors of national wealth, the greater role for the private sector and the diversification of sources of income and employment. In this context, all the factors of Production available will be valued to place the economy on a new level of growth of 8 to 10% per year on average in real terms.

This growth rate will be possible thanks to the development of transport activities, the functioning of Trade and Industry, the expansion of New Information and Communication Technologies and finally the increased activity of the port enabled by the strategic position of the country on major trade flows between Eastern Africa and Asia. This will also be possible thanks to the exploitation of little or unexploited mineral resources, and the new impetus that will be given the development of the economic potential of the regions, Agriculture, Fisheries, Livestock and Tourism with strong an economy and employment.

The development of science and technology has always favoured economic change and social development. Today, developing countries, including those with no natural and financial resources, favour this way through a process of scientific and technological innovations.

Djibouti has constructed a national science and technology centre to boost creativity and capacity for innovation and inventing national researchers. The creation of mechanical engineering, automation and shipyards will be part of the 2035 horizon as a form of boosting the economy and developing the technology. Finally, the realisation of these performances will be based on a vision and a clear direction, with a strong leadership and effective public administration.

In 2035, Djibouti will be developed and designed in a balanced and sustainable way through a judicious distribution of wealth to population and increase the economic activities to boost the country's living standard and to collect as many funds to pay off the public debt. The economic conquest and regional development will be an essential transformation and a major asset to the country. Rural development will be revitalised and strengthened, and will thus increase population incomes.

Ensuring the welfare of Djibouti and Djibouti is the purpose of the long-term development, taking the individual as both actor and beneficiary. Welfare is based on the aspirations of the people and aims to provide adequate solutions to their needs in terms of health, education and employment, housing, leisure and better living environment.The government has adapted various developments of human capital through appropriate initial training, and launch additional development programs to increase the infrastructure and the capacity of the economy.

Developing the society and improving the living conditions are central to the long-term development strategy of Djibouti. The prosperity that the Vision will achieve will reflect into wealth creation that will benefit the entire population of Djibouti. The government efforts on reducing poverty, improving the health and social security, increasing the quality of education, promoting the status of women and youth have soo far produced significant changes to the current situation of the country, however despite these improvements, there are a lot to be done.

Between 1977 and 2010, there was a rapid urbanisation. The consequence of this phenomenon was the rapid development of shanty towns boosted by the rural exodus. The government will put in a development policy to build the city and housing. This will need it to implement actions designed to improve living conditions and environment of the population by promoting urban economy and have access to decent housing and build clean environment for the cities and regions.

As part of Djibouti's 2035 vision, the government will promote regional and international cooperation integration to strengthen the country's openness. The geostrategic position of the country will enable Djibouti to strength its role as the regional hub for trade and possibly make the country the main trade gateway between Europe, Asia and the Middle East including the African continent.

Today's world trade is growing rapidly, and regional trade blocks are continuing to accelerate, a large share of global trade is carried out in regional integration areas. Djibouti 2035 aims to participate fully in control mutations and the building of regional assemblies, regional integration and globalisation. Whether it's IGAD, COMESA, the African Union and WTO, Djibouti will always be an active partner who participates and benefits from trade liberalisation, capital transactions and better allocation of labour to strengthen its factor productivity growth and competitiveness. The development of the Djibouti-Ethiopia axis will be essential to the regional integration from the perspective of creating a single market between the countries within the Horn of Africa such as Djibouti, Ethiopia Sudan, South Sudan, Somali and Eritrea.

The implementation of the vision Djibouti 2035 sets a clear direction and long-term strategy to achieve economic prosperity that provides a decent living standard to the population as a whole and strength Djibouti's role within the region to resolve any constraint or the unprecedented crisis that have undermined the security of the region. The main pillars of this vision are to strengthen the peace and national unit by promoting social justice and cultural identity and national consciousness, develop a comprehensive defence policy to strengthen the country's military capacity, ensuring the safety of people and goods.

Another aspect of the vision is the ideas of promoting good governance to ensure transparency and distributing the wealth fairly to the public. Djibouti as part of the good governance has taken steps to strength the functioning of democracy to allow citizens and collective groups to carry out freely any action or movement that is lawful. The government of Djibouti intends to introduce an independent judicial system which enables and give judges the right to make their decisions based on the evidence before them without any interference from the authorities. Also, the government is seeking to promote diversified growth and a leading role for the private sector, and the establishment of an adequate financial strategy and the preservation of balance sheet.

As part of the vision of 2035, education is at the heart of the government's agenda. For the past decade, the country has witnessed a greater declined in the standard of education as a result of poor performance in schools and examination results, almost 60% of students have difficulties in reading and writing, and there is a huge insufficiency in the French language (the language of studying). Therefore taking considering in these negative factors, the government is ever determined to put in place a platform to tackle these tragic events that have undermined Djibouti's educational system.

The propose plans to boost the national education are to create a sufficient and appropriate budget for schools; raise standards and restoring discipline within the academic intuitions, attracting the top graduates to teaching, Investing the construction of additional schools with the latest technological features so that the buildings and facilities match our ambition for the next generation and more importantly creating a friendly environment system that allows students to maintain a full concentration during the lessons.

On the issue of peace and stability in Djibouti, the vision of 2035 requires long-term development strategy to secure peace and security in the country. Lasting peace is built on social justice, fairness and the rule of law. Indeed, a lack of social justice and equity or an inability of the state to ensure equality of opportunity in the development to all citizens promotes marginalisation and destruction, therefore, it's very important for the Djiboutian authority to take every possible step to ensure a strong security in the country.

The presence of legitimate authority in Djibouti will be the guarantor of the security, preventing public disorder and maintaining the feeling of being under the protection of the state. In this context, good governance and public administration will be strengthened to enable all citizens to fairly access public services. Therefore, the state will ensure the equitable distribution of national resources to all social components but also to conduct a balanced approach to developing the country. The judicial and administrative institutions will ensure equality before the law for all citizens. To achieve this, the country will build an administration with a rational organisation and seamless operation, from the top to the bottom, which ensures efficient management of the state. The Government will provide land administration awareness in relation to peace. It will facilitate initiatives and actions on raising awareness to civil society on the culture of peace and coexistence of peoples.

Institutions and traditional practices have shown their relevance and effectiveness in the maintenance of social peace. They will be integrated into the institutional system of the country. For cultural identity, for the past several years the government led by Guelleh has taken decisive actions to promote cultural identity and national consciousness. The main purpose of promoting the cultural identity in Djibouti is to increase the capacity to disseminate the cultural dimensions of development in all its essential and distinctive features including spiritual, material and intellectuals. Cultural identity is a common denominator of the Djibouti nation and will help the human and civic education of citizens and influence the attitudes, behaviours individual and social.

The defence policy of Djibouti

The government has taken measures to promote a comprehensive defence policy, ensuring the safety of people and goods. The defence of a country is never acquired once and for all. The global changes affecting the defence are not limited only to military and strategic aspects. However, these developments call today and even more tomorrow, a global design defence, combining military defence civil dimension and an economic dimension.

Relying on military and civilian coordinated, such an approach is likely to provide an appropriate response to the diversity of threats. In this context, citizens will be intimately involved in the management of their personal safety and appropriate collective safe reflexes in civic behaviour, accountability and national consciousness.

The overriding goal is before all, to ensure resource security and permanence of their production. Economic goals now extend to service activities including financial services and IT; interruption of the operation of one of the sectors may cause paralysis of economic circuits and disruption of social equilibrium. Finally, the Government will ensure a professional, and an effective functioning of the defence and security features to reassure all citizens, all socio-cultural components of the country. These defence and security elements will be complementary instruments available to the government to maintain this social peace.

On the horizon of good governance, Djibouti is hoping to gain democratic values, strengthen the effectiveness of the institutions that respects and enforces the law, and to this, there must be the presence of real legitimate leadership. Strong institutions play an important part towards the direction of achieving the vision of 2035.

Although the government plays a significant part in strengthening the state's economy, international experiences illustrate that significant development within the private sector can construct a sustainable economic growth, creating employment and overcoming the economic obstacles that have undermined the living standard of the Djibouti population. The economic performance of countries like Dubai Cape Verde shows that small size of the Djiboutian market with the high cost of electricity doesn't represent a constraint to the country's economic development.

In spite of the current growth in the economy, the private sector of Djibouti is still undeveloped and disorganised. Currently, there is deficiency structural conversion of the productive base with the rise of new job creation activities and added value. As part of this, the country's authorities have reinforced, through the vision of 2035, an agenda to transform and diversify the national economy. For this reason, the organisation of this High-Level Development

Exchange not just allow a constructive dialogue between the public, private and civil society in Djibouti, but also allow the exchange of experiences with other states that have similar characteristics as Djibouti in terms of geographic, economics and social.

Considering the greater importance of private-public dialogue in Djibouti and its capacity to help in identifying any obstacle to the economic and social developments, it is critical that serious consideration is given to the recommendations made during the dialogue. The implementation of the five-year plan for various sectors by the government should involve to the degree possible the consultations between the private and public players. However, while the organisation of the High-Level Development Exchange was crucial step towards appropriate South-South cooperation, Djibouti tend to seek to strengthen its economic relations with Cape Verde, Dubai and Mauritius to increase the South-South cooperation.

Now that Djibouti has to come up with plans to develop the sectors, South-South trade is extremely convenient to learn from best practises. The significant development that both Mauritius and Cape Verde witnessed within the space of short term illustrates the importance of strong and valuable governance and the existence of market competition promotes economic diversification and creates employment opportunities.

The strategic importance of Bab Al-Mandeb

The Bab Al-Mandeb strait is situated between Yemen on the Arab Peninsula and Djibouti and Eritrea in East Africa. The Strait also connects the Red Sea to the Gulf of Aden. The Bab Al Mandeb plays a crucial role in today's world as it's the future choke point for much of the global commerce; relatively the vast majority trade between the EU and China, Japan, India goes through the Bab Al Mandeb every day. In 2006, almost 3.3 million of barrels of oil passed through the strait, out of 43 million barrels of world total per day

The Bab Al Mandeb is very strategic geographically, politically, economically and militarily. However, for many years, the region has been suffering from extreme tensions caused by struggle power sharing and the rise of an extreme ideological, religious militant group that has dismantled the functioning of the countries surrounded by Bal Al-Mandeb. This region is globally recognised as a confrontation arena between the world powers that has established a strong military presence and political influence on the countries within the region e.g. Djibouti and Yemen. The countries within the region have attempted to cooperate among themselves to lower tensions and to promote peace and security within the region. However, these attempts still require much more effort to achieve the hoped for results.

The Red Sea considerably upholds geopolitical influences that have made it a main frontal point around which revolve struggles, conflicts and manoeuvres. The Red Sea is likewise a total arena for world powers competition in maintaining a permanent presence to fulfil their political, economic and military interests. Therefore the existence of the Red Sea notifies the greater importance that it has upon world trade and the geopolitical strategic of the region.

The Bab Al-Mandeb strait is situated at the far east of the Arab Peninsula, and on the west is the coast of Africa. The gap between Africa and Arab Peninsula is approximately 22 miles. The strait links the Red Sea with the Indian Ocean and split by Perim Island. The Republic of Somalia is added to Bab Al-Mandeb as it's bordered by the Gulf of Aden. From the geopolitical perspective, the strait seems to be wider than its 22 miles, as to its importance is not subject to political elites that border the Strait, but rather goes beyond to include the political units which are politically, economically, militarily or strategically connected in the same way.

Furthermore, the Western powers have significant interest in the Red Sea to maintain their strategic interest in the Red Sea as they will have clear access to the Gulf petroleum to meet their energy needs. Likewise, Russia can also be included among the countries that have a special geopolitical interest in the Red Sea because the Red Sea is the shortest path that connects its Black Sea with the Indian Ocean. Also, the US is another world power that has major interest in the geopolitical space because through it passes the Gulf petroleum, the production and trading of which are monopolised by the American companies

Taking into account the geopolitical characteristic, the Bab Al-Mandeb symbolise the narrow entrance of the Red Sea, as its width is very unlikely to exceed 22 miles. Also, the Perim Island split the strait into two pathways. The one to the east is about two miles wide, and the other one, the western corridor, is about 16 miles in width. The main use for the eastern pathway is to use small boats between Thobab port in Yemen, and Berbera in Somalia, Djibouti, Assab in Eritrea. As it's not for the use of big ships or international navigation because it is narrow and its depth is about 85 feet. However, the western corridor is the main passage of the Bab al-Mandab Strait. The passage is used for major ships and international navigation due to its deeper and wider, and its depth is approximately 990 feet.

The Red Sea water is extremely remarkable as a result of its high temperatures in comparison to other seas, including those that are located at the same latitude. Usually, the temperature of surface water (600 feet depth) is affected by the temperature of the air. The temperature of Bab Al-Mandeb strait is extremely high during summer, with ranges between 26°C to 43 °C with a greater humidity of 19 °C to 32 °C in winter with medium humidity. The Red Sea is placed among the saltiest of water in the entire globe.

The historical background of Bab Al-Mandeb is certainly regarded as an important when dealing with the established geopolitical fact. The strategic significance of Bab Al-Mandeb can be described into two phases; firstly, in the early 15th century the Red Sea was simply a sea between Africa and Arab Peninsula which continued to connect across the sea. It's clear apparent that the strait is near the Suez Canal on the north, and on the south between Aden in Yemen and the port of Berbera in Somalia and Djibouti. The Red Sea was mainly sea route for trade from the East to West. Trade goods ware carried on the Red Sea and overland on caravans to the Mediterranean Sea where they were picked up by ships operated by Venice and Genova.

Secondly, from the 15th century to 1869, the Portuguese have discovered the route around Africa all the way to the Indian Ocean, and into the Red Sea through the Gulf of Aden and Bab al-Mandab Strait. This pathway was the vital sea route that linked the East and West. This route has largely dominated the trade that used to go through the old route through the Bab al-Mandab. The old route became of minor importance, limited to coastal trade. The consequence of this was an incredible transformation-human movement ceased to pass through the Red Sea. The importance of the ports and countries within the Red Sea worsen. Consequently, this period which took after the finding of the circum-Africa route seen a growing interest from France and Britain.

France attempted to restore this route by acquiring a concession of reducing the customs duties on its goods that pass through Egypt. Its interest in this route was developed by working on excavating a canal across the Suez from the Red Sea to the Mediterranean Sea. However, Britain kept on using the old route to link it to India (former British colonial) to transport supplies and passengers between Britain and India while using the waterway for trading. The effectiveness of the circum-Africa route expanded following the introduction of steam ships in the 19th century. They were more efficient than sailing ships which depended on the propelling force of the wind.

Thirdly, the Suez Canal linked the water routes between the Indian Ocean and the Mediterranean Sea through the Red Sea. This meant that the link between the East and the West was highly shortened. This maritime connection modernised the navigation to communicate the Red Sea. Since then, the Red Sea became extremely powerfully and important than it was ever before. After the Suez Canal had become the quickest route between the East and West, it had shortened the distance between them by almost a half in some instances and by nearly two-thirds in the others. Certainly, this maritime route greatly contributed to the modern industrial. This maritime route brought the distance nearer between European countries and the sources of raw material and their export markets in Asia and Africa at the cheapest costs and shortest time.

Following 1930, which was the start of the stream of petroleum from the Persian Gulf, a fundamental change has happened in the capacity of this maritime route. It was changed from the waterway for goods to an essential oil route which passes through the most important strategic commodity in today's world oil.

Considering the geopolitical distinctive, it's clear that all aspects and characteristics of the strait, which is the southern gate of the Red Sea, likewise applies to the Red Sea waterway that connects the Indian Ocean with the Mediterranean Sea. This ratifies the geopolitical identity of the Red Sea due to its elongated form, limited width and an intermediate position to fulfil the linkage.

The Red Sea as world navigation path has managed to encounter the difficulties it faced such as high temperatures, severe drought and the scarcity of deep-water ports that serve this navigational route to strength its strategic position to serve the inter-regional trade that passes the Red Sea. Previously these negative aspects that damaged the functioning of the navigation, but currently these negative attributes doesn't pose any major threat to the trade. Furthermore, the Red Sea is the ideal sea passage among world navigational routes as the percentage of oil out of the total of the world oil traffic being carried through it in unarmed tankers.

The main responsibility of the international community is to protect and ensure the security and the stability of Bab Al-Mandeb strait and ensure that it's available to all navigation at all times. The straight is extremely important as the Red Sea has always been a strategic interest for world powers, especially the western and its allies.

The geographical coast of the Arab Red Sea composes of 90.2% of the total length of the Red Sea coasts and the Gulf of Aden. The Red Sea is almost located in between the Arab community area in terms of geographically or nationally. The Red Sea is only sea outlet for many Arab states, especially for Jordan, Djibouti and the Sudan. The Red Sea is the primary passage through which Arab petroleum stream to export markets. The economies of most Arab countries depend mainly on petroleum exports, which represent 93% of the total exports of some Arab countries, such as Saudi Arabia, Kuwait, Oman, Qatar, the United Arab Emirates, Yemen and Bahrain.

The possibility of the presence of mineral resources on the bottom of the Red Sea, boost the significance of the Red Sea in the geographic concepts which links to the significance of Bab al-Mandab Strait with the importance of the Red Sea economically through which passes over 40% of world oil traffic tankers. Despite the importance of the Red Sea to the Arabs and their geographical control of its Coasts, the Arabs have failed to maintain a clear strategy towards this area. The foreign powers were the only protector of the strait and the Red Sea. It appears that

It seems that the negativity of the Arab Community is not limited to the absence of a clear-cut formula toward the Red Sea. A most telling example for Arab Community's negative attitude toward the Red Sea is the end of some Arab islands of the Red Sea, such as Sanafir, Tiran, and Small Heneish which came under the military control of Israel by the name of Ethiopia.

The growing interest of the Arab nations within the Red Sea requires Arab community to adopt a common and unified policy to maintain a clear influence in this important strategic corridor. As a result, there is the need to construct a naval fleet to gain the influence in which the Arabs are hoping to achieve. The need for adopting an effective attitude towards the longstanding struggle over the strategic coast of the Horn of Africa, this was highly regarded as an extension of the Middle East struggle between Arabs and Israel.

The demands of Israel and Ethiopia on the Red Sea have begun to meet and coincide since the call to make the Red Sea an Arab lake as part of an Arab strategy to stop the Israeli activity in the Red Sea. It became clear to both Israel and Ethiopia, the only non-Arab countries in the Red Sea, that this call represented a direct threat to their national interests. Although the coast of Israel is less than seven miles, the state of Israel has strengthened its coast to serve itself as an outlet especially as the Suez Canal is closed to Israeli shipping and made its Mediterranean outlet unable to carry Israel to the Afro-Asian regions.

Following the seizure of the Tiran Strait and being permitted to go through the Suez Canal, the main obstacle faced by Israel in relation to the Red Sea usually lay in Bab Al-Mandeb when the war between Arabs and Israel broke out in 1973, and Egyptian and Yemeni forces closed the Strait to Israeli navigation.

In terms of Ethiopia, the Red Sea is the only sea outlet that links her to the outer world. Ethiopia challenged dangers from was threatened by the intention of the Eritrean people to separate itself from Ethiopia which means the separation of the coastal region from the rest of Ethiopia, and the return of this Ethiopia will be a landlocked country cut away from the outer world.

The interest of both Israel and Ethiopia came together when the Arabs developed unprecedented animosity and became the enemy of both. The struggle between Arabs and Israel has always been longstanding tension. The

Arabs have unified under the banner of converting the Red Sea into an Arab lake. The strategic interest between Ethiopia and Israel established various patterns of cooperation against the split of Eritrea and breaking ties with the Arabs. This signifies that Arab nations will tighten their grip over the Bab al-Mandab Strait.

For many decades the so-called state of Israel assisted Ethiopia in various ways including economic and military especially since America stopped its arms supply to Ethiopia in April 1977. The purpose of Israel assisting Ethiopia is that in return, Israel could significantly acquire strategic concessions, including having the privilege to utilise the port of Eritrea for its trade with countries such as Congo, Central Africa and South Sudan. Israel sought to establish a naval military base in the Island of Forma and Haleb, and two other additional bases in northern Eritrea. The Israeli aircraft can fly directly from the bases to Israel, for Israel to have the concession for surveillance and conduct other military operations it will use the Doumeira Island, which is only 20 miles away from the Perim Island.

The state of Israel as part of her barbaric operation in the region has successfully captured the island of Heniesh in Yemen at the entrance of Bab Al-Mandeb. Following their seizure in the island, immediately they've constructed a communication station. The Eritrean situation, along with its strategic weight, has created an obstacle to the geopolitical situation in the southern Red Sea. The Eritrea's strategic position has matched the interest of Israel with the interest of the Soviet Union and Cuba towards Addis Ababa.

For a long period, the Western led by the US had a strong influence on the Red Sea. The Red Sea was a trade route for the West until it transformed into an artery for crude oil. By virtue of its island nature, it offered the West the opportunity to launch at an early time on the field of Colonialism and gain prestige as a naval power. When colonialism pulled out from this area, a vacuum existed and offered other powers the opportunity to fill it.

The geopolitical essence of the Red Sea makes it inappropriate for basing the warships particularly aircraft carriers and fleet submarines which compose of the main strike force of US. The West turned to rely on the conservative regimes in the Red Sea and the use of petrodollars as a tool to gain Western goals and continue with its interest. This certainly makes a hole in the Western strategic network in the region as such strategy depends on political factors which are liable to change from time to time especially since existing regimes in the Red Sea area are unstable and always liable to national, progressive and radical currents. An example of this was the conversion of Addis Ababa, until recently was a fortress for Libyan influence to leftist Marxism after the downfall of the conservative regime of Haile Selassie and the coming of the progressive regime of Mengistu Haile Mariam.

The Western uses the Red Sea as the main passage that imports Persia Golf oil to Western countries which largely suffers from insufficient energy. The West primarily relies on Gulf petroleum to run its factories, acquiring sufficient energy and grow the economy to ensure employment opportunity. The primary objective of the US military forces in the region is to prevent any interruption of oil flow to Western countries and to protect Western oil companies operating in the region and the Gulf area to guarantee the contributions of these companies the balance of payments.

This emphasises the greater importance of Bab Al-Mandeb Strait as a result of its important position in foreign powers strategy for establishing a base to control petroleum as well as the route for transporting it. The Persian Gulf oil streams to Western nations through or from the Red Sea to Europe and Asia. The US has established a very large naval force with immense military equipment such as aircraft carries, nuclear submarines and destroyers in the Indian Ocean, Persian Gulf and the Red Sea. Likewise, the US has several other naval and air bases to serve these naval units.

The main reason for the US to establish such bases is to protect and ensure that US interest goes accordingly in the Middle East, the Indian Ocean and most importantly the Red Sea. The US strategic interest is mostly focused on the use of the naval facilities on the Red Sea and the Indian Ocean to assist military operations during the times of extreme tension. Also, they support the functioning of free navigation through the Red Sea and Bal Al Mandeb, also to ensure the continued of flow of the Gulf oil to US associates in Europe.

The soviet presence and influence in the region had posed a serious threat to the US interest in the region and security of the waterway for US navigation.

Like other foreign powers, France had an unprecedented interest in the free navigation on the sea routes across the Horn of Africa. Previously, France has been hugely dependent on the imports of oil from the Persian Gulf. Regardless of the declining significance of the Bab Al Mandeb as a pipeline for France's oil supplies, this strait remains essential as it lies on the fastest route to French territories in the Indian Ocean. Since France established a permanent military presence in Djibouti, France acquires the ability to react quickly to any threats in the Bab al-Mandab. The French garrison in the Indian Ocean is normally located in Reunion but often visits Djibouti. It normally composes of 12 warships and naval fleet.

The French military in Djibouti is approximately 4,500 troops, supported by military units of 12 fighters. The presence of French military nearby Bal Al-Mandeb strait is presumably adequate to prevent any counterproductive to the security of the Western interest and the strait itself. Furthermore as part of French military operation in the Strait, they are also assigned to secure Djibouti from external enemy, in 1977, when Djibouti gained independence from France; it was broadly assumed that without French military presence in Djibouti, the country would be endangered by the tensions coming from neighbouring states e.g. Ethiopia, Somalia and Eritrea. Djibouti with a population of over 900,000, the country heavily relies on French financial and technical assistance. Currently, in Djibouti, there are approximately 10,000 French citizens, including 6,300 military personnel.

The region was mainly dominated by the British Empire and the colonialism of Italy for more than a century. The junior Soviet state and its ideology strengthen Russian antipathy to British power, looked to a revolution in the colonial empires as the historically ordained fate of this area, as in so many others.

A greater detailed interpretation was developed at the end of World War II when Moscow recommended to its allies that former Italian colonies of Somalia and Ethiopia be placed under Soviet protection. The Soviet Union's primary objective was to challenge British imperial influence as colonialism.

The importance of the Strait and the Red Sea became increasingly valuable, during the war of Vietnam; the Soviet Union supplied huge military equipment to North Vietnam by shipment through the Red Sea passing through the Bab Al-Mandeb strait. The closure of the Suez Canal between 1967 and 1976 illustrated the canal to blockade in the future.

The Soviet authorities sought to secure access to this waterway connecting the southern Red Sea with the Indian Ocean. The increase presence of the Soviet Union's presence in 1960's and early 1970's coincided the British evacuation from the riskier areas like the Persian Gulf and South Yemen. This clearly illustrates the significance of the region to Soviet leaders was completely limited neither to the utility of the maritime route nor to countering British influence.

During the 1950's, the US has launched and deployed submarine Polaris A-3 missile system which posed a serious concern to the Soviet Union. The Soviet military commanders have realised that northern Indian Ocean gave a great location for the deployment of such weapon aimed possibly at the USSR and China. However, Russia assumed that China's interest in the region and the entire Africa would pose a threat to the Soviet interest

The Soviet Union built a presence in Yemen as a result of its increasing interest and involvement in the Middle East, as part of the framework agreement to grant the Soviet Union a presence, the Soviet has finalised a treaty of friendship with the Imam of North Yemen on 1 November 1955. The advocates of Marxism-Leninism in Russia had absolutely nothing in common with the Middle Ages leaders of this poor nation other than their desire to suspend the influence of the British colonialism from the region. Therefore, the USSR was eager to supply arms to the Imam to fight with the British colonialism.

Two years later, in accord with the commercial agreement of March 1956, the Soviet transported eight ships contained arms, anti-aircraft and tanks. Following the revolution in North Yemen during 1962, that conquered the Imam's regime and later established the Republic of Yemen, and during the Civil War which ensued, Soviet aid increased dramatically, reaching a total of $92 million by 1965. Furthermore, hundreds of Soviet advisers were involved in military training. The Soviet began to increasingly compete with China for agricultural and industrial aid projects in North Yemen.

Following the British withdrawal from its position in the region, in particularly South Yemen, and the rise of the radical wing of the National Liberation Front as the supporting element in the Marxist regime of independence. After the independence, it changed to People's Democratic Republic of Yemen (PDRY) which built a closer relation with the USSR. Shortly after felt let down the Yemen Arab Republic assumption for military assistance, the Soviets responded generously to the request of the PDRY. In the middle of 1972, the Soviet was reportedly delivered several military equipment e.g. MIG-17 aircraft and also trained at least 60 South Yemeni pilots.

The turning point in USSR-PDRY relations rose in 1972 during the official visit of President Salim Rubayyi Ali's to Moscow. The meeting has been prepared in advance by high-level of delegations and dealt with a different range of bilateral relations including military, economic, political cooperation. The arrival of a large number of Soviet military experts in Aden and a follow-up visit to Moscow by PDRY Premier and Defence Minister Ali Nasir Muhamad were primary indications of success. The Soviet military assistance to Yemen in 1974 was the total sum of $114 million, provided tangible evidence that strong relations were established.

The purpose of USSR involvement was to gain naval facilities in Yemen and to acquire huge Soviet control over the port Aden and Mukallah. It was clearly important for the Soviet to acquire these naval facilities on the Island of Socotra, the Soviet sees the Island of Socotra as strategic locate to establish a naval facility to maintain its interest in the region.

The Horn of Africa which consist of Sudan, Ethiopia, Djibouti, Somalia and Kenya. This area is globally considered as the most strategic importance forming the southern shore of the Gulf of Aden and jutting out into the Indian Ocean at the point part by which must flow the majority of the oil routes from the Persian Gulf and the Red Sea. So grasp on the Horn means an ability to cut that route and the lifeblood of most of the West and Asia. The Horn has, for centuries, been the scene of wars, turmoil and suffering, but it is an area whose significance has not been fully understood. It is not appropriate to attempt any historical sketch of the countries of the Horn, except in so far as the past contributes to the present.

The Horn of Africa covers approximately 2,000,000 km2 with a population of around 115 million. Up until the 19th century, there were no borders separated the countries within the region. The Ethiopian expansion has reached many parts of the region including the Danakil region, Somali territory and some parts along the border with Sudan. During that time Djibouti was under the French colonial, and the colonial has built a railway from the capital city to Addis Ababa, while its European counterpart (Italy) conquered Eritrea and south Somalia.

Britain was at the time the regional power until mid-1960's, in 1960, following the independence of British Somaliland and Italian Somali, both shared a great vision of reunification as a result of the same characteristic in terms of religion, language, ethnicity and culture. After the unification, the Soviet offered a loan of $32 million and provided assistance in equipping and training approximately 10,000 strong armed force, compared with Somalia's total military budget of $3.9 million in 1964. While the US was in a war with Vietnam, the US president at the time Lyndon B. Johnson chose to cut off assistance to Somalia. Prior to this, the Soviet has supported Somali policy on anti-colonialism and opposition to foreign bases in Africa and aggressive military alliances.

The Soviet Union involvement in Somali had significantly risen when it faced unprecedented pressure from Sudan and Egypt to expel the Soviet advisers from both states, and the growing Chinese competition indicated the significance of an amicable regime in Somalia. Good relation between Soviet-Somalia brought the transportation of Somalia's Kismayu train and Barbera port into the Soviet Union's primary base facilities in the region. The investment of port of Berbera was insignificant since the start when Moscow acquired access to port facilities in Yemen and being evicted from their Egyptian bases on the Red Sea.

Moscow continued its mission to gain influence within the region by undertaking internal involvement in Ethiopia, following the military coup by Mengistu Haile Mariam against the late Emperor Haile Selassie in 1977. After the fall of the late emperor, the country was named Democratic People's Republic.

The Soviet was anticipating leading internal changes in Ethiopia, the real evidence of Soviet anticipation was that Soviet media continued to report the demonstration in Addis Ababa and other parts of the country. When the coup took place, immediately Moscow has expressed its enthusiastic approval and praised the historical importance of the revolution. Following the revolution led by the Derg military junta. The new leadership announced that the country would become a socialist country and strengthen relations with the USSR.

The Bal Al-Mandeb has managed to maintain world's attention as a result of its geographical location and its significance as the southern gate of the Red Sea. Following the discovery of the Strait of Bal A-Mandeb, global competition has begun between world powers to acquire a stake in the region to achieve its strategic military, economic interest. Historically, Yemen had been the main target for many nations since the 15th century. Yemen, just like other countries in the region has faced internal and continued tension. The primary causes for these tensions were political dispute and the rise of extreme terror groups to impose extreme ideologies in their countries. Since the 15th century until the present moment, many world powers attempted to gain control of the Red Sea and Bal Al-Mandeb to protect their interests from other rival countries.

Yemen for many decades took strong initiatives to strengthen its relation with all the countries situated in Red Sea region, in particularly the countries that share Bal Al-Mandeb strait with Yemen to ensure the security of the Strait and prevent it from international conflict. Also, the Republic of Yemen played a crucial role in solving many conflicts that took place in the region and arranged agreements with the concerned nationals within the framework of international law. Also, Yemen demonstrated efforts to secure the strait as it's the only passage in the southern Red Sea, which connects the East of the world with the West of the world that will result in political, economic and military advantage to all nations.

Yemen is anxious if some part of the Red Sea especially the Bab al-Mandab Strait becomes occupied by a world power. As such occupation will have an impact on the security of Yemen as well as all other countries in the region. Yemen has a specific military advantage because this strait is considered as a part of its territorial waters, and in fact, it affects its security. Therefore Yemen continually tries to coordinate its military efforts with countries that it shares the Strait with.

Yemen has designated a policy concerning the strait and this policy is written in the Yemeni constitution which says "The Republic of Yemen confirms its adherence to the UN Charter, the International Declaration of Human Rights, the Charter of the Arab League, and Principles of International Law which are recognized". To achieve economic goals objectives, the government of Yemen wants to create facilities for all ships crossing the Strait to enhance its economic resources. These facilities are extremely important to large ships crossing the Strait to Asia Pacific, Europe and most importantly Africa. Yemen as part of their political interest, considers the Strait as very important as it connects Yemen with all countries, in particularly the industrial countries and superpowers, which no doubt want freedom of navigation through the Bab al-Mandab Strait.

The Bab Al-Mandeb strait is a substantial passage in trade between Europe and Asia as its the transit checkpoint, however since the opening of the Suez Canal and the link between the Red Sea to the Mediterranean Sea, it became extremely important to foreign countries as southern entrance of the quickest waterway that connects the Indian Ocean with the Mediterranean. While the Arab-Israel tension is an ongoing situation, the state of Israel is concerned with having access to free navigation in the Red Sea, especially through the Strait of Bal Al-Mandeb, which is the only passage through which Israel can go to its market in Africa and Asia.

Following attack on the Israeli tanker Coral in the strait in 1971, and the blockade of the Israeli navigation in Bab al-Mandab Strait in 1973 by Arabs during the October war, Israel have paid particular attention to its interests in the region. The Soviet has significant interests in the region. The Soviet interests consist of various aspect, and some of these are crucial to the Soviet national security. The region is the Soviet's southern sea route which is the shortest waterline of communication opened the navigation route between its European ports in the Black Sea and the Indian Ocean, where it has its naval fleet, instead of going through the Mediterranean Sea into the Atlantic Ocean and around Africa. The Suez route makes it easier for the Soviets to support its navy and air force in peacetime and during the wartime.

The USSR had a trade relationship with countries in Africa and Asia Pacific, and intention to protect this route for its trade activities. Furthermore, the Soviet wants to maintain a full control in the navigation on the Red Sea against the Western and its allies as the oil flows from the Gulf States for Europe's Energy and Industry. The soviet interest is to confront the Western influence within the region.

The US strategic interest comprise on various objective, for instance, the naval facilities to support its permanent military operations in Southwest Asia and the Indian Ocean; the freedom navigation over the Red Sea and the Bab al-Mandab Strait; the continuous flow of the Persian Gulf oil to allies in Europe through the Bab al-Mandab; and countering the Soviet influence in the region and safeguarding the sea route against any Arab radicalism for making the Red Sea into Arab lake. Furthermore, the European states had strong interest in freedom of navigation through the Red Sea.

The rise of terrorist groups within the region for the past several years, the so-called al-Qaeda terrorist militia group had been widely seen as an organisation that poses a significant threat to the global peace and stability, since the creation of the organisation in 1988 the group was led by Osama Bin Laden until his death on 2nd May 2011.

In 2009, an affiliated al-Qaeda group was established in Yemen with the name of al-Qaeda in the Arab Peninsula and maintained a radical viewpoint based on Bin Laden's extreme ideology. This extreme radical group rose in the mid-2000's, following its terrorist operation in Saudi Arabia, but the Saudi authorities have successfully defeated the radical group. After this defeat, al-Qaeda Arab Peninsula kept its name and re-grouped itself in Yemen territory, unified with the local al-Qaeda group operating there.

The al-Qaeda Arab Peninsula group had posed a clear threat and strong challenge to the government of Yemen. However, as a result of its increase influence in the country and its growing strong religious ideology, the group had become an independent organisation and totally free from the original al-Qaeda, although it still retains the public veneer of subordination.

In 2011 a wave of pro-democracy demonstration and uprisings took place some parts of the Middle East and North Africa, this revolution has managed to oust several ruthless and brutal authoritarian regimes. During the uprising, protesters have deeply expressed their political and economic hardship faced violent crackdowns by their countries' security forces.

The uprising began in Tunisia after a young unemployed man, Mohamed Bouazizi, set fire to himself after officials stopped him selling vegetables in Sidi Bouzid. In protest of the seizure of his wares and the way in which security forces have treated him and humiliated him, he decided to set himself on fire to express his desperate anger and frustration.

The uprising has heavily affected five particular countries which are Libya, Tunisia, Egypt, Syria and Yemen. The uprising has left some countries in a chaotic situation to the extent that it dismantled the state functioning and placed in a difficult situation to come up with a clear resolution to solve the trace of the uprising in the likeness of Libya, Yemen and Syria. On the other hand, it produced a positive outcome to some particularly Tunisia as it removed the long-standing tyrant and replaced it with democratically elected leaders who are willing to establish good governance and the rule of law.

Nonetheless, as the uprising against the authoritarian governments spread to the remaining Arab world, the revolutions across the Arabian region were seen less successful than in Cairo and Tunis. The tension in Bahrain incited a monstrous government repression which was helped by other Sunni Arab governments in the Gulf and especially Saudi Arabia. The Syrian president, Bashar al-Assad in response to the mass demonstrations, has taken strong initiatives to dismantle public uprising and acted brutality against his adversary to maintain his grip on power, regardless of the end result.

The Libyan government led by Gaddafi has also sought to crush peaceful demonstrations by extreme force, but the regime was ultimately defeated following the military intervention conducted by the NATO alliance. In the southern Arabian Peninsula, the flames of turmoil also inspired the Yemeni citizens, where the Arab Spring quickly assumed many of the same features found in Tunisia and Egypt.

The people of Yemen have shown their determination to ouster the regime of Ali Abdullah Saleh to end the massive corruption and constant repression against the citizens. After 30 years as president of Yemen, Saleh's ability to stay in power was legendary, but the ouster of longstanding dictators like Egypt's Mubarak and Tunisia's Ben Ali clearly gave his opponents hope.

The Yemeni president has heavily confronted the demonstrators who called for him ouster, but the issue he faced was that he didn't maintain sufficient internal resources and the support of Western countries to carry out similar military repression as his counterparts in Syria and Bahrain did. In spite of Saleh's rigorous effort to remain in power, internal and external pressure were imposed on him to leave the office in February 2012. While President Saleh's administration frequently appeared to be very weak, Saleh managed to remain in office for one year after the ouster of Mubarak and Ben Ali.

Since the revolution began, Yemen turned out to be progressively precarious by the violence between the regime forces, the opposition. In such event, the extremist militia, al-Qaeda in the Arabian Peninsula (AQAP), utilised its rebellious arm, Ansar al-Shariah (partisans of Islamic law), to acquire opportunities to seize and retain the country. This exertion took place while the government was responding to demonstrators in a manner that is breaching the fundamental principles of human right.

During this period, President Saleh enforced military activities to allow him to remain in power and prevent the likeness of AQAP from taking over the country. Although the doomsday situation that Saleh anticipated never happened, the terrorist AQAP group have benefited from the Yemeni unrest to achieve its objectives in relation to expanding their control over some province particularly Abyan province. In 2012, following the establishment of a newly elected government, the new regime took steps to dismiss the AQAP and its allied Ansar al-Shariah from their key strongholds. However, the war over the control of Yemen is still subject to substantial uncertainty. The AQAP presence in Yemen represents a major threat to the peace and stability of greater Yemen. The context and the future of this turmoil remain significant importance to the well-being of all states concerned, with the threat presented by al-Qaeda's which is the biggest dangerous affiliate.

For several decades Yemen had faced issues with its governance, as a result of wide corruption and the misuse of public fund. Yemen is a large country in the Middle East and obtains significant resources that have attracted the attention of world powers e.g. the US, the Soviet Union and the Europeans. Yemen has a long border with Saudi Arabia and direct access to key strategic sea outlet, including the Red Sea and the Gulf of Aden.

The country is the only non-monarchy state in the Arabian Peninsula with a population of around 24 million people. Yemen is the most populated country in the region and is currently growing by around 3.45 percent per year. Unfortunately, Yemen is afflicted with several internal difficulties, and a large portion of the Yemeni population has problems with grinding poverty and malnutrition.

The civil unrest in Yemen during 2011-12 has led to soaring prices for food as well as a breakdown of social services according to the United Nations (UN) Office for the Coordination of Humanitarian Affairs. Progressively, the UN agencies involved with supporting Yemen have developed heighten concerns about the potential for a severe drought. Lack of Water and electricity is also another issue that Yemeni faces on a daily basis; the capital city of Sanaa regularly confronts the possibility of running out of water in the years to come.

President Ali Abdullah Saleh was the most influential and pre-eminent political figure since 1978 until his departure from office in February 2012 as a result of internal and external pressure for him to resign. Saleh rose to power in 1978 following the assassination of his predecessor Ahmed bin Hussein al-Ghashmi and established himself as the president of the Yemen Arab Republic. In 1990, after the unification of North and South of Yemen, Saleh became the first president of the Republic of Yemen.

Saleh's considerable ruthlessness as president has helped him to remain in power for three decades, but never permitted him to make himself as the leader of a powerful authoritarian regime as tribes in Yemen were very powerful and well-armed.

The Yemeni government often used excessive force to implement its policies; however, this approach was always the last one as it couldn't be applied effectively due to the strong tribalism in the regions. Saleh's administration was based on a system of intimidation, propaganda, bribing tribal leaders to ease the situation, broken promises and dirty politics Corruption permeated the system from the summit of political power down to poor junior civil servants or soldiers at checkpoints on Yemen's roads.

While Saleh's governance seemed to be inefficient, the leader of Yemen has managed to muddle through until the wave of Arab Spring. To understand the real situation in modern Yemen, it is important to acknowledge how President Saleh lost his reign and the factors that drove the revolution which led to his downfall. In 2011, the Arab world experienced a political tsunami with the developing of the Arab Spring. The remarkable ouster of the Tunisia's Ben Ali in that year overwhelmed the Arab world.

The Tunisian uprising was an aspiration for Egyptian's to remove its longstanding dictator from office on 11 March 2011. Likewise, in the wake of the uprising in the Arab world has had an impact on the Yemeni citizens and expressed willingness to confront their own government after Mubarak resigned. The crisis in Yemen reached a defining moment on January 20, 2011, when protestors across the country took down to the street to demand the downfall of Saleh's regime.

For almost three decades, Yemenis felt let down by the regime and that the government has failed to deliver economic prosperity and better-living standard. Also, the Yemenis were frustrated by the high levels of corruption in their country during the years of Saleh's rule. Shockingly, the government's mismanagement of the economy had no end as President Saleh intended to transfer the presidency to his son. Such a power transfer would have followed the emerging pattern of father-son succession set by Syria in 2000 when Bashar Assad succeeded his deceased father as president.

Similarly in Iraq, before the removal of Saddam Hussein, it appeared that he was preparing his son to succeed him. This system of governance was broadly and negatively seen as a republican monarchy by blunders all through the Arab world. In this situation, the idea of Saleh's family empire was broadly despicable by many of the Yemeni citizens.

President Ali Saleh, despite his weak leadership, was quickly able to recognise the danger posed to his administration by the revolution that is happening other parts of the Arab world. After the ouster of Tunisian dictator, Saleh immediately launched a military operation against his population to prevent the potential for serious unrest escalating to Yemen which had already started to experience large but socially restricted demonstrations consist of mainly university students and opposition activists.

At the beginning of the uprising in Yemen, President Saleh he sought to strengthen the fidelity of the security forces through different promises including pay rises and other benefits. Also, civil servants were promised to be rewarded to decrease the danger becoming a source of discontent. Saleh has also exempted public university students from paying their tuition for the year, to prevent the rise of the university students in the wake of the uprising. After his failure to draw the attention of the Yemenis, he announced on February the 2nd that he would not run for the presidential election in 2013, when his current term expires and that his son would not succeed him.

These final sets of promises seemed hollow as his efforts to erase the presidential term limits prior to the outbreak of Arab Spring demonstrations in Tunisia and Egypt. The people of Yemen have seen his efforts to abolish presidential term limits so he could establish himself as president for life. They also anticipated that he would come back to that priority as soon as it was practical to do so despite any promises he might make at a time of crisis.

Saleh's effort to put an end to the unrest didn't prevent the escalation of demonstrators against him. Growing uprising and insurgency were difficult for the security forces to block; as a result of this, the security forces began to shot fire on protestors in an effort to break the unrest. Furthermore, as in Egypt, the regime has arranged counterdemonstrations designed to show support for the regime and to confront the protestors through the different use equipment such as daggers, broken bottles and even Molotov cocktail.

This retaliation has increased street violence but did not discourage the protestor to carry on with their revolt against the corrupt leader. As Ali Abdullah Saleh prospect to crush the will of people appeared to dim, the Yemeni opportunist president whom he had bribed into supporting him, began to separate them from the regime.

These Yemeni elites had no intention to go down with the collapsing government. The growing opposition has forced Saleh to use any necessary repression against the opposition to remain in power for as long as possible.

The situation in Yemen became worse after the regime violence against the demonstrators increased dramatically on March 18, 2011. Fifty-two protestors were killed in Sanaa when the Yemeni government had used plainclothes and snipers to disperse anti-government demonstrators and resulted in major causalities.

As the tension escalated, dictator Saleh declared a state of emergency and deployed all military branches on the streets to encounter the demonstrators, but all efforts of the president did not discourage the protestors but in fact increased their will to ouster the longstanding dictator. The heavy intensive of government brutality has divided the Yemeni regime.

On 21st of March, General Ali Mohsen, the commander of the northern military region has changed sides and cooperate fully with the rebel groups to bring about a change in the country. General Mohsen was broadly seen as the second powerful elite in the Yemeni regime. In accord with the highly personalistic nature of the Yemeni military system, General Ali Mohsen army stayed loyal to him after his dispute with President Saleh in relation to the mass killings commit by the regime.

Furthermore, several senior officers, including three other brigade commanders, quickly mobilised behind Ali Mohsen. Following the defect of many senior officers, round 60% of the national army had joined the protestors, while other military unites including those in the republican guard remained loyal to President Ali Abdullah Saleh. These armies had the best possible weapons in the ground forces to carry out their operations against the civilians. The troops that were loyal to the president was at the time regarded as rough.

However, there was a wide internal division within the armed forces. General Moshen promised that his army would protect protestors from the government forces. This was a huge blow to Saleh desires to remain in post, the most powerful tribal leader in Yemen Sheikh al-Ahmar, also pledged his support to the uprising to ouster the longstanding dictator.

Hamid al-Ahmar, a multimillionaire and influential political figure in Yemen, who is also the brother of Sheikh al-Ahmar, has emerged with the opposition. The defection has widely escalated and began to hit the national assembly, where a handful of members of the parliament resigned as a result of the mass demonstrations.

Shockingly, President Saleh seemed energised by his decision to make a show of strength on March 18 and was open unfazed by the defections. President Saleh has displayed his full anger and demonstrated his desires to permanently eliminate his opponents. In response to the mass-demonstrations against his regime, Saleh has organised a large pro-regime rally in Sanaa to show the international community that majority of the population are supporting the president with enthusiasm. It appears that Saleh believed he had gained the upper hand at this moment despite the defections due to his heavy repression on anti-government demonstrators.

President Saleh, despite the growing escalation, gave no sign of leaving the office. Neighbouring Gulf States expressed their deep concern about the horrific situation in Yemen and the prospect for spreading instability in the country and the region. Leaders across the Gulf Cooperation Council States initiated that for peace to come back to Yemen Saleh must resign. They also considered that it's necessary for the Yemeni leader to take a comfortable retirement in abroad rather than taking the risk to attempt to stay in power.

In April, the Gulf Cooperation Council drew a roadmap for Saleh's safe exist from leadership. Saleh has several times attempted to fully cooperate with the Gulf Cooperation Council States and promised to sign the GCC resolution on three occasions but refused to do so when promised dates for signing the agreement came.

Saleh's conduct to the Gulf Cooperation Council initiatives was unexpected, due to his resistance to leaving office and his barbaric actions toward his rivals. In April, the Yemeni autocrat made an unsurprising speech inside the capital city where he accused his opponents of unity working with the enemy of Yemen to destroy the sovereignty of Yemen and creating instability in the country, and also accused his rivals of affiliating with the radical extremist group (al-Qaeda).

Contrary, Saleh's refusal to fulfil his promises to sign the GCC agreement feared his rivals and made them believe that he intends to remain in office. President Saleh continued his brutality against anti-regime protestors and hoped that he could oppress the opposition to the extent that international pressure declines if he re-established control over urban areas.

The country's second biggest city, Taiz, was the command centre of the opposition activist and facing significant repression from the regime, including the use of artillery to shell residential areas where demonstrations were being held. In the capital city (Sanaa), there were rare tensions between pro-Saleh forces and opposition armed forces. The fighting's involved the use of rockets, substantial shelling. These tensions were often reduced by various international community truces. The political situation of the country deteriorated on June when the president escaped assassination due to a bomb explosion in a mosque inside the presidential palace.

Saleh was severely wounded during this incident. Several other officials in his regime were affected and eventually lost their lives as a result of the incident. Shortly after the attack, Saleh flew to neighbouring Saudi capital for emergency medical treatment on the basis of not returning to Yemen as Saudi authorities pressuring him to leave the office. After the arrival Saleh, Some Saudi authorities clearly stated that he would either stay in Saudi Arabia or settle elsewhere. The departure of the longstanding Yemeni leader from Yemen had eased the situation in the country.

The pressure on Saleh to return to Yemen was ineffective and insufficient, on September 23 Saleh returned to Yemen to continue with his duties as president of Yemen. He came to Yemen on the 6th day of fresh fightings in the capital, which was the worst fighting since March. As the violence raged, foreign oppositions made a strategy to increase the international pressure on the Yemeni president to resign in accordance with his previous promises. The UN Security Council passed a resolution on October 21, calling the president to fully comply with the GCC agreement immediately and leave the office.

President Saleh had no choice but to accept the agreement as the Yemeni economy heavily depends on international aid. On November 23, 2011, President Saleh has finally accepted to sign the GCC agreement and agreed to resign from the presidency on the basis of not being prosecuted for the crime against the humanity he committed during his time in office. President Saleh had for long-time struggled to avoid this outcome and also feared that the UN would impose heavy sanctions against him and his family members. Such sanctions involved in freezing assets and preventing from travelling abroad.

However, after his resignation from the office many protestors demanded his extradition to Yemen so he could face justice for all the crimes he committed. Saleh has transferred the power to his right hand, the vice president. He kept the position of president as a label until the new president was inaugurated in February. As stated in the GCC agreement, Ali Abdullah Saleh was granted free from all charges against him during his time in office. However, the opposition parliamentary members were able to limit the level of legal immunity provided to the ex-president family and close allies in his regime. Nonetheless, these individuals can still be prosecuted for different charges such as terrorism, corruption and other related crimes.

Many Yemenis were extremely disappointed as Saleh would not be held liable for his brutality and the use of force against demonstrators. Although others accepted that immunity was a reasonable approach to ouster the Yemeni tyrant. The agreement did not request Ali Abdullah Saleh to quit the country permanently, despite the US foreign secretary Clinton declare that there had been an informal agreement that he had to leave permanently. The Gulf Cooperation Council agreement involved various other deals that beyond Saleh's departure from office.

The agreement involved in the creation of a new government which composes of Saleh's party and several other opposition parties. In accordance with the agreement, the new president was to be Saleh's long-service deputy president Hadi, who would be the only candidate running for president in the next presidential election of 2012. Yemen's House of Representatives made it clear that elections couldn't occur in that year as a result of difficulties in the political and economic situation of the country. Instead, a caretaker president with a 2-year term would be installed, and the Constitution would be rewritten, with competitive elections planned for 2014.

The creation of the new constitution is supposed to be worked out in a national dialogue between the ruling party and opposition parties organised in a coalition known as the Joint Meeting Parties. Hadi likewise promised to hold a referendum on a new constitution. The new government led by Hadi was balanced between the opposition and his party; Mohamed Basindwa was appointed the new prime minister of Yemen. Basindwa had previously served as foreign minister under Saleh and member of the General Party Congress but then left the party in 2000. After his departure of the GPC, Basindwa has been independent from any political party. During the uprising, Basindwa strongly opposed Saleh for his brutality against innocent civilians and anti-regime protestors, Basindwa then upheld strong credibility with the Yemeni opposition.

However, Mohamed Basindwa's post as the prime minister was undoubtedly lower position in power to Hadi's position as the head of state who is also the supreme commander of the armed force. Concerning the new cabinet led by President Hadi, the GPC has acquired main ministerial departments including foreign affairs, defence and oil, whereas the opposition took less superior ministries such as the interior, finance and education ministries. As for Saleh, he left the country for medical reasons following the appointment of the new government. It wasn't clear if overseas medical treatment was necessary for him, but what is clear is that many opposition leaders wanted him to leave the country during the election.

While Hadi was preparing to take the office of president, his predecessor Saleh had made a speech before his journey to the US, where he asked forgiveness to the people of Yemen for his brutality during the uprising and declared that it was time for him to relinquish the presidency. Also, he also confirmed that he will retain his position as the head of the GPC and will continue to play a crucial role in the Yemeni politics. One day before the presidential elections, he urged his supporters to vote for Hadi, despite this move was of limited significance since Hadi is the only candidate in the eyes of the electorate.

Hadi was elected as the president of the Republic of Yemen after the official results were announced by the Yemeni interior ministry. However, Hadi acquires the leadership of his political party. Saleh expected Hadi to act like a puppet and kept his loyalty to Saleh. However, Hadi clearly understood Saleh's intention to remain in the political decision making and the fact that he is intending to collaborate with Hadi in leading Yemen.

Hadi at this point showed no interest in associating himself with Saleh. Hadi's efforts to marginalise Saleh clearly reflect on his role in the massacre of March 2011 and his unprecedented violence against anti-regime demonstrators.

The Ministry of Human Right revealed that the heavy casualties on March 2011 resulted in the death of more than 2000 civilians and around 22,000 were severely injured. Hadi has encountered problems on the eve of the presidential election as he was the only candidate running for office. Therefore the electoral process could be seen as huge scepticism. Under these harsh circumstances, the most important question for the new regime's future legitimacy rapidly became what kind of turnout could be expected. Luckily, the electoral turnout was at 65% of registered voters.

This illustrated a good sign as more voters registered despite radical groups including secessionists in the south and the Houthi movement in the north had urged for a complete boycott of the election. Following Hadi's decisive win in the election, the constitutional council inaugurated him as president on February 25, 2012. This moment was a turning point for the future of Yemen and its politics.

President Hadi has both military and political background. Before serving as Vice President, he was general of the Yemeni armed force. Hadi grew up in the southern province of Abyan. He became a military officer serving in the southern army of PDRY before the unification of South and North of the country. During 1986, Hadi and his army escaped to North Yemen as a result of the military coup conducted by his rivals in Aden. Hadi would be executed if he was to be captured by his rivals. His status as an exiled has changed following the unification of North and South of the country. He kept his loyalty to Saleh's regime, and this loyalty was underscored in 1994 when he played a prominent role in crushing the effort by southern Yemen to secede from the unified state.

The main reason in which Hadi was chosen to serve as the vice president was because he hailed from south of the country, Hadi is considerably seen as untrusted in the southern part of the country for his role in defeating the 1994 bid to restore southern independence. On the positive aspect, Hadi was broadly honored by the people as he kept himself away from political and moral corruption. Likewise, many Yemenis believe that due to his wise leadership tribalism selection were replaced by a high level of educated technocrats in high ranking positions.

When he took office as the head of state, he did not begin his presidency with tribal and regional power base which may have been another reason that Saleh was comfortable placing him in his previous position of vice president. The vulnerability could also mean another reason why he was chosen as the transitional president since different political groups might presume that he did not have the backing to go beyond his duties as the head of state and tries to establish an absolute totalitarian regime. In terms of Saleh's perspective, there is a possibility that he viewed Hadi as a weak successor whom he could easily manipulate through the party.

As we know, had is a member of the General Party Congress; however, Saleh still holds the supremacy of the party. In March 2012, Ali Abdullah Saleh used his position within the party to inject himself back into Yemeni politics. In the early months of Hadi's leadership, Saleh has dramatically continued his political involvement in the Yemeni politics despite his ouster. Saleh used to meet on a daily basis with some security and political officials.

Some Yemeni viewed him as the man who makes the country's political decision behind the scene. It was also reported that he made sure that his strong supporters remain in offices and other parts of governmental institutions so they could facilitate him to continue his direct involvement in the Yemeni affairs, and the GCC agreement where he ordered his loyalist within the new regime to ignore President Hadi's presidential decrees when it opposed against his interest. Therefore to prevent this from happening and bringing the situation under control, the US embassy in Yemen, has issued a statement stating that no party has the right to interfere in the implementation of the Gulf Cooperation Council agreement.

Following the statement issued by the US embassy, Saleh has heavily denounced as the statement as it concerned him directly could not be separated from previous threats of sanctions against him and his associates. Hadi formed a cabinet with a significant number of Saleh's loyalist in it and held key ministerial posts throughout the administrative apparatus and security services.

The GCC agreement in relation to the power transfer stated that General Party Congress would hold half of the seats in the cabinet, and some of these ministers were loyal to Saleh than to Hadi. Furthermore, during his time in office, President Saleh had placed the members of his family in several key national security positions to protect the regime. Some of these individuals remained in their positions, despite their political futures were in extreme danger.

General Ahmed Ali Saleh, the oldest son of former President Saleh, was the most important holdover from the previous regime. General Ahmed remained as the chief of Yemen's Republican Guard force for a while, although his command was dissolved, and his future was in complete uncertainty. After the election, Riyadh urgently provided aid to Yemen to assist the new government with the economic difficulties. The US and its European allies also backed Hadi and supported the GCC agreement.

The West alongside the international community could support Hadi if AQAP were to cause insurgency in some parts of Yemen and that Hadi took military efforts against the terrorist organisation. As the political divorce between Hadi and his former chief widen, former head of state Ali Abdullah Saleh continuously accused his successor and the new government of being totally uncertain about the future of the country. Saleh as part of his unlawful actions to cause additional disruption to the new government was working behind the scene to weaken the Hadi government in the hopes that he could return to power.

The US alongside with its European allies and the Gulf Cooperation Council took a dim view of former leader Saleh in relation to his effort to create counterproductive in the Yemeni government. In response to this unlawful role in undermining the government, President Obama issued a presidential order to freeze US-based assets of anyone who attempts to block or interfere with the implementation of the GCC agreement or attempts to destabilise the situation in Yemen. The order was a direct response to the obstacles made by former leader Saleh and his loyalist. This US initiative undoubtedly strengthened Hadi's Leadership.

Hadi's government were very fragile in the fight against terrorism and therefore required strong military support from overseas to assist his government to defeat the terrorist groups. President Hadi has limited internal power and increases his effort to expand his power within the country.

This effort reflects on fundamental change in the country's political system and lessens any future effort at building strong and effective governmental institution. Also, the significant corruption boosted the Arab Spring in Yemen and left other parts of the Arab world in a total mess. In future, President Hadi and his successors could do more to strengthen the Yemeni institutions but any effort in the future would probably be impossible due to Hadi's relatively weak position.

The emergence of terrorist AQAP

The people of Yemen including its diaspora have been prominent in the existence of al-Qaeda and its regional associates; the rise of AQAP has threatened the Middle East and global stability. Yemenis often refer the organisation as al-Qaeda rather than AQAP. The reason why Yemenis refer this group as al-Qaeda is because the group members often pledge their loyalty to al-Qaeda and its principles. Furthermore, following the death of Bin Laden, AQAP leader pledges his full allegiance to Bin Laden's successor Ayman al-Zawahiri. Many see AQAP as a fraction of al-Qaeda, despite the truth is much more complex.

Since the creation of AQAP, the group has been characterised as a ruthless and insurgent force. Ansar al-Shariah acted the head of the AQAP, the group's self-sufficiency has widely been given up, and its lack of independence is no longer hidden. For the past several decades, Yemen has been considered as a jihadi sanctuary by some al-Qaeda writers such as Abu Musab al-Suri and Osama bin Laden. During the war against the Soviet in Afghanistan, hundreds of Yemeni youths joined the fight and rallied behind Osama Bin Laden to end the Soviet presence in Afghanistan. After the war, those Yemenis kept their loyalty to Bin Laden. Yemeni authorities usually viewed this situation as manageable and not particularly troubling in the short-term aftermath of their return. In early 1990, the political culture of Yemen considered the jihad against the respectable Soviet undertaking, and the returning jihadist were seen as heroes.

Furthermore, many Yemeni young jihadists left their country due to harsh economic conditions and the lack of employment opportunities for them. After the war, the international community was less concerned about the conduct of forces that fought against the Soviet, while the Yemeni government acknowledge the potential threat posed by the anti-soviet fighters.

Following the unification of North and South of the country in mid-1990, the Yemeni President Ali Abdullah Saleh considered the Islamist fighters against the Soviet as a valuable counterbalance to southern Marxists in his political approach of creating conflicting groups against each other so he could remain in power.

During the civil war in 1994, the government viewed these anti-Soviet fighters as a beneficiary tool and employed at least three brigades with high experience to fight alongside the government to defeat anti-government rebellions. This force had made a substantial contribution to the Northern victory against Southern militias. The government has rewarded the jihadist force with various positions including military, security and government institutions. Some of the jihadists had left Yemen to join al-Qaeda in the Afghani civil war and sided with the Taliban. The jihadist that remained in Yemen kept their contact with other radical Islamist in overseas and was interested in forming an armed terrorist group to continue their Islamic jihad.

The Al-Qaeda terrorist group, which is believed to have a strong presence in Yemen since 1990's, was increasingly keen to wage jihad against the United States of America and carry out deadly attacks in some parts of USA. The first ever jihadi terrorist attack by these group was in 1992, when they attacked some Westerners in a hotel in Aden, Yemen. The purpose of this attack was to target and kill American soldiers travelling to their duty station in Somalia, but instead killed an Australian tourist and two Yemenis.

Al-Qaeda's Yemen-based agents received were believed to be the perpetrators of the terrorist attacks on the US consulate Tanzania and Kenya in 1998, although it has been confirmed that no Yemenis citizen took part in the terrorist attack. The most notorious attack at this point of the conflict was the al-Qaeda strike against the destroyer USS Cole on October 12, 2000, during this horrific attack at least 17 were assassinated and 40 were severely wounded.

The Yemeni government has cooperated with the US to examine the causes of this strike, but investigators considered the Yemeni government support as resentful and circumscribed as a result of Saleh's efforts to avoid stirring up internal crisis among anti-American ideology in the population. As President Bush was considering if Yemen was a security partner or an opponent in the aftermath of the USS Cole investigation, the radical al-Qaeda launch horrific bombing attacks on September 11, 2001, on World Twin Center (twin towers) and the Pentagon.

Under these dramatic circumstances, President Saleh understood that tolerant treatment to radical militants was contradicting in his own interest. To safeguard his interest, he pledged his full support to the US in the fight against Al-Qaeda and their allies and also expelled Yemen from several suspected radicals who came to Yemen to learn about Islam.

In November 2002, the Yemeni authorities allowed the US to launch drone attacks which killed approximately six al-Qaeda militants, including several leaders in the Marib province, Yemen. Qaid Sinan al-Harithi, the leader of the al-Qaeda branch in Yemen was among the dead. By November 2003, Yemeni security forces arrested Muhammed al-Ahdal, who was then al-Harithi's successor as the head of al-Qaeda in Yemen.

In 2004, with the al-Qaeda dilemma apparently contained if not quenched, the Yemeni government turned their attention on its adversary rebellious Houthi in northern Sa'ada territory, while the US focused on the issues associated with the violence in post-Saddam ouster in Iraq.

After the horrific attack on twin towers, President Saleh was compelled to adapt to a progressive regional violence, including internal discontent made by the US resulted in the invasion of Iraq. Like Afghanistan, post-Saddam Iraq turned into an essential preparation ground for Yemeni radicals. The estimated number of Yemeni jihadist who fought alongside al-Qaeda against the US invasion of Iraq is uncertain. Many observers indicated that approximately 2000 fighters took part in the war for the first few years of the war.

Following the unlawful US invasion, President Saleh decided not to oppose against many extreme preachers, including Sheikh Abdul-Majeed al Zindawi, who publicly influenced young men to go to Iraq to participate in the war. The obstacles for al-Qaeda militants in Yemen rose in 2006 after 23 terrorist members of al-Qaeda committed a mass escape from political security prison in Yemen.

The 2006 jail break has frequently been dealt with as the key event for the revival of a progressive autonomous al-Qaeda in Yemen. On this issue of prison escape, only a few individuals were involved, and these escaped terrorist had the capabilities of causing serious problems after their escape. However, a year later, the government forces launched an attack against this terrorist and killed six of them and brought 11 of the escaped terrorist into custody. Therefore, however, powerful this terrorist might be, there is a need to look for further elements that could revive al-Qaeda in Yemen.

Another component of much greater significance than the 2006 jail break in al-Qaeda revival involved the developments of neighbouring Saudi Arabia. In 2007, several Saudi radical extremists made their way to Yemen after their defeat in Saudi Arabia, to bring many better-financed terrorists into contact with the Yemenis.

The alliance between Saudi and Yemeni al-Qaeda branches in 2009, under the banner of al-Qaeda in the Arab Peninsula, was a huge concern to the Yemeni government and indicated the threat of radical forces in Yemen. The Yemeni government had quickly responded to the threat following the announcement of the terrorist group (al-Qaeda) when the security forces arrested approximately 170 terrorist suspects and forced them to sign pledges that they will never take part in terrorism and were then liberated to the supervision of their tribal pioneers.

While the promises themselves can't be seen as a genuine measure, this was a clear warning to the suspected terrorist, and if they commit any terrorist act in the future, they will face a life sentence and even capital punishment. Also, the tribal leaders of these suspected individuals were required to ensure the good conduct of these individuals. Such actions could prevent numerous radicals from conducting jihadist activities, but are likely of limited effectiveness in encouraging the activities of hard-core terrorists.

The number of Yemeni members in AQAP were estimated around 200-300 in 2011, in early 2012 the number of Yemeni members in the organisation has dramatically increased to 700, including members of the insurgent group, Ansar al-Shariah, which is considered as AQAP branch.

This figure has been justified as inadequate and must be put in a wider context. Previously, such estimates included only professional terrorist and not supporters or sympathisers who might be brought into the organisation at a later time. During 2011, a rise in AQAP supporters and sympathisers seemed to become actively involved in the military struggle against the Yemeni government under the organisational umbrella of Ansar al-Shariah.

Many observers in the region have all indicated that Ansar al-Shariah associates with the AQAP terrorist group, and the government of Yemen sees them as the front organisation for AQAP. Also, several Yemeni military generals have characterised Ansar al-Shariah as a real army with heavy equipment.

Despite the current level of 700 Yemeni members in the group, it's expected that this number to rise significantly as a result of the financial opportunities for the young men to become AQAP fighters. The increasing number in jihadism has frightened the Yemeni government and the local tribal leaders as these young jihadists pose clear threat to the existence of the government and the security and stability of the country.

Also, the Yemeni government were extremely concerned about the external radicals from other countries that are coming to Yemen to join al-Qaeda forces. This process has often occurred in waves, mostly Saudi radicals. Additionally, there is a growing number of Pakistani and Afghani radicals that are moving their operations to Yemen as a result of US military presences in their countries. The Yemeni government has also claimed that some Somali jihadists are continuing to arrive in Yemen to join both AQAP and Ansar al-Shariah.

The Western media frequently characterise the extreme group, Ansar al-Shariah as 'al-Qaeda-linked group. More decisive, the government of Yemen has persistently assumed that Ansar al-Shariah is a branch of AQAP and the government uses the names al-Qaeda and Ansar al-Shariah correspondently.

This interpretation was accurate, as, after some time, AQAP declared that Ansar al-Shariah comes under their command and control large of its forces.

The spiritual leader of AQAP, Adel al-Abab has indicated that Ansar al-Shariah was created by AQAP to convey the straightforward message that these fighters are here to install the laws of God as a substitute for the corrupt Saleh's regime in the country.

This accentuation on internal issues was made to forward the image of a group that was determined to eliminate the corruption and the excessive atrocity carried out by Saleh's regime to undermine the population. Following the establishment of Ansar al-Shariah in Southern Yemen, the connections with AQAP were to be permitted to end up more self-evident. Furthermore, there was a hope that the message would infect the southern people as the people of South openly opposed to the central government.

The people of South felt victimised by the central government as less development were made in southern regions. It is likely that AQAP intended to build Ansar al- Shariah as a mass organisation to make certain it was not left behind by the Arab Spring uprising in Sanaa. The fact that AQAP has used Ansar al-Shariah as a front organisation was useful as AQAP had greater hopes to carry out a heavy strike in Saudi Arabia, the West, and especially the United States.

Such hopes, even if it attracts some Yemen, it could deteriorate the situation in the country. The leaders of al-Qaeda and its affiliate AQAP have strongly concerned about the possible damaging of Al-Qaeda name. Some declassified documents states that the mastermind of al-Qaeda (Bin Laden) was himself concerned if the name and the value of al-Qaeda might be damaged by the campaign against it. Such damage could affect to the regional partners who still pledge their loyalty to the al-Qaeda core, sometimes called al-Qaeda central.

A respective explanation behind the new name might be AQAP's concern about the unpopularity religious fighters in Southern Yemen as President Saleh's use of Islamist fighters in the 1994 civil war. A large number of these irregular armies took part in the Soviet war in Afghanistan, and several of these armies have been affiliated with the al-Qaeda leader Bin Laden. Despite concerns of international terrorism, some Yemeni southerners hold resentment against Laden, al-Qaeda, and AQAP due to the unlawful killings committed by the jihadist fighters during the civil war. Thus, while Ansar al-Shariah showed up on the scene as a jihadist association, its depiction as nearby and unconstrained may have included a push to recognise the front association from some awkward parts of past jihadi history in Yemen.

Battleground casualties are another sign of the extensive relation between Ansar al-Shariah and AQAP. Consequently, after the airstrike against the terrorist group (Ansar al-Shariah) in March 2012, the Yemeni government has indicated that AQAP commander has been identified among those who were killed during the airstrike. This circumstance could be as seen as additional evidence of the relation between the extreme groups. Furthermore, the government has reported that a large number of foreign jihadist were part of Ansar al-Shariah dead.

According to the government officials, the foreign fighters were mainly Somali and Saudi jihadist. Such indications were expected. In February 2012, the leading commander of the African Union forces in Somalia, General Fred Mugisha, clearly indicated that Somali extremist, in particular, al-Shabab jihadist, left Somalia to Yemen as a result of their unprecedented defeat in Somalia. Likewise, the Egyptians and Afghani jihadist were reportedly among the foreign fighters that were identified among the Ansar al-Shariah dead. It's very unlikely that these foreign jihadists would make their way to Yemen to join extreme domestic groups without a foreign connection.

On the other hand, it appears to be beyond any doubt that these fighters could reach the battle zone in southern Yemen by working with an extreme group that has an international connection, for example, the AQAP. After some time, AQAP struggling efforts to characterise Ansar al-Shariah as an independent association appear to have vanished totally. While the Ansar al-Shariah group raised its own flag, in 2012, there were reports that al-Qaeda's black flag is being raised in controlled areas of Ansar al-Shariah. Independent journalist who visited Ansar al-Shariah command centres stated that local people, including Ansar al-Shariah fighters, use the terms al-Qaeda and Ansar al-Shariah reciprocally.

Other sign of the remarkable relationship between the AQAP and Ansar al-Shariah took place after a decisive attack has been launched by the Ansar al-

Shariah against the Yemeni government forces and captured a large number of Yemeni troops. Several tribal have requested reconciliation talks with AQAP about the possible release of the captured prisoners with a promise not to help the antagonist of Shariah law.

Following the agreement, Ansar al-Shariah declared the official release of the prisoners under the authorization of AQAP leader. This clearly showed that AQAP had a strong influence on Ansar al-Shariah decision on important issues such as the release of prisoners and other issues. Before the death of the al-Qaeda inventor, Bin Laden, he and al-Qaeda had a long history of terrorism involvement in Yemen, and many extremist youths have associated with him during his terrorist career. Although, after his death, the operation links between al-Qaeda headquarters and AQAP disappeared due to lack of leadership by his successor.

Several Yemeni al-Qaeda founders in Yemen fought with the group during their youth and were loyal supporters of Osama Bin Laden. The newly leader of AQAP has for many years worked with bin Laden and acted as his right hand during the Soviet war in Afghanistan.

Additionally, Yemen was the most strategic site of al-Qaeda's anti-American strikes, the shelling of the USS Cole. Al-Qaeda terrorist group was clearly behind the horrific attack against the US warship, although some said that the group had used local radical youths to carry out the activity. Bin Laden himself plotted the attack and funded the expenses to accomplish the assault. Also, he disregarded the suggestions from the local people which were to strike against a commercial ship.

In the aftermath of the World Trade Centre and Pentagon attack in September 2001, bin Laden's status as most wanted man on earth would make it difficult to apply strong command over AQAP planning, and he was hence consigned to the position of advisor and letter writer, who communicated unreliably through couriers. Despite bin Laden's advice to his regional allies were valuable to some extent, he didn't have any influence on the final decision.

After some time, the central authority of AQAP characterised him as out-of-hands individual with very extreme views, who had to be humoured to a certain extent. The destruction of bin Laden's influence on AQAP was broadly suspicious before his death in Pakistan. But appears to have been drastically confirmed by documents seized in the raid on bin Laden's house. These documents were declassified documents and gave full details about the locations of the terrorist training sites. While this information was incomplete and some inaccurate, it pointed out several issues in relation to the planned terrorist operations and the ties between him and AQAP.

Also, the documents state that al-Qaeda chief was extremely disappointed that AQAP had waged a war against the Yemeni regime rather than attacking the United States. Also, al-Qaeda's leader declassified letters stated that he believed AQAP was doing similar mistakes that al-Qaeda force in Iraq had made before. Bin Laden was increasingly worried that AQAP sought to seize regions without the permission or consensus of the local people.

Likewise, in an especially revealing decision, Osama Bin Laden has sent his closest associate Sheik Yunis al-Muritani to coordinate with AQAP and AQIM. The visit appeared to be an exertion by the leader Bin Laden to indicate his concerns with the local leaders, but also the objective of the visit was to raise funds for the group.

Although there is no clear indication of the messenger being asked to solicit funds from AQAP, he was told to request a total sum of 200,000 Euros from the typically well-funded AQIM. Such a solicitation shows that Bin Laden wasn't assisting other regional allies with finance. During the time of solicitation, unless AQAP and AQIM were being dealt differently, he was unlikely to provide funds that would have denied him an important instrument, which could somehow or another be utilised to influence AQAP and other regional associate. Without funds to provide to AQAP, bin Laden had almost nothing to offer that organisation, and disregarding his guidance was large without consequences. Shockingly, Bin Laden kept AQAP mastermind and propagandist Anwar al-Awlaki on a low profile and was very concerned if Awlaki would one day lead the AQAP organisation.

This anxiety was allegedly not lessen by Awlaki's Internet advocacy of the significance of attacking the United States, and the Yemeni government forces. The Bin Laden Scepticism on Awlaki could come from the lack of relationship between the two men and their disagreement on different issues in relation to the terrorist activities. It is also likely that bin Laden was to some extent disturbed with the enormous amount of media attention that Awlaki gained and maybe feared that it would overshadow his media coverage. Osama Bin Laden has always endorsed the term 'al-Qaeda central' and was not prepared to allow others to overshadow him within the global of a radical jihadist.

This burden would be particularly clear in the case of Awlaki, as he never met the al-Qaeda leader and could not be considered as Bin Laden senior. The death of Bin Laden appeared to help to increase the downturn of al-Qaeda Central finished whatever remaining influence that the organisation had over branch associations such as AQAP. Regrettably, this was a serious blow to AQAP itself. Bin laden's irregular exhortation was certainty no interest to AQAP as they always ignore his advice, and his failure to provide AQAP with funds indicated that he had no value to their existence.

Following his death, Bin Laden became a martyr to the cause and principles of al-Qaeda and could, therefore, be used as a source of inspiration to AQAP members. Furthermore, in a profoundly symbolic but more insignificant action, the AQAP central authority has pledged their loyalty to Ayman al-Zawahiri (Bin Laden's successor). The AQAP worked essentially as a terrorist association before 2010, yet it later extended its operations to add exertion to seize and govern areas where the Yemeni government had little ability to preserve security.

This approach of capturing and ruling territory was enforced before the Arab Spring uprising, although it was later. In spite of the fact that it was later accelerated because of the Arab Spring violence in Yemen, an early sign of AQAP's increased enthusiasm to fight as a rebellious army can be identified amid the 2010 combat operation in southern parts of the country. When AQAP seized the territory, the local people were almost subjected to strong political indoctrination. Often the AQAP used powerful, persuasive question "why do you oppose the being rule by the law of God?" sadly for AQAP no indoctrination effort was likely to make their rule agreeable to numerous Yemeni tribesman. The implementation of the Shariah law stress severe Islamic punishment for any breach that the organisation believes to have occurred.

The leader of Ansar al-Shariah stated that their aim was to implement God's law in Abyan province. This objective was entirely met in Yemeni provinces controlled predominantly by the AQAP and its affiliate Ansar al-Shariah. Some observe indicated that Ansar al-Shariah implemented a variety of extreme punishment for any action that is contradicting the law of God. These punishments include torture, beheadings, stone death and amputations. One woman was killed under the pretext of being sorcery. Additionally, while it is possible that state media in Yemen exaggerated the cruelty of this extreme group (Ansar al-Shariah).

After Ansar al-Shariah's successful insurgent attacks, the group and its AQAP ally has established a strong presence in Loder, which the Yemeni armed force challenged in August 2010. As part of their strategy, AQAP militants chose to remain in Loder to fight against the Yemeni armed forces rather than leaving the town. These initiatives illustrate the level of their commitments to retain their cause, and perhaps degrade the quality of the Yemeni army.

The government forces had eventually defeated AQAP/Ansar al-Shariah and regained AQAP control towns after days of heavy fighting, which resulted in the escape of a large number of AQAP fighters. There were reports of little casualties on both sides; the AQAP did not consider Loder as crucial enough to launch a bloody last stand of the fighters involved. Such escape was reasonable action as the Yemeni government forces would use heavy military equipment which could demolish the AQAP fighters within a short period, perhaps hours. After the war, the people of Loder certainly did not want AQAP to come back and establish armed resistance to fight against AQAP if they were to return and seize their towns.

The impetus for the establishment of the armed resistance was to capture Zinjibar city by the militants within the time frame, and the concern that AQAP and its ally Ansar al-Shariah would again expand its territorial holdings. The armed resistance fully defended Loder on several occasions, especially when AQAP has tried to re-gain the city but failed to do. After experiencing the savage rule of Ansar al-Shariah, the people of Loder were ready to fight to protect the comeback of AQAP into their city.

In September 2010, the government forces again took part a battle against al-Qaeda forces. But this time the conflict reached the town of Hawta, which has a total population of 20,000. Almost 9,000 inhabitants of Hawta town escaped and made their way to safer zone. Whereas many others were prevented from fleeing by the insurgent groups, so that the terrorists could use the presence of the inhabitants as a shield from artillery and other heavy military equipment by the government forces.

Such behaviour might have been exactly the kind of conduct that Bin Laden and other global jihadist leaders had cautioned AQAP to keep away from if wanted to earn the trust and loyalty of the people. This confrontation was reported to have involved government army tanks and armoured vehicle moving against an uncertain number of AQAP members. In the 2010 battling, AQAP demonstrated its development as an extremist association through the ability to ambush or assault squad and maybe larger units of the government forces.

The police force was also a regular target by the insurgent groups. In September 2010, the al-Qaeda militant plotted an incident in the province capital of Zinjibar, the terrorist attackers on motorbikes used hit-and-run strategy against police targets; there were indications that these attacks were carefully planned and effective execution of a synchronised mission. Also, September that year, the insurgent group AQAP has issued a death list of 55 officials within the government which includes military, judicial and police that was targeted for assassination. Such actions illustrate the insurgency of the terrorist group and this warning meant that unless these official mentioned on the death list, doesn't resign from their posts there is the possibility of being assassinated.

Taking into consideration of the horrific history of al-Qaeda in killing and kidnapping several senior officials in the government throughout Yemen. These insurgent group targets are extremely vulnerable and expected to be killed anytime. Following the withdrawal of AQAP from Loder, there remained some positive signs regarding Yemen's efforts to control terrorism.

In mid of 2010, some Yemeni tribe elders in the areas of Sanaa appeared to be reassessing their perspectives on the costs and benefits of sheltering al-Qaeda suspects in their regions. The harbouring of such criminals led to Yemeni military strikes into their region and undermined to disrupt any support network giving funds from Sanaa or Riyadh. Hence, both a key source of tribal income and general security within tribal areas were undermined. In response to this escalating situation, tribe elders from Abida and al-Ashraf tribes promised that they would stop assisting aid to fugitives that are wanted by government forces. These vows were a positive development, but were not surprising, as no tribal leaders were willing to see a source of authority in their regions that might dislodge them. However, while some tribal leaders were assisting AQAP militants with money and shelter, they have never been keen on surrendering their power to this insurgent group. Seizing such power from tribal leaders was now clearly the main objective of AQAP goal.

The AQAP insurgent group has made enormous progress to deploy its forces dramatically following the division within the armed force over civilian deaths in the massacre of March 2011. Ansar al-Shariah seized the southern city of Jaar in March and Zinjibar in May 2011 and displacing thousands of civilians. This war involved one of the most radical groups, Ansar al-Shariah. On this event, the insurgent militants flew banners with the words 'Ansar al-Shariah'. Around 1,000 forces have seized the city of Zinjibar after coming from Jaar, which previously was controlled by AQAP militants.

A branch of the Yemeni armed force has confronted the Islamists militants but was unable to prevent the city from being captured. The Yemeni army remained positioned near Zinjibar city, by have conducted defensive operations following the defeat. The radicals came close to overrunning this unit in July 2011, but the national army managed to resist the attacks with the help of air force units that were identified as Yemeni.

Yemen's information Vice Minister indicated that the US has supplied with Yemen a logistic support for the armed force assigned to defeat the radicals to prevent the insurgent siege. Offensive operations were conducted by the government forces in 2011 and this operation mostly consisted of shelling the extreme groups with artillery.

There were reports indicating that the government had used tribal mediators to force the extreme groups to withdraw from its strongholds without any violence. The government use of artillery and air strikes led to the huge level of civilian casualties. While it would appear easy to accuse the armed force of lacking an offensive spirit, it should be understood that they were facing major issues in supplying their troops, as a result of the chaotic Yemeni governmental system at the time.

Logistical efforts from Sanaa couldn't happen as a result of the turmoil, and the insurgent group Ansar al-Shariah halt the supply route from the city of Aden to complete the government army solitude. Under these circumstances, the Army leaders feared to carry out offensive operations in which could not finish. Therefore, the insurgent group 'Ansar al-Shariah' remained in control of Zinjibar, Jaar, and other rural areas in the south of the country without genuine hostile activities levelled against them on the ground throughout the rest of Saleh's presidency. The military actions that took place came from the air. When Hadi took the reign, he confronted a strong insurgency that had flourished after the year-long power struggle in Sanaa.

When a Yemeni army lieutenant positioned in the south of the country was asked about his unit's in January, he stated: "we are like an island in the sea of al-Qaeda, we are surrounded in every direct". Under these circumstances, the Yemeni press was anxious that AQAP would gain significantly more ground in capturing regions in the south. These concerns were justifiable. In January 2012, approximately 200 militants captured Rida, a town with a population of 60,000 individuals, about 100 miles of Sanaa. They stayed in control of the town for ten days.

Amid that time, almost few people appear to have been killed although ten police officers were reported to have been kidnapped, and around 100 detainees were freed from the Rida jail, including AQAP militants. It seems that local authorities made an arrangement whereby AQAP could enter the town, free its detainees, and leave immediately. It is possible that the AQAP to understand that they didn't have a sufficient force in the town to hold control if the inhabitants were against them.

On February 2012, the local authority and the AQAP expected the conflict to escalate. President Mansur Hadi took strong measures against the AQAP insurgent as he took the reign, and they had responded with considerable ferocity by hitting Yemeni government targets with suicide bombings and different acts of terrorism. These strikes were made to weaken the government before Hadi could take the reign.

During his oath ceremony, Hadi made it clear that he will continue the war against the insurgents to restore peace and economic prosperity. When he took office, he faced violent challenges from AQAP; a double suicide car bomb was conducted by the insurgent group 'AQAP' which resulted in the death of 26 people in the southern city of Mukallah, at least 20 soldiers were among the deaths. Furthermore, by the time he took office, the situation in the south of the country was extremely dangerous. Ansar al-Shariah militants captured the city of Zinjibar in September 2011, although they had failed to capture the military site outside of the city which stayed under the control of the government forces.

The commander of that unit has told the press that government forces are trying to resupply them had been ambushed and crushed, but the army was able to remain because America sent its aircraft to airdrop food and weapons. The AQAP spokesperson claimed that government forces were able to continue with its operation due to the support that it received from America.

The spokesmen also indicated that the government was able to open a road to supply the army, and this resupply allowed it to prevent another collapse. The spokesman was often referred as the third commander of the AQAP group. After some time, the Yemeni press reported that spokesman had been killed by a U.S. drone.

The 2012 government offensive in Abyan province was a direct interpretation of President Hadi promise to intensify the war against the terrorist group 'AQAP' and to end the existence of the extreme group by all means.

This agenda of wiping out the AQAP was very ambitious since the 2011 division within the Yemeni security forces between pro-Saleh and anti-Saleh forces created less security which the AQAP saw this as an opportunity to seize considerable territories in the South. The objective of the new government led by President Hadi is to continue the war against terrorism despite continuous division within the security forces.

Many of the loyalists believed to remain in their positions, while their critics asked for their removal. President Hadi initially kept many of Saleh loyalists in their positions, although he removed some officials within the military as he regarded them as corrupt and untrustworthy.

Hadi was eager to restructure the military before conducting any military operation against the terrorist group AQAP. Sadly, Hadi's war against AQAP did not begin well. On February 18, 2012, one week before Hadi was inaugurated to the office, but well after Saleh had given up the presidential powers to Hadi, the government forces had considerably suffered from a tremendous defeat by Ansar al-Shariah. Almost 185 armies were killed when the insurgent group attacked a military camp in southern Yemen at night while they were sleeping.

During the attack, the terrorist group had captured 70 soldiers including several officers. As part of their capture, Ansar al-Shariah seized a significant amount of military equipment including artillery pieces and armoured vehicles. After the battle, Ansar al-Shariah militia paraded the military equipment through the streets as a celebration of the victory. The insurgent forces took photographs with the weapons and later posted on jihadist websites to attract more jihadists.

Some Yemeni's were extremely disappointed about the defeat and accused the government forces of being incompetent enough to take the best possible precautionary measures. Various critics also indicated that local army commanders had made agreements with local terrorist leaders who served as informal cease-fires. While Ansar al-Shariah respected the agreements for some time, they appear to have been used to calm the local army into a state of complacency. Such actions would have made the conditions for AQAP to set a trap. Also, while armed force misfortunes were overwhelming, only 32 Ansar al-Shariah fighters were killed in the battle.

Some detainees were reported to have been released to accommodate various Yemeni tribes after mediation by religious scholars and tribal elders. Also, tolerant treatment of detainees might have been utilised to give Yemeni forces an essential motivation to surrender in future fights. If AQAP requested all of their captives killed or savagely mistreated them, more Yemeni government troops might well fight to the death in all future combat.

Unsurprisingly, the AQAP leaders showed no enthusiasm for unwinding their battle after their victory against the Yemeni troops in the south. After Hadi's inauguration, a suicide bomber rammed a Toyota truck into the wall of a presidential palace protected by 45 troops of the Republican Guard in the southern city of Mukalla.

Twenty-six people within the presidential compound were killed, including several soldiers of the republican guard. The AQAP group began to attack the military base in the south of the country with hit-and-run raids. The Yemeni government admitted that the terrorist group had captured some of its strong military equipment including armoured vehicles, artillery pieces, and small arms during the course of these attacks, in addition to the military equipment seizure following the February 18 battle.

After the defeat in February, the Yemeni armed force began to improve its performance in partial reaction to these hard lessons. Almost 200 Yemeni anti-terrorist forces were deployed to help local army to fight against the insurgent group 'Ansar al-Shariah'. According to the Yemeni press, the counter-terrorism Special Forces were sent to help government army in Loder, which was the main target for the insurgent group forces.

The local tribe support committees were vigorously involved in the protection of Loder and engaged in heavy fighting alongside the army units to defeat the extreme groups. Tribal leaders indicated that government forces supplied them with military equipment, and it is possible that tribal militants from other cities received money to take part in the fight against the jihadist.

Furthermore, the Yemeni government forces have used artillery and airstrikes against the extreme groups, while several media claimed that US drones had been deployed to eliminate the terrorist groups. Under this circumstance, the city of Loder was defended, and the insurgents had failed to capture the city for the second time. On 6th May 2012, the deputy leader of AQAP Fahd al-Qusa was killed airstrikes conducted by the Yemeni government, despite the

fact that the world press described the death incident as a missile strike by a US drone. Al-Qusa was a former ally of Osama Bin Laden who was wanted by the US Federal Bureau of Investigation for his connections in the attack on the USS Cole in 2000.

He committed genuine errors in the attack on the USS Cole, despite the fact that he might have increased some aptitude and modernity as a terrorist leader over time. Also, al-Qusa was among the AQAP members who took part in the 2006 prison break and still committed acts of terrorism in early 2012.

The death of such leader had a strong impact on the AQAP resistance and gave a real advantage to the Yemeni government forces to eliminate the insurgent groups. In revenge for the death of al-Qusa, the AQAP militants attacked the military near Zinjibar Media sources maintain that extensive use of drones before Hadi's arranged May hostile bolstered to collect useful intelligence, and disturbed the AQAP control by eliminating key targets.

Al-Qusa, in spite of the errors in his early career, might have been viewed as a key target. On 12th May 2012, after the earlier effort to prepare the battleground, the Yemeni government force launched military operations to recapture AQAP strongholds in Abyan and Shabwa provinces.

The government offensive was conducted with a force of about 20,000 armies, backed by a high number of paid local tribal auxiliaries. It has been reported that the US military advisors took part in the offensive planning Saudi Arabia gave significant financial assistance to support the operation. It seems that a significant share of the Saudi funds may have been utilised to employ tribal militia auxiliaries to help the army. These fighters have been highly effective in this sort of conflict in Yemen.

There are several tribes that have a long history of taking money from Saudi Arabia, and wouldn't have a problem in taking government funds to fight against extreme groups. Just as vitally, the Yemeni air force seemed to have been sent with much more prominent intensity. However, there is some uncertainty in as to how much of the airstrike effort was actually carried on by the Yemeni air force, and how much came from outside sources.

Media sources indicated that the government's standard request is aircraft carry out such operations on Yemeni soil, but they did not take such denials seriously. Virtually the entire Yemeni and international press appeared to believe successful air backing was mostly given by U.S. drone and missile launched from U.S. warships. Media from both US and Yemen have claimed to have spoken several officials from both countries and suggested the possibility of using extensive airstrikes to campaign against AQAP.

Many observers stressed that Yemeni air force were incapable of carrying out a military airstrike against the insurgent groups. Also, others indicated that the U.S. airstrike campaign through drones was too large and significant to be hidden. As the southern hostile proceeded, the insurgent groups struck back rapidly against the regime forces and orchestrated a deadly attack against a military parade rehearsal in the Sanaa Sabeen Square, which resulted in the death of 96 civilians and 300 wounded.

The Yemeni defence secretary, who was planned to visit the rehearsal, was late, and therefore was saved from the suicide attack. The perpetrator of the suicide bombing wore the uniform of the security forces and managed to work his way into the ranks of the soldiers to get ready for the rehearsal.

Following the horrific suicide attack in the rehearsal, the AQAP terrorist group claimed the attack and said that this was just the beginning. Fortunately, the insurgent's awful effort to degrade the local government forces didn't had much impact on the fight against terrorism and radical extremist.

The ground forces launched military crackdown against the AQAP militants in Zinjibar during the first month of the fighting. The push against the provincial capital was portrayed by Yemeni authorities as a "wide hostile" that included military pressure being directed against the city from three sides, utilising components of the armed force, air force, and tribal armed groups. Also, the Yemeni Navy also took part in the fight against the insurgents in Zinjibar as the city is located on the coast of the country and was able block any weapons that was coming to the city through the coastal sea to support the AQAP militias.

The Yemeni armed force liberated the city of Jaar almost the same time they liberated Zinjibar after Ansar al-Shariah fighters fled the city. It was reported that government forces had captured an AQAP ammunition factory in Jaar and killed 50 AQAP militants in the area. On 12th June, the commander of the 31st Armored Brigade, General Salem Qatan, told the media that both Zinjibar and Jaar had been completely purified from the extremists.

On June 14, Yemeni Defense Minister Mohammed Nasser Ahmed visited Zinjibar to demonstrate his safety in doing so and thereby underscore the regimes control of the city. Unfortunately, General Qatan was killed shortly after his announcement on liberating Zinjibar by a suicide bomber in Aden, after the perpetrator went to the General's car as a beggar seeking charity.

The Yemeni government continued their determination to wipe extreme ideologies that will lead to insurgency after the liberation of Zinjibar, and this was widely seen as a turning point. In June 2012, the government has captured the port town of Shaqra which was the last major stronghold of Ansar al-Shariah in Abyan provience. As the offensive undertook in late June 2012, the government forces also captured Azzan in Shabwa province. In addition the Defense Ministry officials claimed to have captured a large cache of bombs and explosives in Azzan.

This constant government initiatives to recapture territories surprised many Yemeni citizens. The Yemeni Brigadier General Mohammed al-Sawmali stated, "This is the end of al-Qaeda's aspirations to establish an Islamic rule in the south. There is no comeback to this." The General al-Sawmali also indicated that he expects the AQAP to continue their fight against the government, with "selective operations targeting key political and military figures." This indication was later turned out to be correct. Additionally, in a last demonstration of ruthlessness before leaving civilians area they had occupied, withdrawing Ansar al-Shariah planted mines all through the area they were evacuating. On June 27, the Saudi press refered to Yemeni authorities as stating that citizens had been killed by mines emplaced by the retreating insurgents

After three days, that number rose to 81, despite Yemeni military authorities stated that their army had evacuated 3,000 landmines from the afflicted areas. While numerous militants of AQAP were killed in the fighting, it was uncertain the number of jihadist fighters who escaped to orchestrate terrorist attacks at a later time under more favorable circumstances. Also, it was reported that some tribal leaders in Shabwa province made considerable efforts to convince some of the defeated Jihadist fighters to surrender and abandon their past affiliation with the militants.

In Yemen, such tribal leaders will ensure the future good conduct of their tribal members in return for some kind of amnesty. Regrettably, these efforts appear to have produced weak results. The insurgent group 'AQAP' have been driven from the urban areas which it previously captured, but many of its militants remained dedicated to the struggle. After these defeats and the loss of territory, AQAP leaders continued to believe that they needed to assert the power and purpose of their group and emphasize their determination to continue the struggle.

However as expected the insurgent group failed to accomplish their planned terrorist attacks including the horrific campaign of urban bombings and killings. The AQAP conducted several dreadful killings targeting key military officials in the case of General Qatan that was killed on June 18 by a suicide bomber; another key military official that was killed by the insurgences was Colonel Abdullah al-Maouzaei on July 19, when he triggered a booby trap in his car in southern Yemen.

However, after awful killings on some military officials, AQAP has attempted to kill another official but has failed to do so. The target was Colonel Yahia al-Rusaishan of the Air Force; he was targeted due to his role in hunting down AQAP members and survived three previous assassination attempts. The Yemeni government responded to these assassinations with serious investigations and to have separated various terrorist cells as a result. On mid-July, an AQAP militant blow himself outside police academy in Sanaa as the police cadets was leaving the academy. The suicide attack killed twenty-two people, who were among the cadets. The security forces later arrested a man whom they accused of plotting the suicide attack on the parade rehearsal and may have been involved with the police academy bombing.

AQAP undertook major operations outside Sanaa, where a suicide bomber killed 45 members of the Popular Defense Committee in Jaar. The commander of this unit, Abdul Latif al-Sayed, was reportedly to be among the dead, and other tribal fighters were wounded in the strike. Another striking attack happened in August when AQAP terrorists killed 14 Yemeni fighters in an explosive and car bomb assault on the security service headquarters in Aden.

Since that time, AQAP has remained proactive, and numerous government security authorities have been dreadfully assassinated in bombings and drive-by shootings from car or particularly motorcycles. Leaders of the AQAP have told that their agents use bikes as it's less likely to be targeted by U.S. drones. Often the insurgent targets intelligent and security forces for assassination efforts, and high security officials loyal to the president were top of the AQAP list.

Beside the military and intelligent official, several leaders of political parties and members of the government were also the key targets. As a result, the security forces had launched major operations to hunt down the perpetrators behind these attacks and claimed to have crushed several AQAP terrorist conspiracy before they were put into practice. The government announced that security forces had arrested several prospective suicide bombers who were intending to attack several governmental buildings, foreign consulates and military academies. Also, as part of the regime forces normal security activities, the Yemeni government approved strong measures against unlicensed motorbikes, in particularly in the southern of Yemen.

Despite the implementation of these harsh measures, AQAP has remained extremely tough and is capable of committing significant acts of terrorism domestically and internationally. They were also interested in future political crises within Yemeni government authority so they could be able to exploit. The AQAP began their terrorist effort against the U.S. during the 2009-12, during this time frame, the terrorist group continued to look for ways to attack the United States, despite their focus on enforcing insurgency in the southern parts of the country and orchestrating major conflicts in that region.

The leaders of AQAP have extremely considered the terrorist attacks against the U.S. and the war against the Saleh regime as their primary objectives, despite the potential for a dissipation of resources with an extreme ambitious agenda. There were some potentially high payoffs for such strategies despite the danger of overreach.

A successful terrorist attacks against the U.S. could endlessly boost AQAP's influence as the front line of jihadi terror so that they could improve significantly their recruiting and fundraising efforts. Furthermore, leaders of

AQAP didn't fear the possibility of U.S. intervention in Yemen after the horrific terrorist attacks and may even have welcomed it. If US were to invade Yemen in response to the dreadful terror attacks, it is completely certain that large number of the Yemeni population would any doubt fight against foreign aggressor no matter how valid the reason for intervention is. In this circumstance, the U.S. administration would have a staggering need to strike back and may effectively choose the wrong way for doing so.

One of the first terrorist operation conducted by AQAP against the United States was in December 25, 2009, when Umar Farouk Abdulmutallab a young Nigerian agent trained by AQAP in Yemen, tried to explode an American airline passenger jet that left Amsterdam, with 280 people on board.

The AQAP agent has failed to accomplish his terrorist operation as a result of the bomb being dysfunctional; he was later handcuffed and restrained by the passengers and airline personnel, so he could be arrested when the plane lands. During his trial in the U.S., Abdulmutallab pleaded guilty to all charges against him about the terrorist attack. The court found him guilty and sentenced him to life imprisonment. Abdulmutallab during the court hearing indicated that he met radical preacher Anwar al-Awlaki and convinced him to oppose the U.S. with Jihad.

After the trial of Abdulmutallab, the U.S. President Barack Obama responded to the unsuccessful bombing attempt by introducing plans to increase the efforts to support the government of Yemen to implement strong initiatives to counterterrorism. In addition, the president has clearly indicated that he has no intention whatsoever to send troop on the ground to Yemen as a result of this incident and declared that "in countries like Yemen, in countries like Somalia, I think working with international partners is most effective at this point." President Obama's announcement echoed earlier comments by U.S. military commanders such as in Admiral Mike Mullen, a former Chairman of the Joint Chiefs of Staff, who claimed that sending U.S. combat troops to Yemen was "not a possibility." In reaction to both the attempted terrorist attack, the Yemeni government has quickly reported that it had captured 29 individuals believed to be members of AQAP in crackdown on that organisation.

The next major operation conducted by AQAP against the United States involved parcel bombs sent via cargo aircraft from Yemen in October 2010, with two American parcel firms including United Parcel Service and Federal Express. The terrorist bomb makers had filled toner cartridges with explosive material and then had the explosives-laden parcels sent to the United States. According to media, the dreadful attack had failed when the packages were ambushed in London and Dubai, due to the information that was provided by the Saudi intelligence.

The plan was evidently to have the packages explode while the aircraft were in flight and make them crash over the sea. If this intelligent effort were to be failed, the packages would be sent to synagogues in the Chicago city where they would kill whoever opened the package.

AQAP leaders have launched an online radical campaign to convince Muslims leaving in the West to conduct terrorist operations as part of Jihad campaign. Previously, internet jihadists posed a minimal threat. A significant number of these individuals enjoy placing blood-curdling postings in internet chat rooms but hesitate at making any genuine sacrifice for radical causes. There are some who are more willing to be serious in accomplishing the Jihadi operation if they were properly recruited. AQAP has been willing to commit time and resources to conquer the issue of recognising potential volunteers from bored hobbyists and recruiting some profoundly dedicated people to participate in acts of terrorism. Mobile phone video of al-Qaeda units fighting in Iraq has been reported to be a vital device for al-Qaeda recruitment efforts in Yemen.

The endeavor to distinguish and promote jihadists from internet radicals is extremely demanding and time-consuming. Some of the issues of incompetence can arise when using internet to recruit terrorists. Moreover, a diverse may have impacted the atmosphere and made it difficult to recruits terrorists over the Internet.

The U.S. withdrawal from Iraq, and the anticipated withdrawal from Afghanistan, appears to have decreased levels of anger in Muslim world that AQAP recruiters have already exploit. One of the AQAP leaders who was broadly suspected of encouraging extremists and hiring terrorists over the internet who is now cleric, Anwar al-Awlaki U.S. Federal prosecutors in the first underwear bomber case believe Awlaki was directly involved in planning this attack.

He is also widely believed to have inspired and helped to radicalise a U.S. Army psychiatrist, who at this time is being prosecuted for an August 2009 shooting attack at Fort Hood, TX, where 13 people were killed and 32 wounded. The psychiatrist is required to plead innocent to the charges, despite the basis for his defense remain unclear. According to some media, President Obama considered Awlaki as an extreme insurgent; the president also told his security advisors that Awlaki posed more threat than the designate leader of al-Qaeda and that he must be eliminate or captured immediately.

This decision was not subjective. If Awlaki was the mastermind of underwear bomber as allege, his plans verged on murdering 280 individuals, and maybe making a circumstance where the U.S. authority would be truly compelled by local public opinion to invade Yemen. Such U.S. aggression would anger significantly Yemeni tribes, who might then increase considerably AQAP fighters. Under these circumstances, it is extremely difficult to envisage such a war prompting a decent result for the United States.

The American forces have the capacity to destruct the Yemeni tribesmen on a regular basis, yet it is difficult to perceive how they could change Yemeni society in ways that would leave that nation a partner after a possible U.S. military withdrawal.

The U.S. emphasis on finding Awlaki delivered results. The radical AQAP leader was assassinated on September 2011, in the town of Khashef by U.S. drone. During the announcement of President Obama in relation to the death of Awlaki, the president called the elimination of Awlaki as a "major blow" in the fight against the extreme radical group 'al-Qaeda', but gave no explanation about the CIA involvement in the operation.

The U.S. Government has never recognized that a drone strike occurred, and the Yemeni government attempted to claim the responsibility of Awlaki's death in public. In making this decision, Obama was certainly mindful of the potential provocative of a U.S. president claiming to target and assassinate a terrorist with a drone in Yemen in contrast to the Yemeni government's desires. The president, therefore, decided to not reveal any details that might shame the Yemeni government.

Many reported that Awlaki death has significantly reduced the attempt of further AQAP terrorist attacks against the United States. Shockingly, this conclusion is a misrepresentation which U.S. leaders need to keep away from. AQAP primarily focused on the internal issues of Yemen due to the 2011 political struggle and the mass demonstrations that ouster the long-standing Yemeni dictator Salah, but international terrorism remained a crucial part of the organization's agenda. AQAP have illustrated that if they were successfully take over the country, this would be the first step to end the royal Saudi monarchy.

Furthermore, any ambiguity over AQAP's plans to continue efforts to attack the United States was immediately put aside as AQAP plot against the U.S. was revealed. The 2012 plot focused on an effort to attack a U.S. airliner again, but this time with an altered and developed underwear bomb. The Wall Street Journal stated that the arranged operation was smoothly revealed as a result of the activities of a Saudi intelligent agent who had formerly infiltrated AQAP and volunteered for a suicide mission on the basis that he would later be able to uncover operational terrorist arrangements to the Saudi government.

The agent's leaders within the AQAP group have agreed on his proposal and gave him the explosives, which were then transferred to Saudi intelligence. Information encircling on this issue was shared with the U.S. The plot didn't go ahead, as the device wasn't seized at the airport and the mission had clearly not been accredited to a particular flight, the Washington post indicated that U.S. authorities have portrayed the bomb used in the attack as an advanced version of the 2009 device, but failed to give further explanation. The Yemeni authorities and security agency seemed to have no information of the plot. Ibrahim Hassan al-Asiri was a notorious AQAP militant who was accused of taking part with the ongoing efforts to strike attacks against the United States.

Asiri is a radical Saudian who has great expertise in bombmaking, for many years Asiri showed great commitment in opposing against the Saudi regime and its western allies. He has been credited with building the first underwear bomb and the device that has been used for the parcel bombs. Taking into consideration about his commitment to AQAP, on 2009 he sent his brother to a mission to serve as human bomb assigned to kill the Saudi interior minister and the head of counterterrorism, Prince Mohammed bin Nayef.

The purpose of targeting Prince Mohamed came after; the prince launched an excessive campaign to hunt down the domestic supporters and sympathisers of the radical group AQAP from 2003-12, and he was critical AQAP target both for operational reasons and for vengeance. Asiri's brother communicated with the Prince with an offer to surrender and bring his supporters with him into the Saudi rehabilitation program. This plot failed when the energy of the human bomb was directed in unexpected ways and killed only the terrorist attacker.

Prince Mohammad was slightly injured; despite he certainly emerged from the circumstance with recently discovered caution in regards to the foe he fought against. Prince Mohammad's adequacy and his commitment to the battle against AQAP were later perceived when he was appointed as the interior minister of Saudi Arabia in November 2012. In March 2008, the AQAP has launched attacks against U.S. and Western targets in Yemen; the U.S. embassy was among the targets.

During the attack on the U.S. embassy AQAP perpetrators fired mortar shells, but the shells couldn't reach the destination (U.S. embassy), but killed a security guard and wounded approximately 13 students at a nearby school. After the attack, the Yemeni security forces managed to capture two main that was reportedly behind the incident and were later sentenced to death. AQAP has prepared a larger and well-planned strike on 16 September, 2008, when several AQAP agents dressed as police officers and attacked the U.S. embassy with car bombs, which killed almost 16 people including one American.

Another genuine assault against the Western diplomatic presence in Yemen took place in April 2010, when a notorious al-Qaeda suicide bomber tried to assassinate the British ambassador by targeting his car in Sanaa. Fortunately, the ambassador was unharmed, despite three passerby were widely injured and the bomber died. The assassination attempt of the British ambassador was huge shame for the Yemeni authorities but not a critical situation as no British national were harmed or killed. Recently in 2012, al-Qaeda has offered three kilograms of gold (equivalent to US$160,000) to anyone who kills the U.S. ambassador to Yemen Gerald Feierstein, and also offered US$23,000 to anyone who kills a U.S. soldier in Yemen.

The issue of drones

As part of the U.S military assistance to the Yemeni government, the U.S. government has designated a plan to help the Yemenis to use the drones, in order to physically terminate the insurgents (al-Qaeda and its affiliates). Furthermore, the U.S. and international press indicates that the Yemeni government forces victories in the 2012 hostile were significantly assisted, if not empowered, by the drone program put in place to assist the Yemeni ground forces. This is a tough case to evaluate, because of the lack of information that has been published in relation to the use of drones. Up to this point, the U.S. administration has been hesitant to concede any utilisation of such aerial weapon in Yemen of yielding to sensitivities especially apparent under President Saleh's administration.

After some time, this policy has been lifted as a result of the extensive Western media coverage of drone use, and the uncertainty of further denials. In April 2012, John O. Brennan who is the counterterrorism advisor to the President of the United States made a public announcement, in which he clearly said that, the U.S. has used the drone to attack terrorist suspects and encounter any terrorist attacks on the U.S., although he didn't categorically specify Yemen as the venue for such activities.

On October 2012, the U.S. Defense Secretary leon Panetta has defended the U.S. government use of drones on the operation in Yemen and said that "noting that such system have played a vital role in government victoriesover AQAP in Yemen", but the Defense Secretary gave no further explanation.

Likewise, the Yemeni foreign minister Abu Bakr al-Qirbi made an statement, where he told reporters on June 2012 during the counter-piracy conference in Dubai that "drones were used upon Yemen's request against fleeing al-Qaeda leaders" during the 2012 offensive. Foreign Minister Qirbi's statement came in a context of the greater American openness about the use of these systems. The remaining Yemeni government secrecy about drone use came to an end in

September 2012 when President Hadi commented directly on the use of such systems.

President Hadi declared he had permitted the U.S. to use drones in Yemen to target suspected terrorist. In doing so, the president began to realise that there was no reason for proceeding with former president Saleh's strategy of denying drone attacks in Yemen as the strikes were broadly covered in world media, and practically nobody trusted the government.

The Yemeni President Mansur Hadi, went on a special visit to the United States, where he told the Washington Post that his country permitted U.S. drone strikes, but it also thoroughly regulated such actions. The Yemeni president indicated during his visit that U.S. drone strikes on Yemeni terrorist targets were not allowed unless he gave the command to do so. Hadi has widely assumed the responsibility for the air strikes, while maintaining that he does not allow the U.S. interest to overtake the Yemeni interests. If the use of a drone is contradicting the interest of Yemen, he will not authorise it.

Furthermore, Hadi believes that using drones will only target the terrorists and its collateral damages are very limited. According to Hadi, "the drone is technologically more advanced than the human brain," indicating that these systems are more precise than manned combat aircraft. The president also indicated that Yemeni air forces were unable to target the terrorists accurately at night, but the drones were doing the job correctly. Hadi thereby asserted that the drones were a better system for avoiding collateral damage. Also, Hadi recognised that some of the drone strikes have accidently killed innocent people, but likewise alleged that his country and the United States took several measures to prevent mistakes of the past.

Hadi's choice to recognize the U.S. utilization of drones in the battle against AQAP drew significant attention in Yemen. Few Yemenis seemed to appreciate his openness and his honesty in relation to the interest of Yemen. Despite the use of drones in Yemen remains significantly controversial, the population of Yemen also appears to have turned out to be to some degree more tolerant of U.S. drone use in the course of last year than it was over previous incidents. This change of Yemeni perception came about as a result of the critical situation in the country, the rise of Ansar al-Shariah and the fact these insurgent groups had the capabilities of capturing many towns and cities throughout the Abyan and Shabwa provinces.

Yet, even significant number of Yemeni citizens who strongly opposed against the extreme ideology of the AQAP, quickly reacted to the use of drones in Yemen and expressed their anger about the innocent people that has been killed following the use of drones and therefore clearly stated that if further operation on drones is conducted, then there will be a serious consequence.

This situation can be extremely difficult for Washington, as serious collateral damages from the drones could create an internal counterproductive which Yemeni government would be unwilling to ignore. Furthermore, several Yemeni politicians including radical clerics have strongly condemned the wide use of drones in Yemen and they are ready to take political actions from further incidents of collateral damage. Such politicians will probably overstate the number of innocents murdered in strikes that involve civilian deaths. The military estimation of the drone strikes is difficult to measure, despite the U.S. and the world press has published large numbers of articles on individual strikes with drone-launched Hellfire missiles. It is unsurprising that the press would latch on to such drama, but drones do more than serve as missile platforms.

Also, the drones could be use as key intelligence platforms by as a result of their capacity to delay over the battleground and other areas of intelligence. This ability illustrates that the drones are a crucial enabler of efficient utilization of ground forces likewise the missiles. In a hostile mode, drones are used to kill insurgent militants that are preparing to strike against the Yemeni army in the battlegrounds. According to the Yemeni media, some insurgent fighters were killed by drones just before they have undertaken deadly attacks against government forces, including some that were found dead wearing suicide vests.

One of the critical issues of drones is that they are very limited as a strike weapon in a situation where enough intelligence about operations on the ground is not accessible. Sometimes it was very difficult to differentiate AQAP agents from the normal citizens simply because of the overflights. This issue clearly a problem, as many civilians who have nothing to do with the terrorist groups are armed and tribal militias have access to weapons, including machine guns and mortars.

The only way to address this concern is through sincere intelligence which permits the drone conductor to differentiate who is the innocent and who the AQAP agent. However, intelligence isn't always precise, and mistakes can occur. Gregory Johnsen, an expert on Yemeni affairs, has always been critical of drone use on these grounds.

According to Johnsen, U.S. forces using drones were enormously depending on information provided by the Yemeni government under President Saleh, and this information were inaccurate. Johnsen also signalled that large number of Yemenis has been angered by drone strikes that have killed innocent people as a result of deficient intelligence. This issue was particularly serious with Yemenis who have lost close relatives in such attacks. However, it seems that U.S. drone attacks in Yemen will never going to stop in the future.

While Hadi and many other politicians may need to acknowledge the political heat for permitting such strikes and deal with claims of collateral damage, this may not be able the most genuine political issue that they could have to address. An issue that would be much more genuine is an inadequate response to AQAP's wide assassination and bombing campaign. While terrorism is typically not as huge issue as an expanding rebellion, it is still an extreme risk, which has killed significant number of Yemeni citizens, and could again increase to the level of an insurgency.

The main purpose of using the drones is that it helps the U.S. to achieve a sufficient strategic result in Yemen and prevents factors that may prompt a more extensive U.S. involvement in a Yemeni war. Moreover, while the use of drone has several political downsides, the possibility that it helped determine of the summer hostile is worth considering. If the insurgent group had conquered the Yemeni army in this effort, the regime may have fall apart at a painful fragile time, and probably leaving the country in turmoil. Such a defeat would also have created the conditions for an even more deeply rooted AQAP presence in southern Yemen, with no countervailing Yemeni authority capable of moving against it. If Yemeni forces had failed, and particularly if they had failed ignominiously, a newly energized terrorist movement could have plagued the region and the world.

The political landscape of East Africa

The Horn of Africa is a great extension of an area that juts from the eastern end of Africa, located between the Indian Ocean towards the east and the Gulf of Aden to the North, extending for hundreds of kilometres into the Arabian Sea. In general, the Horn of Africa comprises of more than 772,200 square miles, most of which brag steppe climate. Despite the horrific leaving condition in several parts of the Horn, the total population that is living in the region is estimated around 160 million.

The horn of Africa is a political region which consists of Republic of Djibouti, Ethiopia, Eritrea, Somalia, Kenya. The Horn of Africa is viewed as a sub-region that comes under the greater region of East Africa. In 500 C.E. the Horn of Africa developed significantly into a major commercial hub, mainly due to the civilisation of Yemen began to move to Ethiopia's Highlands.

The migrants to the region formed the city of Axum, which later became the central Ethiopian kingdom. The city of Axum was mainly a commercial city, as the location capitalised on the trade routes that drove into Africa. The Ivory of elephants was the leading commodity that was passed through these routes as this product were greatly prized around the world for its artistic value. The city of Axum later became a trade hub for the Greeks, who wanted to exploit the resources in the African continent by establishing a strong relation with the Axumites. In fact, the Greeks had so much influence with the Ivory market in the Horn of Africa to the extent that the Greek language was used in some official state documents.

When Axum acquired its autonomy and transformed into a political authority in its own, the city became the centre of expansionary conflicts. The most popular among these wars was the War of the Elephants. The power and the commandments of the Ethiopian kings spun around an assertion made by the royal authorities that all kings could trace their ancestry back to King Solomon. Other crucial goods that were exported from the region were frankincense and myrrh, and these products were prized during the classical antiquity. This is because of the significant amount of fragrant substances accessible for sale in Axum and the neighbouring region, Regio Aromatica.

The people of Aksum have occupied an area within the Horn of Africa which is Eritrea to the present day, close to the coast of the Red Sea. For 500 years BC settlements were established, a combination of farmers and foreign traders who came from South East Arabia. These people concocted their languages and scripts. The sea ports in this region extended and began to monopolise the Red Sea commerce which was starting to challenge on business terms with the city of Meroe. At the start of the 1st century AD century AD, these ports had merged to form one kingdom, with its capital inland on the Ethiopian highland at Aksum. Aksum developed as a result of wealth and its global reputation, prestigious for its enormous stone landmarks and architecture and for its carved multi-layered stone pillars called stelae. During the 3rd century, A.D. a Persian religious leader characterised the kingdom of Aksum as one of the important and influential kingdoms at the time.

In the 14th century, Aksum was highly regarded by foreign traders as a crowing city. The city of Aksum had a glorious temple which was designed with gold. Through this time the region prospered and kept an international reputation. During the Ancient Greek Empire, the people of Ethiopia were seen as a holy people, to the extent that the people of Greek thought that the Gods highly valued Ethiopians.

Military leader Memnon, who was a major Ethiopian warrior who fought in the Trojan War, was incredibly considered as a notable figure and Achilles was the only one to exceed him in the battle. After being killed by Achille's sword, he was seen immortality by the Greek gods. According to the Greek myths, the Ethiopians had got their colour when the sun came close to their country. Herodotus historians wrote about a group of Ethiopian fighters clothed in leopard skins who painted their bodies red and white and who were among the army of Xerxes which invaded Greece in the 5th Century BC.

There was significant trade between the Red Sea, Kush and Egypt for an extended period. There was two leading trade path that was working. One route went from Nekheb to the Red Sea, and the other one went to Qustul in Nubia. Alongside these commercial systems, a tamed agricultural system had been established between the 3rd and 5th millennium BC. Indications of the farming finger millet have been found, and there is a possibility that camels may have had an impact on this culture amid this period.

The roads that went through the district of Eritrea and the Red Sea ports of Azab and Adule constructed commercial links with the Far East, India, Greece and Egypt. There was a trade boom in ivory, slaves, gold, Nubian emeralds and hippo hides and teeth and wild animal. The goods that were imported consisted of cotton, silk, silver and golds, wine glasses and cotton which were produced into plates and solid gold and bronze statues.

This commercial made connections with Kush, Egypt, the Roman Empire, the Mediterranean Basin, Arabia, India and China. The Bab Al-Mandeb was seen as the principal shipping routes of the world at that time. Abyssinia (on the modern day Ethiopia) was the first nation to mint a coin with a Christian emblem. Previous coins had the crescent moon and rising sun. Ethiopia likewise played a crucial role in the improvement and the spread of Christianity around the world. The principles of Christianity embraced by Ethiopia during the Millennium AD are like the same as those which now build the West and had significant Obama's race for President in the USA.

Christianity is a religion which the majority of African countries have embraced; this religion reached Africa long before it came to Europe. Saint Philip the Evangelist preached an Ethiopian eunuch was the financial officer of Kandake. This incident is written about in Acts: Ch8: V26-40. There are numerous references to Africa in the Old testimony. Menelik I was the son of King Solomon and Queen Sheba and the first king of Ethiopia; many Ethiopian believed that he was also the founder nation.

During the leadership of King Ezana in the 4th Century BC, a new Ge'ez writing was created which had an impact upon developing writing scripts spread out from Georgia and Armenia, and this was the first nation to accept Christianity as the country's religion. These contacts illustrate that commercial and diplomatic relation existed between these nations and that Ethiopia had managed to cooperate with the rest of the world.

Aksum had formed a trade connection with the Roman Empire, and this trade links reached all the way to China and probably along the passage of the

Chinese Silk Road. There were commercial routes that were established between the Arabian Peninsula and Aksum and with Japan. Mani who is prestigious Persian religious leader characterises Aksum as one of the most important kingdoms on the globe at that time. Aksum had a powerful influence on the world; Aksum could rely on the region where present day agriculture might have originated.

The people of Ethiopia described how Christianity reached their coast due to a shipwreck. This is coming from the drowning of a Christian philosopher Meopius from Tyre, but his companions on the journey, Frumentitus and Aetius were safe and taken to the Royal Palace. Other sources indicate that both Frumentius and Aetius were Christian merchants that were captured by pirates in the Red Sea and sold into slavery to King Ella Amida. Frumentius later became a minister in the royal court of King Ezana. Ethiopia became the second nation in the world to embrace Christianity and adopted it as the state's religion, following the conversion of King Ezana to Christianity, Armenia being the first nation to adopt Christianity.

Later, Frumentius became the secretary of King Ella Amida, while Aetius took the position of Royal Cup-Bearer. After the death of the king Ella Amida, Frumentius became a close associate to Prince Ezana, who succeeds his late father from the reign. During their time together, King Ezana and Frumentius has conveyed the message of Christianity in the country, and Frumentius went back to Egypt to ask the leader of the Catholic Church to send several Christian missionaries back to Aksum. After the dialogs Frumentius was blessed by the bishop of the Ethiopian Orthodox Church.

He was given the title of 'Abuna Salama' (Bishop of Peace). With the backing and the royal assent of King Ezana, Ethiopia became Christian country and the connection formed between the Ethiopian Church, and the Patriarch of Alexandria remained continuous until the 20th century. Disruption between the links of two bishops arose after the dismal of Haile Selassie, but until very recently the Bishop of Alexandria was in charge for the appointment of all members of the Ethiopian Orthodox Church.

King Ezana has dramatically increased the power and influence of Aksum which they became strategic important during the first century AD. There was a commercial growth in food products and also gold and ivory through the Red Sea port of Adulis while the administrative city of Aksum was built in north-eastern Ethiopia on 7,200 feet above sea level. The port of Adulis linked with commercial route throughout the Roman Empire furthermore went east to India. Trade activity to the Red Sea coast was functioning as early as 100 years BC. Also, the king also built massive monuments to keep his power over the country. The tallest building in which he constructed was 33 meters high, sculpture thirteen storey tower designed with intricately crafted window frames and bolted doors.

The construction was produced from a single quarried stone and was transported from several kilometres to its last site, however once erected it soon tumbled down, caving in onto a close-by cemetery and breaking into three pieces. As yet standing alongside this site is a twenty-seven-meter tall monument. Underneath its base, there were various tombs, buried stairwells, shafts and other objects have been found in the tombs. The monuments were regarded as a staircase to heaven for the previous kings who died. Coming up to the end of the 5th century a contingent of nine priests came to Ethiopia. It's been said that these priests fled from Syria and Egypt for religious persecution. However, they were in charge for presenting a monastic life into the Ethiopian culture which since has assumed a crucial part in the improvement of religious life in this nation to this present day.

The priests were compelled to escape and look for security in Ethiopia due to their Monophysite beliefs which believed that Christ's spiritual and human nature had been joined to form a single entity at birth. The Ecumenical Council of Chalcedon has implemented a different theological approach, considering the difference between Christ's spiritual nature and that of his human nature. Due to this meeting by the council, the Monosyphite views were believed to be unorthodox. This has created a deep division within the church and also separated from the main body of Christian churches by the Ethiopian Orthodox Church, the Egyptian Coptic Church and smaller churches in Syria, Armenia and Turkey. This division happened in 451 years. Until this present day, these churches are non-Chalcedon and made their brand of Christianity within the southern branch of the Christian church.

The nine priests who had escaped to Ethiopia has translated the Bible into Ge'ez, this language of Ge'ez was heavily spoken at that time in Ethiopia, but this ancient language is only used in church services. This interpretation into Ge'ez must represent one of the previous translations of the Bible from Hebrew into different languages and it would good to compare the similarities in this edition to the English translation.

The Ethiopian culture is linked to the world that existed during the Old Testament. At Debra Damo, there is an ancient religious house built in the 6th century on top of a hill. In this compound, females were prohibited as a result of the traditional of the Christian institutions and the existence of the monastic tradition which still exists in today's world. Moreover few of its convictions depend on previous pre-Christian beliefs. Many Ethiopian church rituals are linked to ancient Judaism like the honouring that exists in Ethiopia for the Jewish Ark of the Covenant.

The original Ark of the Covenant was brought back from Israel to Ethiopia by Menelik I, who many believed that he was the son of King Solomon. Their relationship came after the visit of Queen of Sheba to King Solomon to Ethiopia, the purpose of her visit was to see whether King Solomon was wise a many claimed. During the visit of the Queen, she wasn't allowed to drink and myth as she slept with King Solomon so she could quench her thirst. The queen has governed small parts of southern Eritrea.

When Menelik reached age twenty-five, he travelled to Jerusalem where he stole the ark. Therefore today, Ethiopian acts as the protector of the Ark which is believed to be hidden and well-protected on one of the churches in Axum. The second chapter of Genesis in the Old Testament clearly indicates the link between Ethiopia and Judaism, when defining the four rivers which outline the borderline of the Garden of Eden. River Tigris and the Euphrates are among the four mentioned rivers, and they are located in the Middle East, but Pishon River is believed to flow gold fields.

The Islamic invasion in the 7th century has separated Ethiopia from the rest of the world. An Ethiopian religious house in Jerusalem gave a focal point to priests from Ethiopia and connected with Egypt were maintained with a sequence of bishops appointed by the pioneers of the Egyptian Church. At first, the Christian and Muslim communities in Ethiopia lived harmony together. Both towns profited significantly from trading with each other, and there was religious tolerance and accepting the belief and convictions of both sides. This is because of the similarities in their religious practices.

During the 615AD, the wife and the cousin of Prophet Muhammad sought asylum in Aksum with their small group of followers. This group led by the wife of Prophet Muhammad were granted asylum and protection by the Negus Amah who kept them from been forcibly deported to Arabia. Because Ethiopia had provided a haven for this group, Muslims were advised by Muhammad to show admiration and appreciation towards the Ethiopian individuals. It would have been a different case for the history of Islam if the wife of the Prophet had been deported back to Arabia.

There was a greater tolerance that existed and the tribal leaders in the region did not impose Islam on the people. But as the time went the relationship between the two communities become progressively worse, as a result, the Christian community was forced to leave and go to mountains for security purposes against the Muslims. Perhaps the religious community at Debre Dano initially initiated the rope ladder access using protection against the possibility of Islamic invasion. The Christian community kept their Ethiopian culture and identity despite their retreats

For a long time, Islam occupied the whole country, thus isolating the Christians who placed themselves in the highlands regions of the country. The Muslim population initially landed in the area from Saba which lies over the Red Sea on the Arabian Peninsula. Today a considerable number of the Muslim populace of Ethiopia are Sunni Muslims and makeup 25% to 40% of the nation's population. According to some, Emperor Haile Sellasie was a direct descent of King David of Israel.

During the last 10th century the king of Aksumite was assaulted and crushed by an armed group led by a female tribal chief warrior called Gudit. This armed militia group burnt wherever they went and looted any cathedral in their path. During the 12th Century, Ethiopia gradually started to rise against the dark ages and establish a real leadership that works for working people and the interest of the nation. A new ruling class rose to power called the Zagwe

Dynasty; this group was criticized for not been the descent of Menelik I, the child of King Solomon and Queen Sheba.

King Lalibela constructed several churches in the city of Roha which were later named as Lalibela. These newly built churches were carved out of rock faces, and till the present day are a living example of the marvelous masonry skills that this 13th-century African artisan bewitched. The aim of the construction of these churches was to boost and restore the Christian society. In the 16th Century Ethiopia almost went at the hands of Muslim army led by General Imam Ahmad Gurey who launched an Islamic jihad against Ethiopia. After conquering Ethiopia, he was killed in a counter attack led by the Portuguese army. This military assistance given by Portugal has significantly defeated Ahmed Gurey and his army.

During this conflict, John Bermudez, who was a Portuguese citizen, indicated that he was the designated successor of the Bishop of Ethiopia and pressure was applied to the royal court to convert to Roman Catholicism, but these pressures were eventually successfully resisted. King Suseynos who reigned Ethiopia from 1607-1632 converted to Catholicism and intended to forge military affiliation with the West in the succeeding king converted back to Christianity cherished in the Orthodox Christian Church of Ethiopia and began to dismiss all Roman Catholic preachers from Ethiopia

By the 19th Century, Islam dominated the country especially in the south of the country, but the life of monastic has remained the same, as the monasteries were segregated and build in places that were unreachable. In the 20th Century, King Menelik II have successfully ended to the brutal Italian attempt to capture and colonize Ethiopia (formerly Abyssinia). Ethiopia was the only African nation who prevented itself from European colonisation during the European colonisation era on the African continent.

In the 17th Century, Ethiopia experienced an artistic revitalization of Ethiopian culture, as it was unveiled to styles of expression from Europe to Muslim world. This was particularly true during the leadership of Iyasus I, also known as Iyasus the Great. In the wake of succeeding to the crown in 1682, Iyasus was known as an art lover and radiant military strategist. During his reign, he laid the foundation of the most magnificent sacred architecture and the restoration of administrative authority on various provinces in the south of the country that was given to Muslims and tribal intrusion. Following the death of King Iyasus in 1706, the country fall into another period of hardship which led to the collapse of the country into separate regions

The only group remained unified during this difficult period was the Ethiopian church. Following the support of some high officials from the church, Kassa Haile Giorgis a bandit from the northwestern frontier, have designated himself as Emperor Tewodros II in 1855, after crushing several so-called rulers who controlled some parts of Ethiopia. As he took the reign, he began to improve the legal and administrative systems, despite some local governors opposed against this. Tewodros has imprisoned some British officials for opposing him following a tension between him and Great Britain. The British consulate was among those who were arrested. Britain issued a punitive expedition against the Ethiopian Emperor Tewodros II, and just before the arrival of the British Empire armed force, and the emperor committed suicide in 1868 to avoid extradition to Britain.

After several years of a power struggle for the throne, Dejazmach Kassai, who previously served as the governor of Tigray province, took the throne in being crowned Johannes IV, emperor of Ethiopia. Johannes IV attempted to centralize further the administrative system, and this has led to the rise of local government; furthermore, his administration was endangered by external aggression; first by Egyptian incursions, and later invasion by the adherent of the Mahdi in Sudan.

In 1870's Egypt was the main foreign enemy of the Ethiopian empire. In 1875 the Egyptian governor provided significant protection to the Muslim ruler of Harer and began an offensive attack against Ethiopia from the north and east of the country. The Ethiopian emperor has successfully ended the Egyptian invasion; however, the continued occupation by Egypt of the Red Sea and Somali ports reduced the supply of goods to Ethiopia. The opening of the Suez Canal expanded the strategic importance of Ethiopia, and some European powers sought influence in the area. Johannes was killed for defending his western frontier against the Sudanese in 1889. In the wake of his death, he was succeeded by Menelik II, who made Addis Ababa as the new capital and succeeded in uniting the provinces of Tigray and Amhara with Shewa.

Menelik II (1844-1913) had accomplished the vision of Tewedros II had for his country. Menelik took the leadership of Ethiopia following the death of his predecessor Yohannes in the Battle of Metema. Many European powers were extremely determined to capture and colonise territories in Africa. Ethiopia was a prime target of Italy. The Treaty of Uccialli was negotiated between Ethiopia and Italy in 1890. After the agreement, two copies were drafted, one in Amharic and the other one in Italian. On the Italian version, prime minister Francesco Crispi apparently told his European counterparts that Ethiopia became a special administrative region of Italy.

But on the Amharic version, it clearly stated that Menelik II could ask Italy for economic and military assistance when it's necessary, but didn't say anything about Ethiopia becoming Italian overseas territory. When the Ethiopian emperor discovered the Italian interpretation of the agreement, he immediately contacted the European leaders insisting that Ethiopia is still a sovereign nation, not Italian overseas territory. In 1893, Menelik II condemned the treaty, and by 1895 both countries were at war. On March 1896 Menelik's army defeated the Italian troops at Adwa, Ethiopia. As a result of the Italian defeat, Italy recognizes the Ethiopia sovereignty as an independent nation.

Emperor Menelik has expanded Ethiopia by conquest, following his victory in the Battle of Adwa against the Italians. When the emperor died, a large turmoil escalated within the country, which brought his daughter, Empress Zauditu, to power in 1917. Tafari Makonnen became her regent and took the position of crown prince. When the Empress passed away in 1930, Tafari Makonnen was crowned Haile Selassie I as he became the 225th successor of the Solomonic bloodline. Haile Selassie means 'the power of Trinity in Amharic, in 1931 Emperor Selassie drafted the first constitution of Ethiopia. Through his long effort, Ethiopia gained its membership of the League of Nations (now United Nations) in 1932.

In 1935, Ethiopia who was a conventional Commonwealth with the feudal political system was invaded of Italy under the Fascist government of Benito Mussolini. In provocation of the subsequent occupation; Ethiopian demonstrated patriotic resistance to push the Italians out of the country. This war lasted for over five years. While, Haile Selassie, had experienced a considerable diplomatic struggle from exile.

The charismatic Italian leader Benito Mussolini was extremely determined to make Ethiopia an Italian colony and make them pay for the most humiliation Italian defeat by Ethiopia during the battle of Adwa in 1896 when the Italian army was literally wiped out including their four generals in one day. Likewise, few years before the battle of Adwa, on January 1887 at Dogali, few Kilometers from the port of Massawa, Asmara, some Ethiopian forces led by Ras Alula Engida, had attacked another Italian army. This was the first defeat of European power by an African army. The Italian setback in 1896 at Adwa sent a significant shock wave to Rome that remained up until the 1935 invasion. The Italian, during this time, were thoroughly examining ways to come back to maintain its strategic interest in the Horn of Africa despite competition from France and Britain in the region.

In 1925, Mussolini ordered the Italian military to prepare itself to wage war against Ethiopia, but this plan for the conquest of Ethiopia became adequate in 1934. The preparation required a significant amount of money, and large quantities of trucks, airplanes and other heavy military equipment and stockpiling of poison gas to protect Italian military superiority. The primary purpose of De Bono's visits to Eritrea in 1932 was more of a military surveillance than a regular tour of inspection by the Minister of Colonies.

The Walwal incident in December 1934, when forces from both sides (Ethiopian and Italian) confronted inside Ethiopia over the line of the borderline wasn't the principle motivation of the Italian invasion. Mussolini's enthusiasm for the considerable onslaught on Abyssinia (Ethiopia) to construct a massive empire became evident especially when Benito Mussolini claimed that he was ready to wage war on Britain and France instead of given up the conquest of Ethiopia. Satisfied with their triumph at Adwa, the Ethiopians now had to challenge one of the most difficult offensives in their history as a nation.

The prime reason for the invasion was to occupy the land along the Red Sea coast which the Italians conquered for more than four and a half decades before the 1936 invasion, which the Italians had named Eritrea on 1st January 1890. In two years, the last preparation for conquering Abyssinia was achieved under the auspices of Marshal De Bono, Colonies Commissioner. The Colonies Commissioner was sent by Benito Mussolini to lead the war as the Commander-in-Chief of the Northern Front, with nine divisions of 250,000

Italian combatants and approximately 150,000 African armies from Eritrea, Italian Somaliland and Libya, all united under the banner of Askaris. These troops had almost 300 aircraft under the command of De Bono; he had to forward from Asmara into the remote areas of Ethiopia. De Bono had deployed 100 aircraft, under the Marshal Graziani on the Southern front to head northwards.

This strategy was to cross to the Ethiopian capital city, Addis Ababa, within very short amount of time, so that pressures on Italy from the league of nations (now UN) could be avoided. On the other hand, the Ethiopian troops were believed to have approximately 300,000 men, mobilized by regional races or princes whose relationship with one another were deteriorated but often came together when foreign aggressors threaten to invade.

Haile Selassie, the Commander-in-Chief of the Ethiopian armed force, had considerably lacked on moderns means of communication that prevented him from establishing a centralised command to organise the war of defence in the mountainous regions. This tactic would be a great advantage for the Italian forces as they coordinate and concentrate their forces as required. Also, the Ethiopia army had issues with insufficient weapons; it was reported that the Ethiopian army had only 200 light artillery, 1000 machine guns with 150 rounds per person. Transportation and Logistics were self-supported with the exception of small ammunition and hand grenades that were only given occasionally.

Many Ethiopians had not seen armored vehicles nor tanks or aircraft, but what made them united to challenge the external foes was the strong self-image of national pride and patriotism. The Ethiopian showed great determination to remain a sovereign state and defend their unique cultural, and religious values were showed in their prayers and songs, used during the war and the struggle that followed.

On early 1935, the Italian forces moved rapidly towards Adwa, which was 30 kilometres from the colonial borderline that separated Eritrea and Tigray, the northern region of Ethiopia. The Ethiopian armed forces at Adwa were not only outnumbered but also had no capacity to resist the long range fusillade of the artilleries, the deadly machine guns of the tanks and the airstrikes by the Italians.

The Ethiopian army weapons were widely less efficient than the modern Italian armaments. Before any genuine actions, they were told to retreat to save their army for a well-planned defensive plot in the country. On 6 October 1935, the city of Adwa was in the hands of Italian forces. This seizure of Adwa gave the Italians the psychological comfort from the mortifying setback they had faced at Dogali and Adwa in 1887 and 1896, yet for those at the front, the war was merely starting and De Bono chose to advance with the alert.

On November 1935, the capital city of Tigray region, Mekele, came under the command of the Italians. Mussolini was enormously furious about the slow pace of the Italian military operation, had decided to fire De Bono and replace him with Marshal Pietro Badoglio, who formerly served as the Chief of Staff of the Italian Armed forced. Following orders from Rome, Badoglio exerted excessive military crackdown to score a quick victory, including airstrikes and dropping from the air of mustard-gas bombs over Ethiopian troops and civilian areas, although the Geneva Gas Protocol had prohibited the use of mustard gas in 1925. The use of the mustard-gas has resulted in the death of thousands of Ethiopian civilians including the army.

In spite of the use of airstrikes and mustard gas, the Ethiopian militias and resistance fighters, regrouped in their respective regions under their local leaders to fight against the enemy (Italy). Both parties have conducted several battles over a period of three months. These battles and conflicts were extremely intense, and the determination of the Ethiopians was tested against all the odds. Emperor Haile Selassie later said, "although the Italians were superior to us in modern arms, our soldiers had the advantage regarding courage."

On the other hand, Marshal Badoglio reviewed the number of Italian casualties in the Shire region and said "Our losses, including dead and wounded, were: 63 officers, 894 Italians, 12 Eritreans. The losses of the enemy as ascertained on the field were about 4,000; to these must be added those inflicted by aircraft during the pursuit, the total of which was estimated at over 3,000". The combat area in the district of Shire was among the several fronts in Tigray and was led by the Governor of Gojjam Province, Ras Imru, who later withdraw to Gore in the southwest of the country. Almost the whole Tigray region turned into a battlefield for six consecutive months.

At last, on March 1936 at Maichew and Lake Ashenge, the Emperor's primary force set up a cohesive resistance, but the Ethiopian were compelled to withdraw further south towards Dessie, the provincial capital of Wollo. The Italians have captured the city of Dessie, after days of horrific fighting. Failed to reunite the Ethiopian forces and launch retaliation, the emperor and his remaining army headed for the capital city Addis Ababa. The Maychew war where the emperor had assembled his best possible army, but it eventually became the end of the conventional war and the inception of the patriot's resistance movement, which indeed appeared to have started behind foes lines.

The hostiles remained extremely intensified on the southern with the armies of Rasta Desta and Dejazmach Nesibu, also several governors of Harar region, Sidamo and Illubabor has restrained Marshal Graziani's forces from capturing the north of the country, as Marshal Graziani made a solemn promise to make Ethiopian an Italian colonial. This vow was a clear reflection of Italy's colonial policy of relocating its farmers on the Ethiopians fertile lands.

The marshal dismissed the fact that he used mustard gas on Ethiopians, he also resorted to the genocide of civilians, for instance, during the war of Ogaden in 1936. During this time, almost 1000 Eritrean askaris, outraged by such Italian military strategy, forsook to the Ethiopian side, hence testing the fidelity and allegiance of other colonial armies. In December 1935, few hundreds of Eritreans had affiliated with Ras Imru's army on the Shire front. These desertions clearly emphasized that many Eritrean askaris gave solidarity to their fellow Ethiopians and oppose against the colonial power.

While the south-eastern front was under the command of Marshal Graziani, Emperor Haile Selassie was unable to block Badoglio who was coming from the north side of the country. As a result of the several challenges that the emperor had faced, he has decided to withdraw his army from the city of Dessie and instead return to Addis Ababa on 30 April 1936, to prepare his way for exile. By 5th May 1936, as result of the Emperor departure, many

Ethiopians felt they were in the hands of the Italians but amid turmoil and looting rose due to the Emperor's departure.

When Haile Selassie arrived his capital city, Addis Ababa, he quickly held a meeting with his government ministers and several other leaders. During this meeting, the emperor and the participants of the meeting have reached two agreements. First, the emperor had to go for exile to present Ethiopia's case to the League of Nations (now the UN), and secondly the national government should be relocated to the city of Gore and should act as the interim leader. While the first point of the agreement called for a diplomatic and an end to the political struggle, the second aspect indicated the establishment of resistance groups to tackle the Italian invasion and was aimed at reclaiming independence and sovereignty.

Many young Ethiopians were mindful of the consequent authority gap made by the Emperor's absenteeism. The Ethiopian crown prince had told his followers that he should disregard his father and go with them to the hills as shifta. However as the emperor's decision couldn't be opposed, the resistance led by the crown prince also known as the shiftinnet had to begin without him.

The ancient history of Ethiopia as a country began during the third century when it was known as the Kingdom of Aksum. During 340 AD, the king of Aksum has made Orthodox Christianity as the state religion, which escalated quickly to the Ethiopians and gave the symbolism of the royal ideology. Since then, they developed trading activities through the ports of Zeila and Adulis. The empire began to expand over the Ethiopian highlands.

The spread of Islam following the seventh century has constrained the international trade route and weaken the Aksum's regional power. During the tenth century, an uprising led by the Queen Yodit of the Agew people has resulted in the collapse of Aksum state. The monarchy was rebuilt by the Christian Zagwe dynasty situated in the Agew region. In the thirteenth century, the Abyssinian (Ethiopia) state was restored by Aksumite royal ideology. After some time, the spread of Islam from the northern parts of the region and the rise of aggression of Imam Ahmed al-Ghazi in 1527 to 1543 became another major blast to the Ethiopian Christian Empire. Following the defeat of Imam Ahmed al-Ghazi in 1543, the country began to recover gradually. The Oromo's from the south brought another problem by compelling a periodic shift of the political centre. The progressive loss of centralised state led to the emergence of kings and princes who often confronted for over the leadership of the country.

During the 19th century, Emperor Tewodros II created a vision of strong and prosperous Ethiopia. The emperor has built a central state and raised royal income from the Tigray and Amhara regions. While confronting the Egyptian invasion of the coast of the country, he also went to war with the British when he arrested many European missionaries. The British Empire sent a military force in 1868 and captured his mountain stronghold of Magdala. When the British took hold of his fortress mountain, the emperor was encircled by the British troops and his offers to the British were immediately dismissed, he then chose to kill himself instead of giving himself up to the British.

Emperor Yohannes replaced Tewodros II after some time, Yohannes during his leadership from 1872-1889 fought against the Egyptians and later against the Italians in the north of the country. In the late 1880's, the emperor waged war against the Sudanese Mahdist who invaded western Ethiopia. As a result, the Emperor died at the Battle of Metemma in 1889.

Emperor Menelik who ruled from 1889-1913 had succeeded him; many characterized him as the strong and visionary leader who led the victory over the Italians at the war of Adwa in 1896. To confront the strong ambition of the foreign invaders, he quickly took measures to fully compete with Great Britain, Italy, and France to increase its political influence in the entire region, merging with a significant number of previous self-governing regions into the so-called Ethiopian empire. Haile Selassie was the last emperor of the Empire and ruled from 1930-1974, following the death of his predecessor Empress Zewditu. During his leadership, he experienced a major defeat, force to exile and later success in 1941 against the Italian invaders.

The last four Ethiopian emperors were believed to have the same vision of making the country a strong and unified modern Ethiopia and tried to establish a new concept of fidelity and national identity on a distinct population. The impacts of this long history of war and insurgency against several invaders brought a sense of identity and pride connected with previous historical referents that are based on both political and religion dignity.

The Ethiopian defiance was introduced after the Italian army entered and occupied the capital city and the Italian supreme leader Benito Mussolini claimed that Ethiopia became part of the Italian Empire on May 1936. Some claimed that five months after the defeat of Emperor Selassie, the Italian generals (Graziani and Badoglio) ruled only parts of the country. Following the Maychew war, hostility began shortly. Much of the defeated armed groups went into the mountains and began to retaliate the Italian army. During the occupation era, these loyalists stayed active and made life hell for the Italian invaders.

The country was never completely in the hands of Italians. It's adequately clear that during the hostilities, new ideas of politics and governance for the country rose especially during the ongoing disputes and conflicts against the external enemy. Despite continuous pressure from the Italian leader Mussolini to his military commanders on the battlefields to ensure a profound victory over Ethiopia so he could show his adversaries (France and Britain) the Italian strength, the progress made by the Italian army remained slow due to the Ethiopian resistance that Italian army confronted. During the years, the Italians were attacked and ambushed in the hills, mountains and villages by several Ethiopian resistance movements.

Many Ethiopians viewed the Italian occupation and the successive exile of their emperor as loss of their national independence and sovereignty. They also considered the Italian occupation as the complete destruction of their traditional values, and more importantly a major interruption of their history of which they were proud for several centuries. During the conflicts of 1935-1936, thousands of Ethiopian nationalist came together to express their anger by resisting and waging war against the Italian invaders.

While the conventional war was taking place in some areas of south-eastern Ethiopia, the Tigray province was one of the places to be occupied by the Italian army and eventually became the first battleground for the Ethiopian resistance movement. The resistance forces worked in small groups, near to their respective areas.

There were several prominent resistance leaders like Dejazmach Gebrehiwet Mesheha, Dejazmach Abbai Kahsay, Dejazmach Tesfay Medebai and Woizero Kebedech Seyoum who operated from Adwa in the north of Tigray province to Maichew. These leaders engaged in various activities such as attacking Italian troops to take their arms and other military equipment, disturbing the communication system of the Italian forces. As the Ethiopian resistance movement escalated their activities in the Tigray region, the Italian military leaders decided to deploy additional armies to secure to continue their military campaign.

The resistance forces, often referred to as the Italian forces widely hunted shifta. The term Shifta can interpret as looter and bandit, but truly in the traditional Ethiopian context, this term is widely seen as a fighter who is resisting for the establishment of Justice and good governance. Also being a Shifta was broadly considered as a means of bringing hardship to the attention of the people so they could gain sympathy when rulers fail to deliver justice.

In Ethiopia, ambitious and noble people who began as Shifta managed to make their way to kingship, hence legalising the idea of Shifta itself. In the nineteenth century there was two shiftas, Kassa Hailu of Gondar and Kahsai Mircha of Tigray, had gone through this political evolution to become Emperors Tewodros and Yohannes of Ethiopia. Hence the two prominent shiftas were military leaders and later became the centre of resistance by utilising their military expertise against the invaders (Italians). However, a shifta that passed beyond the acceptable norms would be viewed as t'era-shifta and would be seen as a criminal who denied the affection of the people.

The enemy forces clearly preferred to call the freedom fighters t'era-shiftas of the criminal sort. However, to be portrayed as shifta, particular in the presence of the Italian forces, was pride for the Ethiopians. In December 1935, the Ethiopian Defence Minister ordered to all the leaders of the northern parts of the country to work in a manner with patriotism to ensure the Ethiopian independence and most importantly to ouster the Italians out of the Ethiopian territory.

While bush fighters war, which was the main tactics of the shiftas, was ongoing in the north of the country in 1936 where the Italians had control over it, the conventional war was still growing in the center of Ethiopia, especially in Addis Ababa and towards the south. When the emperor's army was crushed at the battle of Maychew and the Italian capture of the capital city on may 1936.

Many notables and resistance fighters including Dejazmaches went to their respective localities but closer to Addis Ababa. They were situated in recognizable and vital villages to recuperate from the exhaustion of eight months of conflict, and to rearrange their strengths for the following period of the patriotic battle.

The villages in which they settled were logistically well located so that the leaders could follow events in Addis Ababa that might lead them to launch retaliation. Many leaders including Ras Abebe Aregay, Dejazmach Balcha Safo, and several others engaged in hit and ran tactics throughout the capital city.

Aberra who was the son of Ras Kassa along with 10, 000 armies was assigned by Emperor Selassie to coordinate the defiance in that region, and this was something that he was doing his very best to accomplish. For instance, in June 1936, he held a meeting where he invited all patriotic forces, including the ruler of Wollo, Abune Petros, at Debre Libanos, 70 kilometres north of the capital Addis.

During the meeting, they have designated a plan to destroy the Italians stronghold areas in the capital; however due to lack of effective communication and transportation have prevented the attack to take place. Irregular attacks by the different armed groups escalated, however, to dominate the battle scene around Addis Ababa.

Gore, Ethiopia, the seat of the displaced government run by Bitweded Wolde-Tsadik Goshu, was far from easy reach and failed to become active in giving national leadership to the resistance groups. The governors had to carry out their resistance without the Emperor. Indeed for many, the surprising departure of the Emperor into exile had resulted in ambiguity and uncertainty. Few leaders like Imru in Wollega and Desta in Sidamo, who had made the long withdraw from the collapse in the north toward the south close Gore, could neither acknowledge compelling ability nor gain the assets to keep their troops in place. However, their withdrawal and their continuous acts of resistance have helped others to join the resistance.

Hence, they had the ability to increasingly distract the attention of the enemy forces, as information about the coordinated assault on Addis Ababa reached the Italians; they encircled the city with barbed wire and cement forts. People easily could come into the city only through several gates. This was symbolic of the need for preventive measure against any act of resistance activity. Practically, as conventional war had shown feeble in the face of the modern Italian conventional army, the need to resist the enemy in another form emerged.

The possibility of conventional war slowly disappeared, but the spirit of resistance continued. A distinct approach of resistance and the means of assaulting started to surface from various quarters. Almost the whole membership of the Ethiopian Orthodox Church and the Black Lion Organisation, as well as several other groups, was on the frontline of the defiance. Their activities ranged from attacking the Italian military leaders directly to providing all necessary support to the patriots in the villages. The Ethiopian Orthodox Church started to play an essential role in widening the extent of the defiance.

The Church took it as a duty to reject the Italian invasions so the country could remain free with a sovereign state. Often verses from the Bible were cited to call national loyalty. The passage 'Ethiopia shall stretch her hands unto God' was cited in daily prayers.

This verse was used to illustrate that Ethiopia has all the right to be a free country as acknowledge by God. Guided by such a profound established conviction, Abune Petros, the Bishop of Wollo, walked through the roads of Addis Ababa condemning the Italian occupation and calling on the people of Ethiopia to persist their resistance for independence. A considerable amount of people came to the streets to express their support to him. But he was later arrested and executed publicly on 30 July 1936, where his statue is now placed.

The execution of Bishop Abune Petros inconceivable in Ethiopia and shocked the country, increase dramatically the anger of the people, particularly the pastorate. The resistance of Italian leaders increased in various forms, but such public reactions didn't prevent the Italians to persist its continuous to execute bishops, clerics, and deacons in many monasteries and churches.

On May 1937, General Maletti had killed 297 clerics in the church of Debre Libanos. A few days later, several other clerics were assassinated near the church of Debre Birhan; other executions took place similarly elsewhere. Despite the continuous repression from the Italian forces, the Ethiopian churches and monasteries continued to be the center of defiance and encouraged the Ethiopians to increase their efforts to secure the Ethiopian independence.

The participation of women in the defiance against the Italian invaders was extremely important. It is hard to calculate their contribution to the armed resistance but their overall support activities, and other forms of assistance to Patriots were decisive. In the Ethiopian history, women had always been active participants in precedent conflicts defending the country.

Not long ago, Empress Taytu and her husband Emperor Menelik led the march towards battlefront in Adwa in 1896 and played a predominant role in the defeat of the Italians. Empress Taytu had grouped thousands of women, including, her stepdaughter and later Empress Zewditu in 1916-1928, and strengthened the defense lines by giving water and taking care of the injured.

The empress was likewise a military tactician whose participation had led to the major defeat of the Italians at the Battle of Mekele one month before the Battle of Adwa. Therefore the Ethiopian women had a historical reputation to assist in defending the country and its values.

Shawaragad Gadle had turned the Ethiopian Woman's Voluntary Service Association, which was under the patronage of Princess Tenagne, daughter of the Emperor, into a secret movement of defiance. The women in this association were involved in wide different of activities, ranging from supplying bandages, clothes, and ammunition stolen from Italian army to the Patriots in the field, to provide shelter and duplicate pass papers for the active Patriots to go through the Italians stronghold territories. Some of the women have managed to collect military intelligence, and some of them went to the extent to prepare military operations.

In the villages, women's were mainly in charge of preparing different foodstuff including dried meat and roasted cereals that could be correlate to 'arid rations' in contemporary military jargon, and also prepare the swords and place them between the areas of the battle and their homes. G. Tafere's indicated that some women sent down from various slopes avalanches of stones, not heeding the shower of bombs that were coming down from the air, and women like Woizero Fantaye fought on the battlefields. It was a tradition for married couples and young men to be part of the resistance movement and often sent to far places from their homes for a very long time.

In April 1936, during the battle of Ogaden Dejazmach Habtemariam was extremely ill to lead the war. Therefore his wife who was also a patriot took over his position and led the army. Lij Bitew and his wife Woizero Wagaye were among the married couples who was together all the way from the northern front of shire to the southern front in Wollega and many of them continued their efforts to ouster the enemy. During the resistance era, the prominent fighters against the Italians were Kebedech Seyoum, Qelemework Tilahun, Sliva Reyed Gadle and Laqetch Demissew.

Many patriots in the capital came together to form an organization called Black Lion Organisation, and this group composes of young students from different schools and colleges including a recently established Holetta Military school. Dr. Beyene was among the prominent leaders of the organization; Beyene was a veterinary surgeon who graduated from London School of Economics.

The aim of the leaders of the organization was much wider than any other organization in the defiance; their group had a set of rules and regulations, and they were ready to launch resistance warfare. Their charter as an organization reflected their political commitment, and their agenda alluded to the period that would follow a successful resistance.

Many Ethiopians told that the interesting features of the Black Lion Organisation constitution were: the assertion of the supremacy of political over military command, the provision of treating prisoners, the ban of exile and the order of suicide as opposed to capturing by the Italians.

Detachments within the group have helped the Italians in various forms. One of their most impressive retaliation was when they burnt three planes on 26

June 1936 in Bonaya, Neqemte, and dozens of Italian troops were killed, including Marshall Magliocco, the Italian Deputy Viceroy to Ethiopia.

The remaining survivor was an Italian priest, whose role was to give blessings to the short-lived Italian expedition in the Southwest, undertaken to exploit Oromo dissatisfaction towards the Amhara region and prepare the way for expansion through Princess Mahisente Habte Mariam of Neqemte. This illustrated that by all Ethiopians in every region within the country indeed supported the Patriots' defiance.

Many showed signs of ignorance for such movement in central Ethiopia. While negotiations in Neqemte were in progress, four members of the Black Lion Organisation attempted to attack some Italian high ranking officials. However, the Italian officers have managed to return safely to their unit, after the attacks became unsuccessful. This attacks has widely angered Graziani and forced him to order drove him to arrange a sweeping siege of Neqemte and its suburbs.

The Neqemte Massacre was a massacre in which almost one thousand people were killed and injured. Therefore, what at first appeared to be a victorious journey for the Italians in an area believed to be favorable for Italian rule ended in catastrophe. However, the effects of the assault and the horrific attitude of the people in the region constrained a large portion of the Patriots to relinquish the territory looking for a more favorable one while the older Patriots began retiring to isolated places.

The son-in-law of Emperor Haile Selassie and Commander of the Southern Patriot, Ras Desta Damtew, pulled back to Arbagoma but was surrounded by Italian troops under General Navarrini. After days of fighting, Damtew escaped to Eya, Butajira where he was apprehended and killed by firing squad shortly afterward. According to Italian estimation, the Ethiopian losses in the wars were approximately 4000. At the start, the Italians believed that the execution of Commander Ras Desta Damtew would crush the motivation of the resistance, but this believe proven wrong and more people began to join the resistance movement to bring to an end the Italian presence in Ethiopia.

The Italians have managed to find some associates among the Ethiopian nobility, not because of opportunism but mainly because of their ambitions to claim power, this for which the Italians might be a stepping stone. Although excessive force was the only means that Italians relied on to maintain their incursion and sustain their presence in Ethiopia, the Italians were searching for associates within the Ethiopian nobility since they have decided to invade Ethiopia.

Their presence in Eritrea had helped them to contact and recruits collaborators in Ethiopia. The Italians had use three approaches that could manipulate the Ethiopians: antagonism among the regional leaders; animosity between Christian and Muslim communities; and the anger of the southern Ethiopia people towards the central government for taking their lands. At first, these approaches appeared to facilitate the occupation, but with the rise of defiance and the Italians unfair treat to the associates, the approaches failed to sustain.

The two close associates of the Italians were Dejazmach Haile-Selassie of Tigray and Ras Hailu Tekle-Haimanot of Gojjam, both opponents of Emperor Selassie. Dejazmach Haile-Selassie, whose great-grandfather was Emperor Yohannes (who reigned from 1872-1889), sought to take back the throne of his great-grandfather with the help of the Italians.

Therefore he put his companions at the service of the Italians. Ras Hailu, the son of King Tekle Haimanot of Gojjam, who highly opposed to Emperor Haile Selassie's ascent to power during the 1920s, had likewise expected to govern Gojjam without any imperial intervention if he associated with the Italians.

Both men had received a huge amount of weapons and money from the Italians for their loyalty and service but not the power they hoped for. Also, other nobles associated with the Italians, prompted by comparable desires. However, Mussolini promised that once Italy takes over the power of the country, he would not rule Ethiopia on a metayer basis by sharing power with the Ethiopian nobles. Mussolini appeared to have appropriately grasped on the profound sentiments of the Ethiopian associates who had their particular separate desires that would not fit in the Fascists' approach.

With the pledge of restoring Muslim dominated states like Harar and re-establishing the kingdoms of Oromo like those of Abba Jobir, kingdoms that were previously part of Ethiopia. The Italians have managed to gain considerable association from Muslim communities and Oromos who were in the south and eastern highlands.

Abba Jobir, who was once a political prisoner to the Ethiopian government for opposing the tax collection in his region, made an Oromo army to join the Italians and fight with the Ethiopian resistance movement. Afterward when Later when he discovered that the Italians would not allow him to gain the autonomous power that he desired, he started scheming with the British councilor who had an office in Gore.

All of these collaborations between the Italians and some Ethiopian nobility, there was the sensation of victimization by the Emperor's desire to centralize power and rule over regional leaders also claimed power. However, these acts of the association have helped the invaders to achieve their prime objectives to some degree, and they were acts through which the associates to protect what they had lost under the reign of the Emperor. Surely these associates worked to secure their particular interest, but these actions weren't particularly seen as opportunistic. Rather, they reflected on the long adversary and conflicting between the center and the outskirts, especially during the times when the center was seen as weak.

On February 1937, Marshal Graziani along with his guests of honor was celebrating the birth of the Prince of Naples, outside the ruler's palace in Addis Ababa. Two young men from Eritrea Moges and Abraham has plotted a deadly attack against the Italians and threw seven grenades, which killed three Italian officers and injured several others. General Liotta, the commander of the Air Force, lost one of his eyes and legs while Graziani, the prime target of the assault, was injured by almost 300 splinters.

Following the attack, Moges and Abraham fled to join the resistance movement in Wolkait, while the wife of Abraham, Tadelech Estifanos, left one day earlier for the church of Debre Libanos. The city of Addis Ababa transformed into a binge of terror. In revenge Marshal Graziani has put forward several retaliatory measures to be carried out and Italian soldiers began to kill almost anyone seen on sight, burning houses and churches, rapping females, even the sick people lying in the hospital were not spared.

The shocking scene provoked Mussolini into action, as he prohibited these outrages measures for fears of pressure from international community. The assaults conducted by Moges and Abraham against the Italian invaders has given substantial force to the Patriots to counteract the retaliatory measures by the Italians.

After February 1937, a new resistance movement has been formed and rose dramatically throughout Ethiopia. Yohannes Saomerjibashian, a young Ethiopian, began an underground press known as the Pillar of Ethiopian light. Blatta Kidane-Mariam established a movement consisted of Ethiopian youth and collaborated closely with the women's organization in resistance activities. The papers were printed by Yohannes and later distributed by youth organization led by Kidane-Mariam, the leaflet was calling for protests and uprisings against the Italian occupation, and these protests began to appear in Addis Ababa's public squares.

The railway connecting Addis Ababa to the port of Djibouti was often raided. In October 1936, the resistance movement had attacked an armored train, escorted by a squadron of warplanes, that was secretly carrying two important ministers of the Italian government, A. Lessona, the Italian Minister of Colonies and C. Gigli, the Minister of Public Works. The train ambushes have increasingly become frequent. A British author Evelyn Waugh, who traveled from Djibouti to Addis Ababa by train in that year, has managed to interview Marshal Graziani directly, he noticed that 'there was a machine gun section posted at the front of the train; another at the rear. From Awash to Addis the line was highly protected.

The defiance in the centre of the country became significantly epidemic in various forms and proven cohesive. Haile-Mariam Mamo was widely known for his hit-and-run tactics around the capital city. In Gojaam, the avowed shifta Belay Zelleke and his opponent Hailu Belaw, despite sometimes conflicting and raiding each other's territory, incurred substantial harm on stationary and portable Italian army. In Begemder, Yohannes and Asfaw were battling the well-prepared foe on numerous fronts. A successful assault in Bellesa forced Governor Mezzeti to withdraw to Gondar, the capital of the Begemder region, where he confronted more unrest.

While the Ethiopian defiance multiplied across the nation, various groups of patriots were operating on their own and using traditional approaches (hit-and-run, attacks) and others adapting modern tactics. There wasn't a unified and central command structural. In most regions, similar acts of defiance were implemented. The Eritreans were also part of the resistance. On January 1936, about 400 Eritreans left the Italians on the shire front alone and joined the withdrawing Ras Imru. Almost 600 Eritreans came to join Ras Desta at Adola on 20 February 1936.

The Italians killed loyalist from Eritrea like Kegnazmach Andom Tesfatsion, Kegnazmach Assefa Bahitu and several others affiliated with the resistance movement on all fronts and almost a thousand of them during the fightings. This historical fact proved false the idea entertained by some Eritreans weren't part of the resistance against the Italian occupation. On the economic side, many Ethiopians have substantially refused to use the Italian currency. Particularly in the countryside, the Ethiopian continued to use Maria Theresa thalers, the initial Austrian silver dollar, for purchasing despite the Italians had announced the lire to be the unit of currency upon their arrival.

However, the Italians had to pay the Ethiopian workers at the platinum mines at Yubo in thalers as they have refused lire currency. Moreover, when the government forced the workers to accept the lire, there was mass abandonment of some local businesses practically stopped to exist as a business and moved to somewhere else. Such immobilize defiance swelled increasing the cost of Italian occupation and severely downgraded the lire. A Maria Theresa thaler could be attained from the Royal Mint in London for 6.50 lire in 1937 and sold for 13.50 lire in Ethiopia.

The soul of the defiance reflected through some parts of Italy as well. Ethiopians who often were taken there either as detainees or translators were anticipated to be shaped in Italian belief system and ways of thinking. Among the 400 notables and their families who were sent to Italy through Massawa in the mid-year of 1937 was the young Zerai Derres, working as an aid. Zerai Derres is an Eritrean translator of the banished Rases, on 13 June 1938, in front of the landmark of the fallen heroes of Dogali in Rome, affirmed words for Haile Selassie. While trying to stop him, some people were injured.

Abdisaa Agga, a suspected accomplice of Abraham Deboch and Moges Asgedom in their endeavor to kill Marshal Graziani, was sent to Libya as a detainee. After the major German army defeat in Libya, Abdisaa Agga, together with several other European prisoners was transferred to prison in Italy from which he later managed to escape. He then took part in guerrilla activities in the mountains of Italy where he met Marshal Tito, leader of the resistance movement of Yugoslav.

During late 1937, Benito Mussolini recognized that defiance was increasing significantly in Ethiopia despite Marshal Graziani's dreadful suppression. Mussolini had later replaced Graziani with Viceroy U. Amadeo, as he replaced Graziani, he believed that pacific approach would ease the situation and would contain the end of the insurgency. With an effort to attempt an alternate approach, the new leader held talks with rebel leaders, expecting to negotiate their capitulate.

Amaedeo has offered the rebel leaders money, titles and positions in his administration and implemented the approach of divide-and-rule among the Ethiopian resistant leaders. Indeed, several leaders and some low ranking chiefs reacted decidedly, which emphasized that the Ethiopians reaction to the occupation and the chances of the new circumstance was neither uniform nor universal.

However, many Ethiopians remained resistant. The resistance movement, the churches, woman's organization and the youths were among those who remained resistant, and many of them continued with their normal resistant activities. Some patriots joined the negotiation talks, seeming to associate with the invaders but only to buy time until a more convenient moment to reciprocate. For example, the preeminent patriot Abebe Aregay negotiated his capitulate with the Italians, but many historians interpreted this case as an absolute diversion to get breathing space for his weak army

Guerrilla groups, led by the great warriors like Zewde Asfaw and Abebe Aregaay, kept on making the well-established Italians in the Ethiopian capital city feel insecure at all times. Furthermore, the regions remained unstable and insecure for the Italians. Ethiopian loyalists like stationed in several fronts, commanding almost 3000 armed resistance and made the countryside complete dangerous for the invader's troops. Only in the south was more or less stable and secure, and road-building and administrative services could be established.

As the negotiations failed to reduce the resistance, the General of the Italian armed forces at that, General Ugo Cavallero persuaded the Duke of Aosta that the approach used by Graziani was very effective and would eventually bring the desired outcome. This meant the implementation of a heavy military campaign and excessive use of force. General Cavallero began to construct road connections between strategic ports connected with chains of forts, which still is a visible Italian legacy in Ethiopia today. From 1939 to 1938 Cavallaro's troops implemented the Graziani's approach in what appeared to be an endless conflict of terror.

In 1940 Mussolini embarked the most horrific venture of his career. He signed a treaty with Germany to went on the European war on 10 June 1940. France and Britain, both acclimated to diplomatic contest with Italy in the colonial separation of East Africa, were currently set to become the main adversaries of Italy, as they were of her Axis associate Germany. This new association of world powers came as an excellent gift for Ethiopia.

Emperor Selassie, who repeatedly requested for help during his five years of exile, has been completely ignored by foreign powers and the League of Nations (Now UN); found backing from his twist of events. Various types of support to the Ethiopian cause and the resistance began to stream in, not just from Britain where the emperor was granted exile but also from other allied forces. The emperor returned to Ethiopia with the belief that British intervention would drive the Italians out of the country.

The British planned Haile Selassie's trip via Sudan, where he began to mobilize Patriots and resistance movements in exile and advance towards Ethiopia. When he came to the capital city of Sudan in July 1940, he received a warm welcome and support from the resistance leaders in the field. But, he was unsure the people he left with the Italians in 1936 would welcome and treat him. The possible uprising in Gojjam, the Ogaden and Eritrea and other regions, the Republican principles of Takele Wolde-Hawariat and the vigorous thinkers in the defiance against the fascist Italians were some of the dangers that the Emperor needed to address. The resistance movements had made their political force, with claims and suggestions for the post-war era in Ethiopia.

The role of the defiance in representing this sort of political challenge to a liberated Ethiopia is possibly worthy of a different case, but mainly the ideas of rebellion, social justice, and individuals' rights that rose up from the resistance were an improvement which Ethiopia, and particularly the new government, needed to manage.

From June 1940, a well-orchestrated propaganda campaign on behalf of the Emperor attempted to enhance the conditions for his arrival. On 30 January 1941, when the Emperor crossed the border from Sudan, escorted the General Orde Wingate, he declared that there would be no striking back against the Italians. This affirmation was viewed as the official suspension of the resistance, despite that no one was certain how the Italians were going to respond.

Later the Duke of Aosta and his troops withdraw to the strategic pass of Amba Alagie in Tigray region, quitting Addis Ababa to resistance movements, who were in the mountains and inside the city and to the British general, Alan Cunningham, who was making his way up from Kenya to Addis Ababa. On 6 April 1941, Addis Ababa was liberated and a month later, on 5 May 1941, Emperor Haile Selassie entered the Addis Ababa. His reign was re-established, and he remained in power for the next 33 years.

Despite units of British troops, combined with the Ethiopian resistance forces, ended the Italian occupation of Ethiopia, this period left a remarkable remembrance of native Ethiopian resistance. At the time, it was acknowledged how much the invasion and the occupation had disrupted the traditional culture and the myth of the divine Emperor. Many patriots associate their patriotic resistance to the European war where the same enemy had to be destroyed completely. What Ethiopians clearly remember up to this day is the appalling conduct of the Italians and the hardship and the courageous struggle of the patriots.

Following their considerable defeat and withdrawal from Ethiopia, the Italians were expecting the Ethiopian, who considerably suffered from brutal repression for over five years, to take vengeance. Defiance and revolt, is indeed is a response to injustice, and the Italian's excessive use of force was perceived as beyond tolerable limits.

Such activities or conduct had no model in Ethiopia: the mustard-gas bombings, the mass killings, arbitrary detentions. However, with Haile Selassie's assertion not to perpetrate harm on the Italians in departure, following his declaration, the U.S. president at the time Franklin D. Roosevelt sent a message of gratitude, and the Ethiopians chose not to take revenge against the Italians.

During the five years of the occupation, the Ethiopians opposed the Italian invasion and violations of the Ethiopian rights and the mass injustice. Once the occupation came to an end, two aspects allay their reactions and their indignation to retaliate. Firstly there was their traditional diligence based on the religious culture of tolerance and pride, and in this respect, there is a distinction in religious culture between the Europeans and Ethiopian. Secondly, the global political spectrum and the reliance of Ethiopia on foreign diplomatic and material assistance may have assumed a part in softening the Ethiopian reaction at a higher level.

The Italian incursion of 1935 and occupation of 1936-1941 of Ethiopia was led by a modernized and powerful European army that couldn't be coordinated by Ethiopia at the time. Conventional military speculations and diplomatic actions were widely used utilized in high structures against an Ethiopian armed force that did not have the working central command structure, not to mention contemporary weaponry systems or political support.

The Italian unleashed an excellent campaign of fierce submission both from the ground and from the air, which the Ethiopians had no defense capacity and which resulted from significant death toll. At the start of the occupation, the destruction of the Ethiopian armed force before Mussolini's war machine followed by the exile of the Emperor persuaded that the fate of a long-autonomous country was doomed. Any possible emergence of patriotic resistance also looked far-fetched. 'Mussolini's dream, one shared by the Italian people and constantly reiterated in the press, that millions of Italians would be able to find land and work in Ethiopia then seemed to gain ground.

But the Ethiopians were ready to defend their sovereignty. The vast majority of the cities and towns were in the hands of the Italians, but they couldn't get control over the countryside where the defiance was gathering momentum. Although the excessive Italian use of force them to capitulation, most Ethiopians render their sense of freedom and dignity as a nation and were ready to oppose any superior force that violated their rights as an independent state and their historical identity and traditional. Ethiopians have chosen to fight back and protect their independence without the Emperor, who some believed that he should present as a symbol of unity.

Hence the formal Italian war of occupation was challenged with community-based resistance. The customary form of defiance, shiftinnet, had found another territory to spread to and another foe to counter, and they have enjoyed a much wider popular support. Unlike the old shiftinnet inspired by a rebellious noble or a few politically ambitious individuals, anti-Italian resistance drew upon all sectors of Ethiopian society: the peasantry, the nobility, the clergy, intellectuals, women and the youth alike.

'From this point, resistance was no longer an aristocratic affair' but in fact 'serendipitous,' as Schaefer rightly observed – gifted with the ability to find novel ways of revolt and action. For the Italians, however, resistance was an act of violence by irrational outlaws or t'era-shiftas who deserved to be hunted down, flogged, publicly hanged or executed by firing squad to create a state of fear and submission. Despite the repression and atrocities against the resistance fighters, the Italians never achieved the desired result.

While the resistance expanded in scope and tenacity, the Italian human and material costs were growing, and driving the Italians to a state of increased fury. Not only was the whole objective of their occupation thwarted but also 'never in their quinquennium of the rule did the fascists feel secure in Ethiopia, and their anxiety came to border on neurosis.' To the relief of Ethiopians, Italy entered the Second World War on the side of Germany, and the Allied forces began to pour in support to bolster the resistance movement in Ethiopia. After the Italians were defeated, resistance, which had become nationwide, came to an abrupt end.

The five years of Italian occupation shook feudalist Ethiopia and the impact the occupation created in traditional Ethiopia was significant. As McClellan put it: 'It was an event that swept away old myths and created the opportunity for Ethiopians to re-examine the nature and meaning of their state.

For Ethiopia, the war highlighted a need to move fully into the modern world'. The fact that Ethiopia had failed to repulse the predatory Italian invasion in itself proved to many that the country had a long way to go, among other things, in building a modern system of self-defence. But, given the whole purpose of the invasion and occupation, there was another aspect to what the 'modern world' constituted in the context of the Ethiopian conception as a free and sovereign nation that had to face unprovoked aggression.

While the need to move into the modern world was deemed essential, there also emerged a rethinking of why and how the occupation was conducted and how resistance had been organized. In the first place, there was no doubt that it was Italy's authoritarian, nationalistic and greedy colonial ambition that led to the invasion and occupation of Ethiopia. For most Ethiopians, the invasion and occupation were executed in the most barbaric and violent manner. The perception was that if this were the guise of the 'modern world,' few Ethiopians would be attracted by it.

Second, the essence of the resistance was to safeguard the independence, religious values and cultural identity of Ethiopia, all taking inspiration from the domain of the past as heritage. Given the violent 'present' defined by the Italians, the Ethiopians naturally oriented themselves to the past, i.e. all that defined their historical and cultural identity. In both cases, the reason for the motivation for change was negative. Italy's modernity can hardly be seen to have positively transformed Ethiopia's traditional society. The only thing remaining and still referred to by Ethiopians is the 'heritage' of Italian road-building.

After 1941 Ethiopia moved towards modernity at its pace within the contours of the old imperial order. The Patriots' contribution to the freedom and independence of the country was highly valued, and many of their leaders were rewarded with public positions. However, the social and political aims of the resistance – ideas relating to social justice, equality and more openness in the political system – were not followed up.

Patriot leaders were also expected to be loyal to the Emperor again, and those who dissented or actively conspired against him were removed, and in some cases (like Belay Zelleke) executed. While the Emperor promulgated a newly revised constitution in 1955, installed a parliament, allowed limited non-party elections, embarked on far-reaching judicial reforms and developed the education system, the old property relations and the lack of democratic rights, such as a free press, free elections, and political parties, remained unaddressed. In this respect, the Patriots' program was not realized.

Modern Era of the Horn of Africa

For decades the Horn of Africa has witnessed an intra-state and inter-state conflicts. This region is considered as the most conflicting region in the entire African continent, and as a result, the region has confronted major hostilities and ongoing conflict which had a major impact on the relationship between some countries within the region e.g. Eritrea and Ethiopia. Also, the rise of the terrorism and piracy in the region has led to the establishment of military presence of world powers. The most recent intra-state conflict in the region was the second North-South civil war in Sudan from 1983-2005, and the inter-state conflict of the two neighboring countries Ethiopia-Eritrea war of 1998-2000, which devastated the stability of the region.

Since the horrific attack in the history of America in 9/11, Horn of Africa became the center of the global war on terror, driven mainly by issues related to the collapse of the Siad Barre's government in Somalia and the rise of the so-called Al-Shabaab extreme group and the rapid expansion of piracy in the coast of Somalia.

The conflicts destroying the region are underpinned by historical and socio-economic issues which can be categorized into two sections: intra-state and inter-sate. Moreover, they have been intensified by intra-regional and global intervention. Apparently, such interventions have been compelled by competing for national interest and other factors such as the strategic linked to the war on terror and global concerns about the escalation of piracy.

Interventions by the international community (mainly the U.S.) have contributed to the provocations of the conflicts and the instability of the region. The geostrategic importance of the Horn has attracted world powers in terms military and economically, especially the proximity of the Horn of Africa to the Middle East region. Furthermore, Bab Al-Mandeb strait and the Red Sea is the prime shipping route for merchandise from the Middle East to the Far East and Europe. The finding of natural resources, greatly desired by transnational corporations and states, also the region offers the external actors an unprecedented interest following the establishment of the global war on terror and the present of naval forces off the Somali coast due to the piracy.

The U.S. strategic interests in the Horn of Africa focus on keeping Somalia from turning into a command center for al-Qaeda and its domestic affiliates. In seeking its counterterror technique, the United States has discovered common cause with Ethiopia. The Ethiopian government has since quite a while dreaded the restoration of Somali irredentist claims on its eastern border, or that a strong Islamist movement may blow tension among its Muslim community and feels besiege both by a strong indigenous separatist armed group in the Ogaden region and unprecedented border conflicts with its neighboring Eritrea.

But the long outrageous behavior of the Ethiopian regime, both home and in neighboring countries, poses a major obstacle for the U.S. and its strategic interest in the region. The U.S. government must be prepared to push their regional partners to change its strong-handed strategy to political disagreement and counterterrorism. Ethiopia has long struggled with internal issues since the downfall of Mengistu in 1991. The country's economy has significantly grown despite the high level of poverty and unemployment; recently the government has attempted to adopt measures to institutionalize a system of multiparty democracy, but critics say that this move has failed. As a result of internal disputes.

In 2005, Ethiopia held its most free and fair elections. Before the polls, there was a significant opening of political space. The opposition parties were able to participate the contest and hold campaign rallies; the press has managed to publish critical political analysis and raise the voice of the oppressed opposition activists, and sympathizers and both local and international observers were present to monitor the election outcome. But the regime's provisional efforts to open up the political space were not remunerated: after a series of distortion in the vote and tallying procedures were found, several position parties have ultimately rejected the election outcomes and accused the government of perpetrating bias results. The Ethiopian government led by Meles Zenawi declared a state of emergency and responded with unprecedented measures that led to mass arrests and the disappearance of the main position leaders.

The country dove into a period of civil unrest and turbulence, during which the TPLF government detained and prosecuted thousands of civilians and arrested hundreds of preeminent opposition figures, including several journalist and actors from the civil society. Many of these government measures against protestors have been legislated, and as a result criminalized public support by foreigners and enforced harsh criminal penalties on terrorist acts, including disturbing public protests.

Impact on U.S. Policy Objectives

For Washington, collaboration with such totalitarian Ethiopian regime indicates rising challenges to U.S. policy objective. First, the Ethiopian regime attempts to reduce widely the political contest in the upcoming election of 2010 as the government feared the occurrence of fan ethnic tensions in the country. The Ethiopian ruling party, EPRDF, is believed by the vast majority of the population to be controlled by a single minority ethnic group, the Tigre, and its grip on power have significantly angered the majority ethnic Amhara and Oromo communities. General public discontent with the government is extremely high following the 2005 election results and the government's actions in breach of the human right.

Secondly, the Ethiopian war with neighboring Eritrea and the extreme radical groups in Somalia, and with the powerful separatist groups in the Ogaden region, have a jihadist sway. While the United States and Ethiopia affiliation has had temporary tactical advantages, it may be sabotaging the wider U.S. counterterror objectives.

Ostensibly, U.S. dependence on Ethiopian military and intelligence has served to aggravate instability in Somalia. Ethiopia's incursion of Somalia, and the long presence of Ethiopian troops in Mogadishu, rather than subduing struggle, has prompted a local resistance that has served as an encouraging point for local terrorist militias. It was the development of an unpredictable rebellion against the Ethiopian army presence that successfully shot a periphery jihadist youth militia, the Shabaab, to power. Global jihadists have now taken advantage on the local resistance, and on the U.S. backing of the Ethiopian incursion, as an as a chance to globalize Somalia's conflict.

The presence of foreign expertise, fighters and financing have helped to tip the balance of power for Al Shabab, Somalia's radical group. Also, there are Ethiopian government concerns that the conflict in Ogaden could lead to jihadist movements. While the firm alliance between America and Ethiopia has advantages to some extent, it's sabotaging the broader U.S. strategic interest in the region as there is a considerable anti-America sentiment in Somalia, and stems in many parts of U.S. conspiracy with the Ethiopian incursion and reported Ethiopian violation of human rights in Somalia. Also, Ethiopia has reportedly taken part in human right abuses within the Somali region in Ethiopia (Ogaden), which shares a border with Somalia, where the Ethiopian regime engaged in a counterinsurgency actions against the ONLF (Somali separatist group).

Although the EPRDF government denied human right charges, Amnesty International, and other Human rights organizations, have published crimes and violations against the human right carried out by both the Ethiopian regime and the separatist groups.

The U.S. decision to remove their military personnel from the Ogaden region in April 2006, and the subsequent failure of the international community to pursue responsibility for these crimes and atrocities, has solidified a widespread of public perception in both Somalia and Ethiopia. The U.S. has therefore turned a blind eye to these human right abuses in exchange for collaboration in the counterterrorism campaign.

The border dispute between Eritrea and Ethiopian is another complication on U.S. efforts to help restore the central government of Somalia. For long-time, the Eritrean authority has argued that Ethiopia has refused to respect the decision of an independent border commission on the separation of the common boundary and has requested a mediation from the international community. Ethiopia has accused Eritrea of supplying weapons and finances the extreme group in Somalia. The government of Eritrea has rejected these accusations, and some particular allegations leveled by the UN and the African Union against Eritrea were later proven wrong.

The request for sanctioning Eritrea is still growing, some comments made by former U.S. Secretary of State Hillary Clinton on a visit to Kenya on 2009, in which she associated Eritrea to Somali radical extremist suggests efforts by the U.S. government to engage in an active political dialogue with the Eritrean regime may be obscure.

These factors show that the U.S. government's ability to influence issues in Somalia will require some measures on diplomatic efforts to solve the border dispute between the two neighboring states to address the issue of human right in Ethiopia constructively.

The U.S. government is unwilling to pressure the Ethiopian regime to adopt democratic reforms and open up the political space for more transparency in the Ethiopian political spectrum, and this could be for various reasons. According to many experts and policy makers, the regime in place is extremely fragile and on the brink of collapse.

Some diplomats are anxious if the Ethiopian population engage in protest and other actions which could potentially lead to resistance that it may destabilize the regime. Therefore the U.S. can't afford to disturb or cause obstacles a country that has collaborated with them to achieve its strategic interest in a region where conflicts and extreme groups have fractured.

Another significant obstacle for the United States is the absence of an international agreement on one crucial question: Is Ethiopia a democratic state, or is the administration of Prime Minister Hailemariam Desalegn and previously Meles Zenawi is heading towards authoritarianism? The idea that Ethiopia is fundamentally democtatic state where the rule of law is respected remains solid, especially among European countries. The absence of any consensus would require the United States to take the lead and possibly confined part in compelling Ethiopia for reform.

At last, the U.S. government efforts to promote democratic reforms in Ethiopia are obstructed by the absence of willing associates on the ground. The Ethiopian civil society and democratic activist are anxious, and fear for their security as well as economic security and they have no intention to organize and engage in public protests. This means that local effort will not support Washington's effort to prevent the oppressive actions conducted by the Ethiopian government. Several international organizations that have supported or raised the concerns of the opposition parties have been expelled from Ethiopia.

U.S. STRATEGIC INTEREST IN SOMALIA DURING THE COLD WAR

The U.S. involvement in African affairs was much narrowed before the World War II, except several commercial treaties signed with some West African countries. In general, U.S. was not keen on African matters and did not express any concerns to the European colonization of the continent. But, there was some thoughtfulness regarding Africa when, on January 18, 1918, President Woodrow Wilson issued a fourteen points declaration to the Joint Session of Congress in which he stressed the importance of self-determination and the establishment of governance. The Atlantic Charter, signed by both the U.S. President Franklin Roosevelt and British Prime Minister Winston Churchill, was another action to encourage peace and stability across the globe by compromising colonialism.

Both leaders acknowledged the devastation that colonial cause to people's right to self-determination and self-governance. Later, U.S. President Wilson wanted to counter the dangers posed by German Nazis which had changed the U.S. attitude towards European Imperialism. His position had clear implications for the African people who suffered from foreign colonization.

After the World War II, the Soviet Union entered the global political spectrum to oppose the Western influence and imperialism. Subsequently, the Western became more proactive in promote democracy in the former colonial nations.

The end of the World War II marked the start of decolonization in Somalia vigorously. The process was not always at its best. At the time of Somalia independence in 1960, British Somaliland and Italian Somaliland joined and unified under one flag, yet colonial boundaries granted Ethiopia, Kenya, and

France control over regions in which ethnic Somalis make up the majority of the general population. While these three countries were allies of the United States, the U.S chose not to deteriorate its relation with Somalia due to the threats and dangers posed by the Soviet Union and the strategic importance of the Horn of Africa. As a result, the U.S. government has promised to the new Somali government a financial and military assistance. However, the Soviet also offered a similar deal to the newly established government of Somalia in pursuit of its strategic location.

In this manner, the Republic of Somalia became the winner during the Cold War era; even the U.S President at that time John F Kennedy acknowledged the increased development that Somalia is reaching and as a result met with the Somalia's Prime Minister Abdirashid Ali Sharmarke in 1962. However, the Soviet Union eventually offered Somalia what they most wanted which was more military hardware.

On 21 October 1969, following the assassination of Prime Minister, Abdirashid Ali Shermarke, during a visit to LasAnod District, in the northern part of Somalia by his security guard. The military-led Major General Siad Barre staged a coup, the day after Shermarke's funeral, and took over the office. The military government has quickly adopted scientific socialism, dissolved the parliament, suspended the constitution and nationalized major private firms. The U.S influence concluded after Somalia signed a friendship treaty with the Soviet Union.

On November 1969, President Siad Barre introduced the Supreme Revolutionary Council (SRC). The SRC announced to abolish tribalism and favoritism, the major issues to develop and growth during the nine years of Prime Minister Abdirashid Sharmarke. The country's economy was in a deep recession and was dependent on foreign aid to run the country. When the military seized power, many Somalis have considerably welcomed as the regime pledged to wipe out corruption, tribalism, and favoritism and introduce a fairer society that works for all.

Mainstream acceptance encouraged Barre's initiatives like the establishment of scientific socialism and the fight against tribalism, as it was regarded as the real cancer of Somali society. The military government formed a slogan stated,

"Tribalism divides where Socialism unites." The military regime had gained the trust of the people by encouraging self-sufficiency and self-reliant mentality. This initiative helped to promote a national, instead of clan awareness, for it reduced on dependence on traditional tribe ancestry for survival. The prime vision for all Somalis was to be united, including those under the Kenyan and Ethiopian rule.

During the first couple of years of Barre's leadership, the Somali-Soviet relationship grew dramatically, and both nations formed a military alliance. Both Somalia and the Soviet Union signed a comprehensive agreement which brought the Soviet military equipment to Somalia. Various, advanced Soviet weapon systems appeared, such as MiG-21 jet fighters, T-54 tanks, SAM-2 missile defense system.

In exchange, the Soviets were granted a military base at the port of Berbera port, near the Red Sea and the Indian Ocean. From this strategic position, they could counter the U.S military operation in North Africa and the Middle East and control trade. A more threatening feature of the agreement saw the Soviet secret security agency KGB instructing and training their Somali counterparts, the National Security Service, which could arrest people anytime for perpetrated allegations.

The vision of a stronger and greater Somalia came about when President Barre invaded neighboring Ethiopia to free his Somali brothers in the Ogaden region in 1977. Incidentally, the 1977-8 conflict between the two neighboring states Somalia-Ethiopian, allowed by Soviet backing, was the separating point in the friendship between the Cold War countries. The Soviets chose to betray his long-term ally who granted him a base in the strategic location and vowed to support his Ethiopian orthodox counterpart to counter President Barre's nationalistic plans. The Somali army had lost the battle when Eastern coalition bloc (consist of Cuba, East Germany, Libya, South Yemen and the Soviet Union troop) connect themselves to the Ethiopian belief and principle.

Indeed, Somalia was not destined to drift out loose. In a captivated world, a friend of the U.S was inevitably an enemy of the Soviet Union. The Soviet assistant to Ethiopia gave the U.S an opportunity to revive its relations with Mogadishu government. The U.S administration offered up-to-date military equipment to Somalia so it could counterbalance the soviet and Cuban assistance for Ethiopia. Somalia that was built by the Soviet aid joined the Western Bloc in 1978, hence verifying the old overused that there are "no permanent friends no permanent enemies."

During the cold war era, the U.S had a history of supporting Africa's ruthless dictators who extremely violated the principle human rights of their people in return for accessing the African resource. It was only necessary that these ruthless thugs somehow suit the wider interest of the United States. This policy has long compromised key principles of the constitution: respect for individuals rights and freedom, organizing free and fair elections, free market economy, abide by the law accordingly.

However, such opportunism remained at the heart of the U.S foreign policy. Somalia has managed to fit the trend. In spite of Siad Barre's bleak human rights record and bad governance, the U.S persisted its financial and military assistance to his government to protect Somalia from Ethiopia's communist regime.

This is one of the American-Soviet proxy conflicts was undertaken where commonly guaranteed destruction prevented a direct conflict. Like many other African dictators, Siad Barre profited widely from America's backing and the blind eye. His government survived the 80's, after they received grants, bailouts and flexible loans from the World Bank and IMF, and food aid through USAID, which was distributed between camps and displaced people, due to the refugee flood from war zone Ogaden region in Ethiopia.

In return, the U.S gained what they most wanted which was the permission to build a strategic naval base at Berbera. This was a win-win situation between the U.S. and Somalia. However, President Barre's dark shadow delayed the American integrity. President Barre who often people considered him the East African dictator has neither accepted the existence of political oppositions and creation of democratic reform. Instead, he chose to conduct himself as a thug, using excessive force against anyone who showed sympathy to oppositions or engaged with anti-government protest. His armed forces carried out mass killings some parts of the country especially in the north, where they slaughtered hundreds of innocent people, raped the woman and create animosity between clans.

Siad Barre was exceedingly contradictory to what the United States was evidently seeking after. It is no wonder that during the 80's, increasing opposition groups requested a fair share in the government. At the point when Barre disregarded this demand, the opposition groups armed itself and launched armed resistance against Barre's regime and called itself Somali National Movement (SNM) with the intention of removing Barre from the power.

The SNM insurgent group has managed to seize two major cities in the Northern parts of the country (Hargeisa and Burco) in 1988. President Barre and his generals used their sophisticated US-made weapons against the SNM insurgent group to wipe their existence. He virtually leveled the rebel cities. Following the collapse of the Soviet Union in 1991, the U.S interest in Somalia came to an end. Therefore the U.S. has retreated all their support and assistance to Somali's regime that enabled the long rule of Siad Barre.

When the US government suspended their entire financial and military assistance to Siad Barre's regime, his security machinery had eventually collapsed. Sensing the government's weakness, insurgent forces formed a movement called United Somali Congress and appointed Mohamed Farah Aideed has the movement's secretary general. The group has later stormed the capital which forced the President to flee Mogadishu in January 1991.

As the insurgent began and the legitimate president fled the capital, hundreds of civilians lost their lives and thousands more fled their homes as the insurgency escalated and the situation was worsening day after day, water and shelter became extremely short. With the shared enemy eliminated, so too did any reason for the resistance movement to be unified. The same warlords that overthrew the president continued to fight among themselves for power and control; as the situation got out of hands, tribalism came back to Somalia at the worst possible time.

America decided to heavily neglect its former Cold War East African partner until the worst horrific event of the US history on September 11, 2011. Now involved in another major international conflict, the U.S. government found new strategic interest in Somalia and across the region.

This time, the US government offered significant assistance to Somali warlords and former Somali opponent, Ethiopia, to fight America's proxy war. The US President at that time, George Bush reported that Ethiopia could be a major partner to fight against the international terror network. In 2005, he gave a $450 million donation in food aid, engineered by the US Department for International Development

The Rise of Warlord in Somalia

The warlord phenomenon began after the collapse of the central government in 1991. This was the period of the United Somalia Congress insurgent movement, characterized by much unfortunate chaos and violence. When USC leadership (mainly from the Hawiye clan) could not adjust its political differences, it slid into a conflict which took the form of outright war, given that the USC was, in fact, a tribal militia at heart.

Two sides from the Hawiye clan conflicting among themselves: one side was supporting to self-proclaimed president Ali Mahdi Mohamed and the other side to General Mohamed Farah Aideed. For many years the conflict-afflicted the Somalia people with lost property and lives. These two men were complete problem for everyone as neither of them could claim victory or take control over the government institutions. Therefore, peace and security in Mogadishu were downgraded. These two leaders were captured in Somali tradition. They misused that culture and tradition while bearing the guise of contemporary diplomacy. They adequately transformed the struggle for control of the USC in a conflict for tribe supremacy.

The insurgent group recruited fighters from their tribe and dedicated themselves to their tribe, rather than the national interest of the country. Both Aideed and Ali Mahdi were competing for the post of presidency of Somalia. Although their association had previously ousted former president Siad Barre, both men did not understand the importance of compromise. Now they had worked together to remove the authoritarian regime; each chose to become a local political leader of his respective tribe in the hope he would eventually take the leadership of governmental institutions for the sake of his sector of the population. What's more interested is that both men hail from the same Hawiye tribe of Mogadishu, Somalia.

Aideed hails from Habar-Gidir sub-clan, whereas Ali Mahdi belonged to Abgal sub-clan. Hence, General Aideed and Ali Mahdi divided the Hawiye into two sub-clans over which they govern as warlords. This development marked a dangerous slant which was inconsistent with the contemporary nation state. Thus, Warlord became an accepted part of the political culture of Somalia. With so many dangers posed by other tribes in the country, major tribes had to increase its military strength so they could protect themselves.

Ultimately, the regime itself was pervaded with warlords. The country's security fractured and good state of governance was fading. In summary, while clan elders were in charge of clan family affairs in villages and towns, warlords were the prime players upon the national stage. They kept their distance from clan affairs as it could create tension with tribal elders. The warlords focused themselves with warfare but knew no other alternative of dealing with the situation. In effect, they brought and plunged the country into turmoil and gave the ordinary people a complete nightmare.

U.S. Support for Somali Warlords

The US government has reassessed its foreign policy after the collapse and later the end of Cold War. Somalia marked one of the changes, as there was no real significant importance to the Horn region, the US administration suspended all of its assistance to Barre's, left him to face the armed resistance by himself. Energized, guerrillas rose armed resistance against the very fragile national army. Abruptly, Barre's regime resembled a pushover. It immediately stopped to existed, yet the transition was less ideal. Somalia went from one leader to several; already in conflict mode, warlords took to fighting each other although Siad Barre was ousted from power. Therefore, chaos and hostility replaced peace and security. The country went back to dark ages and clan warfare.

This kind of disorder was part of the old nomadic culture but incompatible with the needs of a contemporary state. The clan system took its toll. Major clans gathered behind the warlords with Enthusiasm. They were all pursuing their interest and territories; they ended up encroaching intensely upon each other, instigating a continuous civil war in Somalia. A large number of citizens, as a result, lost their lives and much more fled their homes. More severely, the level of starvation has dramatically increased to the extent that in 1992, the country saw its worst famine in the history of Somalia. A quarter of the Somali population has experienced a significant malnourishment.

The UN responded this crisis with an emergency humanitarian to help those who have severely affected by the famine in the countryside. This was easier said than done. It became obvious that U.S. could not assist aid to Somalia without involving itself in the civil war. Often the warlords were obstructing UN aid shipments from reaching those in need. The U.S. President George W. Bush's administration designed a new initiative called "Operation Restore Hope" before he left the power in 1992.

This effort saw the United States ally with the UN Secretary General Boutros Boutros-Ghali in the deployment of 30,000-strong peacekeeping army to ensure effective delivery of humanitarian food aid to the Somali population. The United States president had visited the town of Baida, which many labeled as the "city of death", to see the effectiveness of the humanitarian aid. In 1993 Bill Clinton was elected president of the United States and continued his predecessor's involvement in Somalia.

The humanitarian mission turned into a national building effort, however, in search of the best possible government, officials from the United Nations and the US helped to sow the seeds of animosity by pitting one warlord against the other. One good example was when Belgian peacekeepers helped warlord Mohmed Hersi Morgan to capture the city of Kismayo from Aideed's partner, Mohamed Omar Jess. This action enraged Aideed and his army. Several violent protests escalated against the UN humanitarian effort.

The US policy went from humanitarian mission to military mission and issued the arrest warrant of General Aideed. This showed that the US has completely failed to comprehend the clan politics of this country. Without a doubt, General Aideed was a ruthless warlord who has absolutely no humanity whatsoever; but the UN and the US coalition began to hunt him down and bring him to justice. Aideed was widely seen as a national hero because he stood up and opposed world superpowers.

In Somalia, despite constant tribe conflicts, compared to when a foreign enemy invade the country, old tribe rivalries give way to unity against the foreign enemy. After all, the tribes are just separate pieces of one shared, regional culture; and this is where they become Somali. Aideed's tribe and his rivals resisted against the US-led mission in Somalia. In response, the US and the UN increased the conflict, and as a result, eighteen American soldiers lost their lives and the shoot down of the two Black Hawk helicopters. The process of state building has failed as result of a misunderstanding of Somali culture and deluded foreign policy based on military intervention instead of peaceful talks and political resolution.

The conflict became a huge embarrassment to President Clinton especially when the corpses of American soldiers were being dragged by the Somali fighters in the streets of Mogadishu. Shortly afterward, the US President Clinton has admitted that US policy towards Somalia had failed and announced his intentions to bring the US soldiers home.

The al-Qaeda chief Osama Bin-Laden claimed the responsibility for the US defeat in Somalia. Also, the terrorist leader affirmed that he supplied with Somali fighters with sophisticated air missiles that had shot down the two Black Hawk helicopters. In 1994, U.S. and international forces left Somalia, having been defeated by militias a few-hundred-strong. Bin Laden clearly insisted that US army had no strength to fight in such wars. Somalia has always been a strategic location, but the US has widely neglected it between President Clinton US troop's withdrawal in 1994 and the beginning of War on Terror in 2001. The United States expressed anxiety about the impact of growing terrorism across the world. Bin Laden vowed to continue his fight Until the US interest is ruined around the world. In this manner, the new threat of terrorism has effectively replaced fifty years of Cold War. However, this was another kind of enemy especially in failed countries such as Somalia and Afghanistan.

The terrorist organization (al-Qaeda) threatened several times the US and its regional ally, Ethiopia. In response to this threat, the United States made another foreign policy mistake, as partners approached some of the warlords who starved the country. Thus, against its policy, the US legitimized their reign of terror. In the process of continuous for control of regions within the country, some warlords designated two semi-autonomous government;

Somaliland and Puntland. Where Southern Somalia, including the capital city Mogadishu and Kismayo, remained chaotic and reckless.

George Bush came to power on 2001, promised to promote compassionate conservatism. The United States effort to build a new association in Somalia: The Alliance for Restoration of Peace and Counterterrorism. This consisted of regional warlords. The Bush administration paid each warlord a sum of $150,000 per month for their cooperation. This foreign policy quickly changed after September 11, 2001, Al-Qaeda attacks on twin towers and the Pentagon. From December 2001, President Bush chose to increase the US involvement in the Horn of Africa once again.

During a press conference by President Bush, he declared that Ethiopia would be a key regional ally against terrorism. Just as Somalia benefited from US economic aid during the Cold War period due to its strategic position in the Horn of Africa, now neighboring Ethiopia as the favoured country, benefitting from Aid from the US Department for international development. In this manner, both Ethiopian government and Somali warlords were widely hunting suspected terrorists in the region.

This unilateral action extremely weakens the new transitional government by further legitimizing states within a state. This was unnecessary for Somalia; the President of Somalia, Abdullahi Yusuf Ahmed continuously repeated the need for US humanitarian, political and military aid for his government. The US policy failed, as Somali people widely rejected the coalition between warlords and Ethiopia. The former only brought anarchic and insecurity; the latter was opportunistic, and more likely a potential colonist. It is no surprise, then, that when strife started between US-backed warlords and the Islamic Court Union (ICU), the vast majority of Somalis were backing the ICU as they were the only hope for a peaceful Somalia.

The United States policy have only escalated tensions by calling the ICU as a radical extremist, and approaching Ethiopia, a major beneficiary of American arms since the Cold War ended, to fight against the ICU in a kind of proxy war on the pretext of the War on Terror. Apparently, the US government rejected to specifically address the subject of supporting the Somali warlords, who styled themselves as a counterterrorism coalition in quest of continued

American backing. The US state department spokesman Sean McCormack explicitly told reports "The United States would work with responsible individuals in fighting terror."

The US bet on the warlords failed after the ICU defeated them. The ICU took control of the capital and many parts of southern Somalia after their decisive victory against the thugs supported by the US. This became a complete dreadful blow to US anti-terrorism action as a whole; it uncovered its Islamist character. The ICU established harshly interpreted sharia which virtually punished all criminals, banned the use of alcohol and the khat, imposed woman to wear hijab, and banned movies and televised programs.

The ICU brand of Islam might have been an abomination in better times, but most Somalis saw no better alternative. The US had failed to internalize just how insecure Somalia ended up when it sided with the warlords who committed this problem. As a reward, it now had a staggeringly hostile governing body to deal with. With the Islamic Court Union in power, Somalia's weak transitional government has been operating largely out of Kenya and southern city of Baydhabo.

A large portion of Somalia was in chaos, ruled by savage warlords who had no humanity, Mogadishu was unsafe to the extent that Prime Minister Ali Muhamed Gedi could not visit the capital. The Prime Minister described the US government involvement in the fight between the ICU and the warlords as dangerous and argued that US involvement would undermine his government. The Prime Minister said "we would prefer the US to work with the transitional government and not with criminals", he also added "Somalia is not stable place, and we want the US in Somalia, but in a more constructive way. Clearly, we have a common objective to stabilize Somalia, but the U.S. is using the wrong channels".

The Rise of Islamic Movement in Horn region

After the fall of Siad Barre in 1991, opportunistic warlords brought the country back to dark ages. Their militias destroyed the country during the civil war, as they fight for strategic regions and towns. Anyone with an army or militia could gain some piece of Somalia. Therefore, an Islamist group in the northeastern quickly captured the city of Garowe in 1992. While 99% of the Somali population are Muslims, the country had maintained itself without a religious thrust. Religious leaders and clerics have always been respected dignified simply because of their knowledge of Islam, but the Somali culture usually draws a line between their realm and those of state, and clan.

Religious leaders have never interfered with clan politics nor requested any particular political position other than teaching. For centuries, the pastoral society in Somali has propagated its religion tradition. Fundamentalism held little appeal for it. Tribe society experienced harsh restrictions in Salafist ideas. Especially grating among these were tough laws, rank-and-file leadership which could challenge and weaken the clan system. This is why the Somalian pastoral had rejected militant religious enthusiasm in the past.

It saw insecurity instead of tranquillity in the confiscation of power from the fundamental social units. It was not easy for hardcore Islamism to survive in the Somali society without the help of tribe leaders. The Islamic part of the Somali society and its leadership initially came from various tribes and regions. But only one objective unified all of the aspects, and this was to rule the country in Islamic law. The group was completely opposed to all of Somali history. Often built as ancient, fundamentalists think themselves continuous.

The people of Somalia believed that the old clan system was un-Islamic and needed not change but to eradicate. This thought was reckless and extreme. Its fate in the town of Garowe shows an underlying rift with the Somali people. The tribe system reduced the Fundamentalist after communities from north-eastern of Somalia learned that the movement's main leader, Sheikh Hassan Dahir Aways (prospective leader of the Islamic Court Union), hailed from the same tribe as former warlord General Mohamed Aideed (Hawiye). General Aideed achieved a bad reputation as the infamous warlord who led the rebel resistance which ousted former president Siad Barre and promoted a mass genocide against the Darood clan in some parts of the country.

Hundreds of the victims left their homes in the capital for refugee camps in neighboring Ethiopia and Kenya. A prominent East African historian Said Samatar characterized the link between Somali tribe and Islam as follows "Somalia will never be a breeding ground for Islamic terrorism. The reason why the Somali politics is shaped as it is now is that of the extraordinary degree, by a central principle that overrides all others, namely the phenomenon that social anthropologists refer to as the segmentary lineage system."

Looking the phenomenon further, Samatar agreed completely with what Professor Cassanelli argued about the systematic division of Somali society: "My uterine brother and I against my half-brother, my brother and I against my father, my father's household against my uncle's household, our two households, against the rest of the immediate kin, the immediate kin against non-immediate members of my clan, my clan against others and, finally, my nation and I against the world."

Therefore, religious leaders regularly lost the fight amongst religious and clan loyalty. This was the exact fate of the north-eastern Islamists in the city of Garowe. Sheikh Aweys looked beyond his tribe to recruit an Islamic army, but he failed. Local tribal leaders and inhabitants described him as a foreigner and foe of the Darood who needed to dismiss the peace that they had enjoyed after the collapse of the Somali government. When he and his militants lost the backing of the general population, tribe warlord, and future Somali president Abdullahi Yusuf Ahmed gathered his militia to expel the Islamists from Garowe. That is the best example of the old tribe system overwhelming the invasion of hard core Islamic thoughts.

However, it was extremely difficult to crush radical extremist as it was to destroy the tribe system. The group did not die. Instead, it came up with alternative approach and point of attack to the southern parts of the country where there was significant violence and chaos to exploit. For many years, the Islamist began to reorganize under the radar quietly. In 1996, they announced a new movement called Al-Itahad al-Islamiya, based in Gedo in the southwest, near the Ethiopian and Kenyan borders. The tribal leaders and warlords had only a free handle. The group Al-Itahad al-Islamiya recognized a power vacuum and took advantage of it.

Sheikh Dahir Aweys formerly defeated by warlord Abdullahi Yusuf Ahmed in 1992, restored as the group's leader. The Al Itihad began to collect weapons and enforce Shariah on local people without tribe leaders' consent. Al-Itahad al-Islamiya had placed its regional authority contrary to existing clan leadership. With the growing threat perpetually premonition, local leaders attempted to negotiate with the Islamists, encouraging them to lay down their weapons and continue quiet teaching duties.

The militia group widely rejected the proposal and started killing some influential members of the tribe to assert that they were serious. During the negotiations, tribe leaders confront Islamist's rationale, and logic was beyond their ability to grasp, as their adversaries truly believed that they haven't had any hidden reason other than God's message and convey his words to all people.

There was a long debate occurred as the southern Somali clan looked for suitable strategy. Omar Haji Mohamed, a Mareehaan warlord, and former Defence Minister helped drive the discussion toward Ethiopia. It decided to look for military assistance. Now Sheikh Aweys committed another mistake by working outside his Hawiye clan region. Jointed home forces and Ethiopians continued to crush to religious groups in the Gedo region. Al-Itahad al-Islamiya was invalidated as a danger to southern Somalia. Twice-crushed, Aweys and the remaining of his army withdrew to Mogadishu, where his Hawiye tribe controlled. It could no more fight against any armed clan close to the Somali-Ethiopian border.

The Islamists were counteracting, but all was not well. Old obstacles and problems kept on distressing Somalia. As warlords fought one another for territory, the United States kept its distance from the people of Somalia, who went through a decade of severe war and famine which forced many of the Somali citizens to go to refugee camps inside and outside Somalia.

The international community had no longer considered Somalia as a country because the country began to disintegrate and split into mini-states ruled by tribe leaders who were protecting the interest of their respective clan and territory rather than national unity government. Putland state was created as an autonomous region in the northeast of the country, while Somaliland located in the northwest of the country declared its independence as the Republic of Somaliland.

The southern part of the country has remained extremely violent and chaotic. The regions hardship empowered Islamic pastors to make a return as conveyors of peace and security. Without a doubt, the establishment of the new Islamic court system fulfilled their promise by bringing justice to Mogadishu.

The Islamic clerics addressed many issues such as real estate and many other civil disputes which tribe conflict had resolved. Mogadishu and southern regions saw a massive drop on tribe disputes and the enforcement of unlawful activities. As a result, the Hawiye tribe, which previously suffered significantly at the hands of warlords and related criminals, began to support the Islamic priests as a possible check to hurtful warlords' influence inside the tribe.

The Islamic group ability for stabilization was evident, seeing that their fundamental objective was to progress and ensure the interests of the tribe. Shockingly, radical extremist has indicated over and over that this is too much to hope for. While Islamic clerics dedicated themselves to the Somali cause and to establish fair justice that serves the interest of all, they had a greater objective than their tribe as a top priority: to introduce Sharia and to rule first Mogadishu and afterward all of Somalia by Islamic law.

With the help of their clans and its leaders, the clerics had an opportunity to organize former members and sympathizers of the Al-Itihad al-Islamiya into a court militia, in charge of enforcing rulings and arrest escaped criminals. The arming of the court gave it enormous autonomy and justification, bordering on martial law. In 2006, Muslim leaders and business people progressed more towards forming a political organization called the Islamic Court Union (ICU) to unify all Islamic forces. They have designated their parliament and elected approximately 90 members to legislate the interest of Islam. After the designation of the parliament, they elected former Al-Itihad al-Islamiya leader Sheikh Hassan Dahir Aweys as president. In previously, Aweys had failed to Islamise large proportion of the country. Now, with a political party and established court behind him, he once again pushed into the south.

Since Somalia was classified as failed state and began to lose their territorial integrity following the ouster of former president Siad Barre, the US administration distressed to this development by hiring criminal warlords to fight the American proxy war under the pretext of the War Terrorism. President Bush warned about the potentially of Somalia become the new haven for terrorism. Al-Qaeda and non-state actors are in favor for chaotic and violent atmosphere so they could train militants, operate their financial network and plot targets. In Somalia, the al-Qaeda group has recruited militants and delivery their "destroy and kill" philosophy.

The U.S. accused and branded the Islamic Court Union as a terrorist organization without knowing the complex relationships between Islamic clerics within the ICU. In reality, the ICU, just like other groups, is very multifaceted. Apart from the distinctive groups loyal to the particular ethnic group, ICU militants and leaders sought and supported different ideologies within Islam. These include the Salafist, Brotherhood, Islamist, and Jihadist Muslim. The United States had failed to recognize these differences and chose to take their actions and judgments. By accusing the whole organization (ICU) of terrorism, Washington estranged Somali Muslims almost and created a much more enemy in the process.

The Islamic Court Union organization rose to power following the unprecedented military intervention led by the United States to Somalia. There were three main factors that led to the rise of the ICU: violent tensions and chaotic situation which led to the death of thousands of Somali citizens and denied all their rights; the greater absence of the international community in addressing the need for stability and national reconciliation in forming a credible government from the people; and for the people and last but not least Washington and its partner Addis Ababa in characterising and framing all loyal and devoted Somali Muslims as radical extremist in need of destruction

Due to the U.S. failure to comprehend the greater importance of the real issues that Somali's are facing, missed the chance to enhance its global image and in Somalia. Addressing the issue of ICU with appropriate way via diplomacy and political consensus could have been the only way in easing the U.S. notoriety for stereotyping and not trying to understand Muslims (or worse, being their enemy). The Islamic countries along the Arab League and several African countries came with efforts to stabilize Somalia, but, the United States chose to take the route of creating more conflicts and gave no space for peace and stability

By financing both the Somali warlords and the Ethiopian government in their fight against the ICU, the people of Somalia and many officials with the transition government recognized that the U.S. is in fact part of the problem but never part of the solution. In reality, the deceitful plan of Kenyan-based CIA agents made the radicals much more popular, increasing their reputation as spiritual warriors among the extremist and traditionalist alike. It is presumably not coincidental, therefore, before the Somali capital city was under the control of the ICU and enforced a strict understanding of Sharia law. Washington was worried that Somalia had gained its version of Taliban.

Ken Menkhaus, an associate professor of political science at Davidson College in North Carolina and expert in Somali affairs, mourned the results of the turn in U.S. policy for Somali: "This is worse than the worst-case scenarios – the exact opposite of what the US government strategy, if there were one, would have wanted". Washington quandary increasingly developed and reduced some more urgency when Sheick Aweys, leader of the Al Itahad al Islamiya movement took the leadership of the Islamic Court Union.

Previously, the Al Itahad al Islamiya movement was added to the list of terrorist al-Qaeda-linked groups. The United States, have for long been complaining about problems that they have created themselves. They've paid little attention to a long decade of humanitarian crisis in Somalia, violent and turmoil.

To this present day, the United States Department of African Affairs web page has not included Somalia as unrest spot in sub-Saharan Africa in need of support and attention. In Brief, Washington has no internal political and economic interest in Somalia which needed to intervene for peace and stability. However, as the radicalism and extremism come forward, Washington move its policy and seeks a quick-fix defaced war and further increasing of the crisis. Often, many ask this question of: Is the United States involved in Somalia for Somalia's sake, or for its own?

The Ethiopian regime orchestrated mass accusations against Al Itahad al Islamiya and its leader Sheick Aweys and accused of plotting a series of bombing attacks in Ethiopia. During a congressional meeting, the Assistant Secretary for African Affairs, Jendayi Frazer, told the U.S. legislators that Washington should control the situation and coordinate a response through a new body called the Contact Group.

The Contact Group comprise of the African Union, United Nations, European Union, United States, Italy, Tanzania, Norway and others. Frazier made it clear that the ICU seizure of the Somali capital and other cities in southern parts of the country as an expansion of al-Qaeda mission: "The U.S. government remains deeply troubled by the foreign-born terrorists who have found haven in Somalia in recent years.

Washington has drafted a U.N. resolution that would allow the African Union to intervene in Somalia and requested the international community to finance this peace effort. On December 6, 2006, the United Nations Security Council passed resolution number 1725. Predictably, the Ethiopian armed force, with complicit U.S. support, rushed in to protect the United Nations-sponsored Transitional Federal Government (TFG), based in Baidoa, a small town in the Northwestern Bay region.

After twenty years of failed state, Somalia began to construct a Transitional Federal Government (TFG) in 2004, with the objective to promote peace and stability in the country and to strength the national sovereignty. After two years of international mediation led by the Intergovernmental Authority on Development (IGAD), the TFG was the fourteenth attempt to stabilize the country and establish a functioning government after the fall of former president Siad Barre in 1991. Following the formation of the Transitional Federal Government in late 2004, the transitional government was based in neighboring Kenya until July 2005.

The federal parliament did not meet on Somali soil until February 2006; on February 2006 the federal parliament holds its first parliamentary session in the western city of Baidoa due to security fears on the capital city Mogadishu. In July 2007, after months of delay, the transitional government held a reconciliation conference. Main political parties including moderate Islamist were invited to the conference but instead they chose not to participate. As a result, many observers regarded the conference a failure. For some time, the TFG governed from southern Mogadishu, where the situation remains critical.

The negotiators who formed the Transitional Federal Government tried to give reasonable representation to each tribe through the 4.5 formula. The four major tribes which consist of Darood, Hawiye, Dir and Rahaweyn, each received sixty-one seats in the parliament, while the remaining tribes together received thirty-one seats. Following the structure of this formation, the minority clans argued that they haven't received a reasonable share within the parliament.

When President Abdillahi Youssouf Ahmed was forming his cabinet members, he deliberately chose people from different tribes who shared his pro-Ethiopian views. Thus, President Abdillahi Youssouf choice of prime minister, Ali Mohamed Gedi, a technocrat without political summon, was considered as an attempt to underestimate the Hawiye, which widely opposed the Ethiopian presence and influence. In 2007, Prime Minister Gedi had resigned following considerable pressure from both the U.S. and the Ethiopian government, alleging differences of view with the president. According to many, President Abdullahi Youssouf and Prime Minister Gedi conflicted over the control of oil contracts for Somalia. During the struggle, both men mobilize tribe support in an attempt to keep power. This move has divided the Transitional Federal Government apart

The clannish politics have made numerous Somalis disillusioned with the TFG. Many believed that the Transitional Government was divided into three parts: one headed by the president, another part by the Prime Minister, and a third by those who controlled armed forces.

President Abdillahi Youssouf Ahmed had a long decade of political experience, before holding the highest office of the country, he previously served as president of Puntland, the autonomous region in the northern part of Somalia. Abdillahi Youssouf was educated in Russian military school and later served as military commander during the late 1960's. Following his imprisonment for rejecting to take part in the 1969 military coup, Abdillahi Youssouf led a failed coup against Siad Barre in 1978 and later fled to Kenya.

During the 1980's, Abdillahi Youssouf served time in Ethiopian jails, but when Mengistu was ousted by the TLPF armed resistance group in 1991, he was liberated and later made strong ties with the newly Ethiopian TLPF regime. Abdillahi Youssouf had such great animosity and rivalry with Sheick Hassan Daher Aweys, the leader of Islamic militant group and former chief of al-Itahaad al-Islaami (an anti-Ethiopian resistance movement). President Abdillahi

Youssouf went for health reasons in 2008, and many indicated that due to his poor health he was unfit to lead the country.

In 2007 following a tension between President Abdillahi Youssouf and his Prime Minister Gedi, the president published a presidential decree on November 2007 to appoint Nur Hassan Hussein, a former chief police officer, the new Prime Minister, replacing the outgoing Prime Minister Ali Mohamed Gedi. Prime Minister Nur Hassan Hussein hails from the Mudulook subclan of the Abgal, Hawiye.

When Nur Hassan Hussein took office, his cabinet appointments were widely criticized for making the government too large. In January 2008, after a series of criticism, he reduced the number of the cabinet from seventy-tree to twenty members. Many argued that President Abdillahi Youssouf chose Nur Hassan Hussein as prime minister as he lacks a political support from his Hawiye tribe.

Prime Minister Nur Hassan Hussein expressed enthusiasm to sit and negotiate with the Islamist but was in a weak position to do so as he lacked control over government budget and the armed force.

Mohamed Dheere, the mayor of Mogadishu since 2007, controlled the customs revenues from the port and had his armed group. From 2001 to 2006, Mohamed Dheere was the warlord of Jawhar, a town situated in the north of Mogadishu. In 2006, Mohamed Dheere joined the Alliance for Restoration of Peace and Counterterrorism, a CIA-backed coalition of warlords opposed to the spread of the Islamic Movement. Dheere hails from the Abgal, Hawiye.

On December 29, 2008, President Abdullahi Yusuf Ahmed officially announced his immediate departure and handed his resignation to the federal parliament over the dismissal of Prime Minister Nur Hassan Hussein and his cabinet which was not approved by the federal transitional parliament. After the resignation of the head of state, the Speaker of the Parliament Adan Mohamed Nuur Madobe, as stated in the constitution, assumed officially as the interim President of Transitional Federal Government until the federal parliament is electing a new president based on the Transitional Federal Charter within 30 days.

Delaying the election until a new interim parliament, which could potentially include moderate Islamist movement was widely considered from the both the international community and the internal political actors, but the interim President Aden Madobe declared that a new President would be elected within the constitutionally mandated 30-day period. On 11 January 2009, Ramtane Lamamra, the African Union Peace and Security Commissioner told that the presidential election is set to take place on 26 January 2009, with preparations including nominations of candidates starting on the 20th January.

On January 2009, Sheikh Sharif Sheikh Ahmed was elected as President of the Transitional Federal Government by the Transitional Federal Parliament, after the resignation of his predecessor Abdullahi Yusuf Ahmed. President Sheikh Sharif Sheikh Ahmed, a moderate Islamist and former leader of opposition Islamist armed group, was elected as the country's President following UN-sponsored talks in Djibouti. When he officially took office, he appointed Omar Abdirahid Ali Sharmarke as the Prime Minister of the Transitional Federal Government in February 2009.

Prime Minister Sharmarke was broadly considered as the bridge between Islamist within the federal government and the international community. His father was the country's second President, who was later killed in 1969 by his security machinery in the northern district of Las Anod. Sharmarke hails from the Majeerteen Harti Darod clan. After the appointment of Prime Minister Sharmarke in February 2009, the federal parliament increased significantly the mandate of the Transitional Federal Government for a further two years to 2011 and increased the parliament to include another 200 Members of Parliament from the opposition Alliance for the Re-liberation of Somalia and 75 MPS from civil society, making the size of the transitional federal parliament to 550 MP's.

In May 2009 violent clashes took the streets of Mogadishu between the Islamic armed group resistance and government forces, which led to the death of 100 people and displaced approximately 50,000 innocent civilians. This violent continued throughout 2009 and 2010. The transitional government, supported by the African Union troops, managed to control some part of Mogadishu and chunk of northern parts of the country. The remaining parts of the country were in the hands of warlords, al-Shabab, and its affiliates.

Many hoped that the withdrawal of the Ethiopian army and the recently elected moderate Islamist Sheikh Sharif Ahmed as president and his imposition of Shariah law would widely reduce the tensions within the country. But unfortunately, this wasn't the case, as the two main resistant Islamist group al-Shabab and Hizb al-Islam, have dramatically increased their insurgent military actions in 2010.

Al-Shabab, a radical Islamist group that rose up out of the remaining parts of the Union of Islamic Courts (UIC), a group that was annihilated by the Ethiopian troops that invaded unlawfully Somalia in 2006, was controlling large parts southern and central parts of the country. Al-Shabab and its internal affiliate Hizb al-Islam considered the recently elected President Sharif Ahmed, a former leader of the Islamic Court Union, as a U.S. puppet, who is aiding the interest of the Somali enemy. Both Al-Shabab and Hizb al-Islam follows an extreme form of Wahhabism and tend to avoid traditional tribe based fractional divisions that have characterized the social order of Somalia.

While 5,000 troops from the African Union have stationed in Somalia to help and protect the transitional federal government, the central government command was very restricted to a few districts of Mogadishu. To fight against the Islamic militant groups, in September 2010 President Sharif Ahmed imposed heavy pressure to his Prime Minister Sharmarke to resign from the post after a conflict between both men over the draft constitution. On November 2010, the President appointed Mohamed Abdallah Farmajo as the country's prime minister and was later approved by the Somali lawmakers.

Farmajo, a historian and a professor at the State University of New York at Buffalo were appointed as the country's Prime Minister following a protracted dispute between the president and his predecessor Sharmarke. Farmajo hails from the Marehan Darod clan. He was appointed as Somalia's Prime Minister on October 14, 2010, and was later approved by the federal parliament by a show of hands.

The appointment of the new Prime Minister (Farmajo) has had a mixed reception. The majority of Somali citizens have welcomed the appointment of Farmajo due to his honesty and his ability to restore peace and stability in Somalia. However, a handful group in parliament have widely opposed against his appointment because of suspicions he is against the 4.5 system and his position against the Ethiopian influence in the Somali political spectrum.

The reduced eighteen-member cabinet appointed by the new Prime Minster Farmajo was the bravest reform of President Sharif government has undertaken. Most ministers in his cabinet were Diasporas, well-educated and technocrats. However, accusations of favoritism have been leveled at President Sharif for promoting two close aides believed to key Aala sheikh figures to full ministerial posts, and many claimed that 4.5 tribe systems should be abolished as it instigates division among the ordinary citizens.

However, this government seems to be the initial step towards remunerating merit, as opposed to political convenience. Several like the finance minister, had a managerial and administrative competence. Most of them lack political experience and the connections with influential tribe constituencies must be effective. Late experience demonstrates that politicians who have no political support are more vulnerable and their influences are widely restricted. Critics say that they have similar qualities the president wanted so that he could tighten his grip on power.

President Sharif ambitions appear to have been to pacify both foreign and domestic critics, re-establish his image as a reformer and overshadow his main opponent, Speaker Sharif Hassan Sheikh Aden, a former ally and a friend who needed to abandon the new government entirely and used procedural tactics for weeks to delay its approval. Given the increase high-stakes political challenge and with the end of transition which is six months away, in August, the new cabinet ministers have no time for maneuver restricted prospects of fundamentally changing the government's distressing situation.

The transitional federal parliament was the most influential institutions in the country, despite its power to function accordingly was restricted. Lately, its powers and influence within the political landscape have dramatically increased, in light of the fact that quarreling senior leaders often takes their disputes to federal parliament to resolve it. The additional power and influence they have acquired have its price. Factionalism is disease, corruption overflowing, and alliances in steady flux.

The federal parliament is situated in an old police institute in a turbulent area of Mogadishu and always faces attacks from radical extremist and other insurgent individuals. The location of the parliament was extremely insecure, and many members of the parliament were highly feared for themselves, a majority is normally obtained when critical issues are to be examined, and AMISOM troops have made a huge security cordon. The security issue and the logistical difficulties required in organizing an effective session genuinely hamper successfully. There are approximately 150 MP's that are based in Nairobi, Kenya, as a result of the insecurity in the Somali capital city.

After the extension of the federal parliament in January 2009, the transitional parliament was resolute by a long authority crisis that based on the mandate of the previous speaker, Sheik Adan Madobe. A framework agreement made in Djibouti between the old TFG and the Alliance for the Re-freedom of Somalia, kept Madobe in his position, despite efforts by some members of the Alliance Re-freedom of Somalia to elect one of their own.

In August 2009, Adan Madobe refused to resign, when his term was about to end, he argued that his mandate would automatically be renewed for the two years to come. However, Speaker Adan Madobe has underestimated his fellow clansman, Sharif Hassan, who was working behind the scene to replace him.

To make the situation more difficult for Adan Madobe, President Sheikh Sharif and his ally Sharif Hassan worked closely to find a common beneficial deal, under which Sharif Hassan would use all his powers and influence to ouster Prime Minister Sharmarke in return for President's backing for his speakership candidacy. However the first attempt to achieve this plan was partly failed, in May 2010.

Although Madobe left office, Prime Minister Sharmarke kept his position. Much of the following turbulence within the TFG comes from the increasing power struggle between the President and his past associate and power broker, the new speaker of the parliament, Sharif Hasan. Assumptions are widely divided on why the once close individual relationship started to deteriorate. What is not in dispute is that it is hopelessly broken. They are presently pushed by oppositely opposed political counts and aspirations that add to developing factionalism and insecure state of flux in politics.

Speaker Sharif Hassan and his former allies such as Mohamed Abdirizak Osman "Jurille" and Abdurahman Haji Ibrahim Aden "Ibbi" are well-established businessmen who widely represent the interest of a group of business elites in Mogadishu. Speaker Sharif Hassan has been cautiously campaigning to get his presidential ambitions. A talented and persuasive operator, he is able at preparing support from his tribe, he frequently uses his money uses and his political influence to gain advantages. His impressive move to secure the prestige position of the speaker was excellent.

Ethiopia and other foreign actors were supporting him; he widely orchestrated suspicions of Sharif and his Aala Sheik supporters to project himself as a secularist and the only person that could prevent the radical group of al-Shabab to take over the Transitional Federal Government.

While his reputation is significantly growing among the international community to the detriment of the president, his history is, however, ambiguous, and he exercised an obstructive and devastating influence within the transitional government. The president of TFG Sheikh Sharif was broadly under international pressure to make reforms and to make significant changes within his government, particularly from a faction of reform-minded figures alias the Kutla that became extremely important within the parliament. He realizes that he needs to develop them in his battle with Sharif Hasan. However, a few individuals progressively see him as a part of the problem.

The Kutla is an interesting phenomenon, they are cross-tribe and opposed to the political landscape. The group is led by Abdi Hashi, a well-respected man hails from the north of the country who, despite his age and illness, had mobilized reformers and put forward a program that has hit an emotion with knowledgeable parliamentarians of different ideological influences. Efforts by the president and the speaker to blackmail and co-opt members of the Kutla have failed, however, the high-stakes recommended that the strain on its cohesion will soon escalate.

The Transitional Federal Constitution of Somalia submits the TFG to a decentralized system that is based on federalism. The Independent Federal Constitution Commission was in charge making the correct federal structure, while the federal government pledged that the process of federating Somalia will take approximately a period of two to three years. However, critics have argued that the federal government controlled the process, and dialogue with other political forces was very minimal. The Transitional Federal Government has shown neither the will nor longing to transfer power. Indeed, under President Sharif, there has been an inconspicuous shift away from the federalism thought that official rhetoric cannot cover.

The Transitional Federal Government made strong efforts in the first few months of 2009 to reach out to few within the hard-core extremist. As the president intended to show his sincerity about the national reconciliation, but sadly these efforts later failed. By April, the new government lost the will intention to proceed with the attentive exploratory talks. Certainly, the insurrection, floated by Ethiopia's army withdrawal, had turned out to be more intense, had no encouragement to satisfy Sharif's suggestions and was ruining for a decisive battle.

The few who seemed agreeable to make an agreement with President Sharif, like Al-Shabaab chief Mukhtar Robow, were regularly pulled down by more urgent political considerations. Sharif's effort dilemma was a well-known one. A president of a weak and uncertain government, with minimal territorial control and without a viable armed force; he was in no position to dictate a peace settlement and had little to offer an insurrection that felt it was winning. He was reluctant unwilling to abandon ministers and other senior authorities who did not contribute to the government and gave their posts to others. His approach was only to engage honorable feelings and values of Islam, forgiveness and most importantly Somalinimo.

Many considered whether President Sharif was considerably lacking military means to transfer the power and subsequently force grant should not have done more to construct a wider, a better national reconciliation approach, yet his choice to rapidly drop the project as opposed to keeping on working on the resistance of the numerous disappointed Al-Shabaab leaders was at least a strategic blunder.

The failure of the power-sharing agreement with the ASWJ shows clearly that the Transitional Federal Government's inadequacy in shaping political alliances and encouraging compromise. The ASWJ started as an alliance of tribes that wished to ensure their traditional form of Sufi Islam and is the main faction in central Somalia ready to mount powerful resistance to AlShabaab. Despite the fact that it was a characteristic associate, territorial states and other international allies needed to apply significant pressure to bear on the TFG before it brought the group into a formal power-sharing agreement.

After the power-sharing agreement, many members of the ASWJ were appointed ministers and their army commander, Abdikarim Dhego-Badan, was also appointed as deputy commander of the TFG army. However, ASWJ's share in the cabinet was not compatible with its military authority and regional control in respect to the beset TFG, which only held few areas of the capital city. That showed the ASWJ that the regime was not genuine about power sharing. The agreement between the government and the ASWJ has practically collapsed; despite government officials denied it. There is an enormous division within ASWJ itself, and virtually nobody knows which group speaks for the old organization.

The transitional government was not willing to save the agreement. In fact, it is an open mystery that regime hardliners are content with the obstruction in the agreement and forced Sharif to abandon the deal.

Several leaders of ASWJ organisation have widely accused neighbouring Ethiopia of interfering in the Somali political affairs and encouraging the TFG not to collaborate with the ASWJ for the common interest. Some of the TFG leaders were often seen as naïve and seemed to lose the public support. However, most blame for the internal disputes between TFG and ASWJ was due to leaders from both sides failed to resolve their differences and compromise for the interest of the country. The president and his associates remained profoundly uncertain and often used postponing strategies to restrict the agreement.

Leaders of the ASWJ have failed to remain as one and manage their internal differences, this mass division and crisis within the ASWJ, has fractured the organisation and obstructed their desires to utilise the TFG programme to realise their goal of crushing the so-called al-Shabaab terrorist group permanently. It is most likely difficult to revive the agreement now, given the gap that has opened in the "moderate alliance" so precisely join in mid-2010 and once touted as the best device which to overcome the insurgency.

While it might be too late for the president redress that error, his government or any other upcoming government must prioritise national reconciliation to overcome the long-term crisis that has undermined the well-functioning of Somalia. The initial step must be to revive the hopeless compromise committee, restore its participation, widen its mandate and give it the all the necessary resource to draw up a comprehensive national plan.

The committee should likewise contact the moderate leaders of the al-Shabaab that are willing to relinquish their terrorist activities and work with the government to stabilise the country as a whole. In the past, there has been a strong atmosphere of antagonism to federalism within Islamism in Somalia, whether regarded as moderate Islamist, conservative, or extremist. Most Islamists tend to support a stable central government. Many of Sharif's associates are totally against the idea of conducting the federal system in Somalia, which they consider a secularist programme they were forced to agree in at the Djibouti talks.

The president's indecision is a component of this unresolved tension and needs to pacify the two camps in the transitional federal government. Members of the cabinet who have accepted TFG's federalism promise to truly do not last long. For instance, when Ex-Defense Minister Mohamed Abdi Mohamed Gandi negotiated with Ogaden patriarch in the Jubba region of the south with a perspective to obtain their support for forming a regional state called Jubbaland, with the support of Kenya, he was quickly underestimated and ousted.

No place has indecision, if not hostility, to dispersal been more obvious than in the relations between the Puntland regional state and the TFG, which have been deteriorated from 2009 and has always been poor. Puntland argues that the TFG doesn't give them mutual and common support, and TFG is inflexible antagonistic to its federal ambitions.

The region is broadly marginalised in the federal institutions and hardly acquires their fair share for the entire country. Friendly states and countries have provided scholarships for Puntland students, training opportunities and technical support remain the monopoly of Mogadishu. The Galkacyo compromise in August 2009 between the Federal government and the Puntland authorities have recognised the validity of these discontents and complaints tried to address the issue. However, Puntland acknowledges that the transitional government was dishonest, and the agreement made nothing concrete. Recently Puntland's anti-Mogadishu rhetoric became more blatant, and it seems determined on growing the tensions.

During January 2011, the government of Puntland was deeply frustrated by the composition of the new government and the fact that their region was marginalised in the cabinet; therefore the Puntland government declared that it would not work with the TFG until a legitimate and representative federal government is formed and recognised by the stakeholders in Somalia.

A few days later, Puntland took decisive measures against the TFG officials by prohibiting them from coming to the region. The TFG viewed this as a persistent and aim on withdrawal. The failure of finding a solution to this issue is part of managerial inexperience and political inability. But the growing tension is not a periphery-centre power struggle. It is symbolic of the fundamental issue at the heart of the issue of devolution, and the major contradictory understandings of federalism. The individuals who from the beginning have been distrustful of federalism refer to Puntland as a wake-up call and verification of why the nation shouldn't take that path. Instead, a large number of individuals accused the leadership of disturbing the resistance from Puntland by its conflicting positions.

They contend that pro-federalism position would have made an atmosphere more helpful to calm the talks. A perspective predominant in reform hovers tends to accuse both sides: the TFG for lack of authority and Puntland for "careless posturing" to redirect consideration from its poor record. Both governments seem to incite hostility and escalation to proceed, to create political capital. Puntland sought to dishonour the TFG's official pro-federalism position, while the TFG seems to anticipate Puntland as a devolution test gone too far, its government as problematic in the battle against radicalism and its image of federalism as an obstruction to developing the central government's writ throughout the nation.

The challenge undermines to revive clan deficiency lines and resuscitate bullheadedness. Stereotypes about Hawiye "awkwardness" and Majerten "egotism" are being restored and starting to colour discourse. As the TFG has failed to lead the devolution procedure, active communities on the outskirts began to organise and making their local government. Somalia is encountering major rebellion against the centre chaotic, unilateral, clan-driven process.

While many welcomed the endeavour by different communities, particularly in central Somalia, to make their administration, the nature of that process is discretionary, and its direction is alarming. An intra-clan and inter-clan race to cut out fiefdoms unmediated by any impartial agency that eventually prompts a hard to reverse fait accompli is not the sort of federalism most had as a top priority. In the meantime, various diaspora factions are looking to capitalise on increasing global interest for decentralisation and are making briefcase administration that have no local constituency or even on-the-ground presence.

The two government-controlled areas in north-central of the country, Galmudug, and Ximan and Xeeb have made significant progress in promoting stability, rebuilding the greater structure of local government and providing the basic necessity to ordinary citizens. Both regions (Galmudug and Ximan and Xeeb) should be encouraged to continue with these efforts, but political disagreements and animosity thrived in both regions and endeavours to make the semi-democratic or consensual system of administration remain insecure, so it is hard to hold up them up as models. Despite efforts to reach out to different tribes and expand the number of their administrations, they remained under the control of single clan: Galmudug by the Sa'ad and Ximan and Xeeb by the Saleeban, both sub-clan of the Hawiye/Habar Gedir tribe

There are immense territorial disputes amongst them, and Galmudug region began to have tight relation with Puntland that occasionally caused armed conflict. Crime association involved in piracy and kidnapping are active, al-Shabaab and its extreme allies posed significant dangers; and the late fighting in Adaado, the seat of the Ximan and Xeeb government, shows that any stability is questionable.

The two districts have previously engaged in lengthy but promoting negotiations to form a greater, and more reasonable, local government. The conflict that erupted in late November 2010, apparently over field and water for animals after a long drought, was to a great extent over the post-agreement dispersion and accelerated by spoilers looking to abandon the negotiations. The districts are famished of resources and greatly rely on upon the goodwill of their families in overseas and the volunteerism of their people to work. The international community should bolster their efforts, and also needs to make more incentives for such administration to merge.

A major fundamental problem is starting to openly recognise: the deficiency by the Transitional Federal Constitution to correctly describe the separate the entire scope of government powers between the president and the prime minister. These were regularly challenged by the power centres that were meant to be correlative yet have a tendency to be antagonistic. The outcome feeds a dangerous hostility and adds to the weakening paralysis that has contaminated every government since 2000.

The Transitional National Government negotiated in Djibouti 2000, inaugurated the mixture power structure that has turned into the most remarkable and incapacitating component of all consequent transitional governments, however, the struggle between the President at that time Abdiqasim Salat Hasan and his Prime Minister Ali Khalif was agreeable compared with what followed. The most paramount struggle between President Abdullahi Yusuf Ahmed and Prime Minister Ali Mohammed Gedi in 2004-2005 partitioned the regime into severely hostile camps and was resolved after Gedi was compelled by his Ethiopian allies to leave office.

The leadership dispute, particularly the periodic triangular conflict between the president, the prime minister and the speaker were mainly responsible for the government's deadlock. But, efforts and debates to reform the Transitional Federal Government solved the issue.

Adjusting the structural issues of the TFG needed boldness and strong leadership that yet the president did not show, nor does there seemed to have been the will of the leadership to an ever-lasting solution. Domestic interests are served by state of affairs, however, precarious it might be, while the international community is wary of the dangers, and expenses, of reviving the Djibouti compromises. There is the existence of captivating reasons for making a single power centre covered temporarily with full constitutional powers, to only improve decision-making and implement fully and accordingly the transitional agenda. There isn't an easy solution, but reforms have its unforeseeable complexities.

The political crisis that always occurred within Somali's political landscape often lies on the system of selecting leaders that naturally opposes the good governance and well-established democratic state based on values and the rule of law. Often these drastic leaders are chosen to ensure greater clan balance and representation, and this system of 4.5 has kept competent individuals from office, created clan extremism and prevented the emergence of issue-based politics. For as long as this extreme and dangers system exists, democratisation and good governance will remain a pipe dream.

Those in favour of this 4.5 system argue that this system is designed to calm the current tension and will function within the transitional period, yet this does not clarify why such system that is verifiably defective and create crop after crop of clumsy leaders should be seen as an impermanent solution. Many argue that clan representation is only forward, but it's very crucial to adapt regular debates to establish a fair system that works for everyone. However, the sooner as Somalia disregard this extreme radical clan representation system for democratic-based politics in which leaders are elected based on competence rather than clan affiliation, the sooner the country will move forward and progress.

The failures of Sheikh Sharif's government

Sheikh Sharif was elected as president of the Transitional Federal Government on the 31st of January 2009 in Djibouti, in a hotly contested, overnight by the Transitional Federal Parliament. He was predeceased by a man often viewed as a ruthless authoritarian military leader, Abdullahi Yusuf, whose aggressive style and close relation with savage warlords had harmed his leadership. His government was widely despised, and his rigorous style isolated regional powers, particularly Ethiopia, and in the end brought a campaign that ousted him from the political spectrum.

Nobody questioned the difficulty that lies before the new president when the Transitional Federal Government move back to Mogadishu. Saddled with unmanageable and irrational government and parliament, with no strong army and massively under-resourced, Sharif had his work cut out, but most of Somalis are extremely disillusioned with the incompetent secular political leader, seemed tentatively supportive of his desires to make a radical change with the past and launch a new era of clean politics. There was a practically delighted hope that Somalia has the chance to create a workable transition and re-establish peace.

Most of the public support for President Sharif come from his previously leadership of the UIC (Union of Islamic Court) Executive Council and his role in instigating and coordinating the 2006 uprising in Mogadishu that toppled the warlords and introduced a brief rule of calm and peace in the city and much of the south and central Somalia, until the unlawful Ethiopian invasion in December 2006. Many critics downgraded his role during that period, claiming that Sheikh Sharif was simply a leader in name but the real power and command came was vested in Sheikh Hassan Dahir Aweys and the chief financial backer of the Islamic Courts Union, Abukar Omar Adani, was later deserted. Indeed, the choice to place him in charge for the UIC may have been, to some degree prompt by the yearning to have a less polarising leader than Aweys, ready to mobilise public support for the Islamist project.

Deficiencies of government experience of the Transitional Federal Government's political progression, but, have poorly undermined his presidency. Concerns to project himself as consensus-builder running a tight ship and able to hold the coalition government together, he gave soo much powers to those with high experience. By surrendering control at an early stage mostly to Sharif Hasan and his advisors, he coincidentally created a new power centre that later dominated his own. Consecutive efforts to reclaim his power were deftly defeated.

Opposed to an emergency, mindful of his weak position and not able to summon the strength to resist the insurgents, he played along a strategy that conveyed a powerful political price. The marriage of convenience with Speaker Sharif Hasan obstructed his desire, halts greater reforms, isolated large portions of his support base and eventually damaged his moral standing.

In light of the Transitional Federal Government's bleak record, the decision of numerous is unflattering, even cruel. Previous key associates, diplomats and senior ministers have all hold Sharif accountable for the failures. To understand the negative implications on the body politic and public moral, it is vital to review the hopes with which he came to the leadership. That a professed Islamist regime, which was the first in the history of Somalia and could so rapidly prove incompetent and, more awful, become involve in infighting that has increased public despair and brought frustration with the whole transitional administration model to an all-time high.

President Sheikh Sharif has widely failed to design a broad vision based on his moderate Islamist values. He failed to take advantage of the momentum of his election to make a message able to arouse a public that was for the first time approachable and with it the opportunity to regain control from the radical extremist, whose radical programme was starting to separate the society.

Public tension began to escalate, trust in the government disappeared, and enthusiasm rapidly gave way to cynicism. President Sharif's has cultivated the public image as a reformist, and moderate Islamist leader is now under attack.

The secularist and radical groups, who previously supported him, see him with increasing suspicion. The Sufi faction that initially gave huge support to the TFG and fought alongside the government to defeat the extreme radical group of Al-Shabaab have become increasingly anti-Sharif due to the political disagreement between him and the Sufi's.

President Sharif's failure to make contemporary vision cast the large defect of the modern Islamist groups in the country. In the Somali political spectrum, there is no culture of systematic theorization on the socio-political and economic aspect, for instance, ambitious Islamist factions have made use of elsewhere. Apart from the traditional appealing expressions, "Islam is the truth, and the solution" and "the holy Quran is our constitution" there is little that they have offered to the people Somalia and the current horrific situation in Somalia.

No figure has developed within the group to dominance Islamism, which in Somalia, therefore, lack of the principle anchor is based on impersonation. President Sharif isn't the only one to blame. Nobody from the Islamist movement has provided a clear explanation of the moderate Islamist vision are and its policy implementation. Sharif is widely contradictory on democracy and devolution in some areas within the country.

President Sharif's political thoughts are set of expressions that repeat in his public speeches, such as sinaan, talawadag, adalat, (equality, consultation, justice). The doctrine of shura (council) governance in Islamist belief is particular from democracy. It implies accord based governance. Modernisers Islamist always indicate that shura doctrine is consistent with contemporary democratic principle, and there is no inconsistency amongst Islam and modern democracy. However, moderate Islamists are regularly wary of the idea of modern democracy, which most likely clarifies why Sharif abstains from using the word democracy.

Since it had no larger policy framework, the government has rapidly fallen into policy obfuscate. There was little to guide senior cabinet ministers and armed officials, so they improved strategy in a discretionary way. On some occasions, authorities sought egotistical interests which they called national interests. At the point when few others, disappointed by the inaction and asserting devotion to what they believed was the TFG's initial mandate and programme, acted, they rapidly crossed paths with the president and his associates. No place was this policy voids more harming in the national security area. Military officials had no clear orders on the offensive of re-capturing the capital city from the extreme groups. New recruits were sent to the battlefields without any sufficient psychological and military preparations.

In the absence of an inspiring message that theirs was a cause worth dying for, morale rapidly fell apart. An enormous amount of abandonment have proceeded; many soldiers switch sides, worked alongside the enemy, sell their weapons, uniforms and equipment.

Former minister Abdirahman Abdishakur Warsame indicate that if President Sharif were more serious on the issue of government state building and national reconciliation and tried his very best to improve the situation, and failed, many would have to respect him and forgive his failures. The truth is: this is the president who never tried any attempts to create success. Former associates of the president and diplomats characterise him a mysterious leader, remote and untroubled by the increasing public speculation about his true convictions. President Sharif was completely uncertain on the main issues, and this was harming the TFG politically, escalating rumours and created a deep mistrust within the cabinet.

ASWJ leaders have openly called Sharif to build an exclusively Wahhabi state. Supporters call him a patriot who is intending to prevent sectarian issues, however, it's difficult to see what the national interest his indecision serves. The deputy prime minister and finance minister at that time, Sharif Hasan Sheikh Aden struck a deal in April 2009 for $17 million worth of new Somali banknotes to be printed in Sudan, without consulting his colleagues.

Governor of the Central Bank Bashir Isee argued that was not consulted and opposed the deal because the regime did not have the ability to implement a currency change. The North-eastern regional state of Puntland has also widely rejected the deal. The arrangement met hardened resistance from international donors, and the divided government adjust it in January 2010 following a significant pressure the Federal Parliament Sharif Hasan and President Sharif. The first printed note was printed was introduced in some places of the capital in 2010.

In the northern regional state of Puntland as a form of rejection has collected the new banknotes and burned it. The government of Sudan have pulled itself from the deal following its analysis indicated that it was not entirely above board. Yusuf Mohamed Siad, former Defence Minister of the Transitional Federal Government, took the government offensive against the insurgent too serious. His armed forced took frontlines in northern and central parts of Mogadishu, the Minister himself led some of the fightings against the insurgent Al-Shabab. He later lost his patience after successive demands to the prime minister's office for assistance were rejected; Yusuf Mohamed Siad announced his resignation in June 2010. After some, he stated that the government had no capacity to face and defeat the extremists.

African Union Mission in Somalia (AMISOM) officials argued that Yusuf Mohamed Siad demonstrated more resolve to persist the battle than his associates. He and his small armed group have affiliated themselves with AMISOM. In 2010, President Sharif and his Prime Minister Sharmarke had declared a major offensive that never emerged. The president often wore the military uniform as a form to express his complete commitment to destroy the armed insurgent group permanently. The government's failure to carry out the operation to force the rebels out of the country increased the negative public perception of the federal transitional government and weakened military capacity.

There is an increasing awareness that the political and military crisis is as a result of the weak leadership from the president. The Transitional Federal Government performance had significantly disheartened those who hoped for strong and sustainable new Somalia with a dynamic and energetic leader. But President Sharif's ambition to counter the early friction inside the coalition left him defenceless against the conspiracy of a powerful group of the old order drove by Sharif Hasan. In effect, he turned into a rubber-stamp head of state, confronting for the interests of his new associates. The friendship of Sharif Hasan estranged old friends; particularly the more conservative components now alluded to as Aala Sheik. Quite a bit of his time was spent in unnecessary outside travel and long talk local tribe leaders and lawmakers.

The then deputy prime minister and finance minister of the TFG, Sharif Hassan Sheikh Aden gained unprecedented powers to the extent that he is gradually exercised some of the presidential duties and eventual became the de facto head of state and government. Many officials within the TFG and the Somali population as a whole who needed regime favours had to obtain Sharif Hassan's authorisation.

The broad impression he is not his own man has profoundly harmed president Sharif. The idea that he remains most appropriate to lead the transition is still ahead by a lessening circle of supporters yet is currently unpalatable to many Somali citizens and few of the international community. Although the president has lately turned back some of his powers, Sharif Hasan kept on using his position as Transitional Federal speaker to increase his influence. The performance of Prime Minister Omar Abdirashid Sharmarke was not better.

President Sharif's promise to initiate a new period of clean politics and establish a system that would tackle the significant corruption that is existing in the country and propel good governance that ruined the previous regime remains displeased. Expectations that President Sharif would take measures to clean up the government were immediately rejected.

The transitional government talks to bring about ways to dismantle the corruption was discarded, as an annoy Sharif, desperate to continue the affiliation with Speaker Sharif Hasan's strong faction, sacrificed principle to practicality. As a result, corruption has increased dramatically to the extent that it became serious than ever before, managed by powerful elites and permeating every tier of government. Favouritism jobs culture, wide corruption and total absence of reliable records add to the problem make even the best forensic audit attempt difficult.

The vast extent of the corruption centred on the Aden Aide International Airport and the port Mogadishu. AMISOM army heavily guarded the two facilities. Despite efforts from Prime Minister Sharmarke to clean the corruption and build a strong administrative system, they remain tenaciously hostile to reform. Financial aids from bilateral sources were another source of corruption, although it wasn't as bad as during the leadership of President Abdi Qasim Salat Hassan and Abdullahi Yusuf, where millions of dollars of government money would quickly disappear without any trace.

The way in which aid was dispensed to the Transitional Federal Government has significantly changed, and a strong system was put in place to create measures of deterrence. The PricewaterhouseCoopers was hired to act as trustee for the transitional federal government from the international donors to overlook of these funds were used, and there was also foreign presence to observe the utilisation of these funds.

The agreement with the TFG was amended to reinforce the international community ability to conduct regular audits. In any case, this would be strongly opposed by those in the regime who opposed the deal from the start, contending it's destroying the national sovereignty and creating a new form colonialism.

The disorganised and deregulated free market system that came into enforcement following the ouster of former president Siad Barre's administration was broadly credited for publishing the entrepreneurial energy of people of Somalia and creating a compelling business model that has transformed a large part of the Somali speaking Horn, but it was mainly blamed for instigating corruption. Most companies paid no tax to the government but often bribe some senior government officials, often to attain signatures on legal documents connected to the external business, support for international business agreement or essentially as protection to keep the administration on their side.

Similarly, the telecommunication is reported to have been corrupted. With several cellular networks, it was increased considerably in the past several years, as demand for mobile phone and internet services increased. With a yearly turnover of hundreds of millions of dollars, the telecommunication sector is the most profitable commercial venture. Both current and previous government officials have considerable share in some of these companies. Although these firms pay no taxes to the treasury department, they often offer money and stake to officials in the government.

Minor corruption, particularly in the immigration and security services continued to escalate. A large sum of money was spent on useless foreign travel and luxuries, and some officials went as far as abusing the state asset and not differentiating the state asset and their personal asset. The transitional government's response to the corruption has disappointed many Somalis and forced them to lose faith in the government.

The government's culture of allowing corruption to exist, minimising its significance and disregarding it as an unavoidable life stays intact. The President of the Somali transitional government seemed to be too relaxed on the issue of corruption, in spite of his promises to end the corruption. The fight on corruption is unrealistic to highlight the cause for reform the transitional government following the resignation of Prime Minister Sharmarke. Indeed, the intentions and timing of the initiative are arguable. All signs are that the president is presently in survival mode, vivified by the ambition to outmanoeuvre his opponents and to increase his term office.

The newly appointed finance and economy minister, Hussein Halane, has made sincere efforts to put in place transparency into the revenue collection and cut significantly the bureaucracy within the customs and treasury department, as well as to reinforce internal system controlling the distribution of government revenue. So far he seems to have a free hand to revitalise and renovate his ministry and make a more open and responsible fiscal and monetary system, but he is going carefully, and very cautious if powerful interest were to resist and introduce radical reforms that contradict his policies.

The international community alongside the foreign donors like the IMF gave the TFG considerable assistant to put in place a sustainable mechanism in both the TFG and local governments to end the endless corruption that weakened the credibility of the TFG. These mechanisms by the international community have helped the TFG to improve the management and the revenue collection and strengthening internal auditing efficiencies.

The international community and the IMF were extremely concerned about the significant corruption that is taking place in the government and ministerial departments. Several prominent foreign advocates led by the EU and the US expressed deep concerns, cautiously showing increase frustration to government officials and demanding actions to put to an end the corruption.

The investors have no intention for public conflict with a regime in which they funded could provoke a major crisis that could easily aggravate the situation it's already battered image and hand the extremist a propaganda triumph. However, this tactical fragility lies down at the hands of the corruption. The partners of the transitional federal government have adopted a more strict approach, which included the pressure to the president to fight against the graft firmly on the agenda; they have themselves supported the institutional reforms and started to put forward heavy sanctions against corrupt senior government members.

The political leaders in the Transitional Federal Government are fighting ever than before to remain in the political life and keep their posts so they could access to the different advantages available to the officials. For long-time, president Sharif was significantly under pressure from Aala Sheikh, which forced him to share the power with his former secularist allies, who it believes have thwarted his true Islamisation programme. They've accused President Sharif of empowering his new ally Sharif Hasan and contend the president had made a huge mistake by picking Sharif Hassan as his new associate.

The president is at this time thinking to increase his mandate as president beyond August 2011, when the official date of the Transitional Federal Government came to an end, many argued that the country has had many short-lived transitional administrations. Many of Sharif's advocates thinks that the reforms he is currently putting in place, such as considering who shall be the prime minister and accepting the appointment of new technocrat cabinet, as it will strengthen his post as the country's president.

The president has built an immense war shield for his political campaign for another term as president with a sum of millions of dollars from the Arab investors. The federal parliament has moved. Quickly after a careless decision from the IGAD to call for a two-year period postponement of its term, they've voted to increase its mandate for three years.

Main partners and investors denounced this unilateral act. The newly appointed prime minister Mohamed Abdullahi Farmajo and his eighteen-member cabinet have been widely welcomed by the UN, foreign actors and donors but controversial internally, as both the president and his prime minister farmajo criticised of being bias and avoiding the 4.5 clan system. Speaker Sharif Hassan and his advocates will without a doubt drain this dissatisfaction to maximum political benefit.

There is spreading resistance to the president Sharif desires for the second term, and rumours are overflowing that an active quest for his ouster is in progress. Neither President Sharif nor speaker Sharif Hasan has kept their leadership positions after August 2011, unless the TFG implement considerably, tough reforms, including giving more powers to local governments and explaining the roles and division of power between the president and the prime minister.

The government officials, as opposed to helping establish the peacebuilding efforts, they've instead weakened it, and they've likewise failed the people of Somalia by not taking decisive actions against the high record of corruption. However, amusing that it was difficult to increase the writ of the regime or deliver a comprehensively accepted constitution by August, reform of the transitional government is considerably more important than new administration.

One of the top priorities of that new government were to make the transitional federal institutions much more representative of regional governments. The practice in which they used of choosing parliamentarians from a small fraction of people with as a means to engage in UN-sponsored peace conferences which led to the appointment of countless members with few local constituency and little connection to local authorities administrating the districts they claim to represent.

The international community has recommended two alternatives which were that local governments to appoint the member of parliaments that would represent their areas and the clans of who lives there or create another chamber of deputies with the objective to represent those regions and local governments working with the central government.

The second alternative proposed by the international community was to decrease the size of the parliament from its original and unmanageable 500 members. This would have been done by either the Parliament at the time to form a mechanism for cutting their distended ranks, or the central government negotiating a suitable mechanism by which the local governments would choose a new body to represent them.

One of the issues that the Transitional Federal Government had faced was a security service which completely lacked structure; the systemic corruption entirely weakened the security intelligence. Pressure from allies and international partners have led to the significant failure to produce sufficient progress to meet the needs for strong security. Two years after the training of the transitional government troops, it seemed to have some modest progress, and they are to some degree clearer. However, the TFG wasn't able to seize and hold substantial radical controlled areas of Mogadishu. It is to a great extent AMISOM and militias partnered that drove the war against Al-Shabaab and gradually increased government control. Due to the TFG's impediments, any future AMISOM offensive would most likely be able to take territory bit by bit.

It appeared that TFG and its AMISOM partner had learned lessons from the previously failed training initiatives. There was a joint operation, and the military recruitment process was getting better, more efficient instruction from the EU Training Mission in Somalia (EUTM) and troops from Uganda in Bihanga (south-western Uganda), and AMISOM in Mogadishu, although they are yet to be examined on the combat zone.

The Spanish-led EuropeTM was initially intended to orchestrate and give structure to random security sector reforms already gave by few Western countries. The purpose is to train almost 2,000 transitional government fighters in two stages, to simply facilitate AMISOM's training burden and free assets for its counter-rebellion efforts. The first batch of 700 recruits finished basic training in October 2010 and is to experience a cohesion building exercise led by AMISOM at the Jazira training camp in the capital before being integrated into units and taking an active battle role.

However, there are many issues that continued to persevere. The selection process supports some tribes, particularly the Abgal. Since the TFG gives recruits, and a few components of the training took place in Mogadishu, regional governments and political factions like the ASWJ have widely rejected to participate. This has increased the impression that Sharif is constructing an armed force which is loyal to him, rather than a cross-clan national armed force loyal to the central government.

Strong personal interests and corrupted officials were predominantly the drawbacks to reform and transparency. Attempts to give the armed force better and stronger military equipment were slow and resolute by claims that officers sold some equipment. AMISOM undertook some initiatives to construct a comprehensive structure for the divergent armed groups and whip their members into a fighting structure which was a huge problematic. There remains defiance to the formation of a compelling leadership, coherent military formations. The former chief of staff of the Somalia armed force, General Gelle, attempted to improved things but was underestimated, was later fired from his position.

The political failures of the transitional federal government, and the army's problems restricted the power and the strength of the new force. Despite the European Union Training Mission haven't tackled the greater issue and crisis, its general record will be measured not just by how great the training was, but also by the use made of it and the end it served. The essence of this was that the national army was still very weak to take over the roles of defending the government and the institutions and defeating the insurgence.

The Ugandan-led AMISOM armed forced were stronger with better equipped. In late 2010, the UN Security Council has passed a resolution to allow the deployment of additional 12,000 armed forces; however, AMISOM together with IGAD refused and argued that 20,000 were rather required. Funding gaps continued to be a significant challenge to the TFG, and the needs for specialised battle equipment were deeply perceived.

While some perceived that it was very unlikely that these issues would be resolved in a short matter of time, the UN showed their will to support, as it considered the mission as the last line of control against Al-Shabaab. Regardless of the criticism of its occasionally aimless use of force, there is a reluctant appreciation for AMISOM's success to fight against the radical extremist who intends to overthrow the UN-backed transitional federal government.

One of the biggest problems that AMISOM faced was that they had not had enough support from the international community to achieve their objectives to eliminate the insurgents and had absolutely no road map to achieve the end goal. This is because there was a lack of appreciation amid the planning stage of the difficult aspect of the task, although optimism encircling the Djibouti peace process influenced several diplomatic and political decisions.

Uganda's lack of peacemaking has aggravated this. The outcome was a conventional UN-style peacekeeping plan to ensure the transitional government institutions and to allow the interim government to make any strategic political decisions. This was insufficient from the begin, and efforts to reconstruct it so AMISOM can face any new difficulties and specifically practice more prominent battle adaptability have caused long battles within the UN and AU.

A wider comprehensive process has helped the African Union Mission in Somalia organisers to predict enormous post-deployment complexities and get a more flexible mandate and time-consuming debate. However, the diplomatic efforts over the command were not clear between the advocates of conventional peacemaking model and those covetous of a more coordinated and strong mission to respond better to post-Cold War conflict.

Many in the Security Council were extremely divided on the issue of launching a broad offensive against the insurgency inside the capital city Mogadishu, but many feared that if this took place during the Ethiopian presence, the Somali population would turn against all foreign and oppose their presence.

AMISOM begin to misuse the flexible interpretation of their mandate in Somalia. Both Burundi and Uganda troops have increased their footholds in the southern parts of Mogadishu and later constructed additional bases in places dominated by al-Shabaab. As part of this, AMISOM began to work and associate themselves with different militias and provided with arms and ammunition to keep safe recaptured areas.

The new stations give AMISOM tactical benefits consistent with even a tight interpretation of their mandate. The objective of their mandate is to free Mogadishu from the insurgent and to strength government forces so they could take in charge of their affairs and defeat al-Shabaab if they were to come back again. However, there is hypothesis the more activity indicates forthcoming effort to retake the city and afterwards move the military efforts to southern and central parts of the country.

One of the reasons for which the Ugandan forces are so eager to destroy al-Shabaab reflects on their anger and their desires for vengeance following Al-Shabaab's suicide bombing attacks in Kampala, in July 2010 which killed more than 70 Ugandan citizens.

Such wide offensive activities without the approval of the UN Security Council would convey dangers for AMISOM and provoke political and diplomatic conflict, but this might be part of broader plan silently backed by foreign actors. The Somalia government officials totally remained secretive about the details of the planned military operation by the IGAD (International Governmental Authority for Development), but Kenya and Ethiopia have supported and backed few offensives carried out by Somali units trained in Kenya and Ethiopia.

However, Ethiopia cautiously thought about launching a strong and irresistible attacks to put the extremist "al-Shabaab" into significant pressure to retreat, but AMISOM and the Somali government forces gave no indication of making a political strategy for stabilising and recaptured territories. However some tribe elders have secretly supported the planning of southern regions of Jubba and Gedo, and the central regions of Galmudug, Galguduud and Hiraan, popular supports in the south have made the situation more optimism. History has long suggested that Somalis have always opposed and resist against any foreign military aggressions, including those that have served their long-term interests.

For long-time, the insurgent group "al-Shabaab" were working solidly to make the Somalis go against AMISOM as the Ethiopian forces withdrew. They have long used firing mortars from civilian areas into AMISOM bases which triggered several counter attacks and later resulted in the deaths of many civilians. Al-Shabaab has also orchestrated a mass propaganda against AMISOM and carried out significants attacks against government officials and AMISOM personnels. The dangers of a particular military strategy were clear but worth repeating.

Crushing al-Shabaab and its affiliates were believed to be possible, but after so much effort to do so, the insurgency still exists and has widely undermined the sovereignty of the state of Somalia. Some militias backed by regional actors have regrouped and used the Kenya and Ethiopian involvement to throw the nationalist belief, also the increase of international jihadist and many youths recruited from both in and outside Somalia.

Radicals who felt cornered were extremely required to amplify their irregular benefit, going forward to commit terrorist attacks across the region beyond. AMISOM efforts have in some way succeeded as the political system of Somalia have slightly moved towards the international required direction and government have focused on restoring law, order and governance of liberated areas as a form of partners with assurances that they wouldn't be dominated by the center.

It was once believed that the transitional federal government would provide that political structure, but without a more coordinated from the international community, important reforms wouldn't occur at the time. But there was great deals disparity among foreign actors on the issue of restoring peace and stability in Somalia, with continued attempts to a peace process led by the government of Somalia.

In September 2012, Somalia marked a milestone with the formation of a new federal government led by the newly elected President Hassan Sheikh Mahamoud. Almost all Somalis were deeply happy and hoped for real change that serves the interest of Somali and its people, as the end of Somalia's long political transitional.

On 17 January 2013, following a meeting between President Hassan Sheikh Mahamoud and the U.S. Secretary of State Hillary Clinton, she officially announced that for the first in 20 years, the United States have recognised the government of Somalia and vowed to support Somalia with their full capacity to bring about a real change. Several weeks later, the President met with the EU High Representative for Foreign Affairs and Security Policy Catherine Ashton, during the meeting, Catherine Ashton on behalf of the European Union has declared that Somalia is no longer a failed state.

Several foreign governments and international organisations have since followed and restored diplomatic relations and started to open embassies in the Somalia capital city. The creation of a new federal government has given Somalia a real cause for hope, for the first in time in two decades. The President nor his Prime Minister Abdi Farah Shirdon has taken any role in the long bloody civil war that has destructed the Somalia and left thousands displaced. Both men were successful businessmen, while Hassan Sheikh was a researcher and head of the technical institute of Mogadishu.

The newly government consisted of intellectuals and technocrats individuals rather than former warlords or discredited political entrepreneurs from the past, transitional governments. The new members of Hassan Sheikh's government were extremely committed to reviving the hope of the people of Somalia and restoring the national institutions to bring the country back on its knees and genuinely fight against the extremism that is destabilising the country.

The new administration led by Prime Minister Abdi Shirdon moved rapidly to assert policy positions, including the six-pillar strategy that distinct particularly from the program of previous regimes in their integrity and pragmatism. The president and his newly appointed Prime Minister Abdi Shirdon have pushed for the implementation of national dialogue, the creation of credible justice system and clear transparency of public finance management.

The elected federal parliament of Somalia indicates a step forward. It was the first time that the parliament to be elected in the country, and its membership was broadly seen of a higher gauge than its corrupt predecessor, which was for the most part preoccupied with the measure of their sitting allowance than the passage of legislation.

The elected speaker of the Somali federal parliament, Mohamed Osman Jawari was considered to be the most suitable candidate to hold the office of federal speaker. Jawari, a constitutional expert, has greater knowledge of Sharia law and Islam more than the Islamism groups. After his appointment as the federal speaker, he led the way to create parliamentary committees and developing the parliament agenda for the future of the country and holding the government accountable for any misconduct or mismanaging the public finance.

The SFG has been supported by a remarkable development in security inside the capital city, the arrival of a huge number of residences to their homes, a huge inflow of investment, and the restoration of peace and stability within Mogadishu. Some of the gradual progress made was due to the effort of the genuine friendly partners of Somalia as the UN-backed African force in Somalia (AMISOM) has produced a little effort to bring peace and order to the city due to the opportunist interest in Somalia. Many believe that AMISOM forces are prolonging their mission in Somalia for self-interest and better salary. Previously there were serious criminal activities committed by some of the AMISOM forces such as rape, killings, raiding homes and even on several occasions of looted local businesses. Despite the little security development in Somalia since the deployment of the AMISOM in 2007, the insurgency and the terror attacks by extremist is still having an enormous impact on the security of ordinary people and the country as a whole.

The real issues that Somalia is currently facing are the deceptive efforts by the international community when it comes to the political affairs and reconciling the state of Somalia. It's clearly obvious that key regional actors are reluctant to see a stable Somalia and therefore taking every necessary to step divide, disintegrate and create animosity between the different clans so the country could remain in a turmoil atmosphere.

The Lost Road Map

Despite the Somali federal government merits, the country has still a long way to go. In 2012, following the establishment of the federal government, Somalia was ranked as one of the failed and corrupted countries in the world. The newly elected federal government was neither permanent, broadly based nor democratic. This was an interim government, formed by provisional constitution for four years. It believed to be the government for all Somalia, but truly it's the de facto authority over the capital city and some parts of the south of Somalia. It is also a government that represents a country that for more than two decades faced civil war with the fractured central government.

Since the federal system was introduced in the Somali political spectrum, Somalia split into various regional states, and since then, many regional states were established and gradual the power and the existence of the central government of Somalia swift away. Some of these regional states chose to cooperate and work with the central government in order to keep the country going, whereas the others e.g. Somaliland and Puntland kept their distance from the central government to the extent that they banned officials from the central government to enter their regions.

The Somali federal government attributes contradictions says little regarding the new government than about the process through it was formed. The road map had involved a long series of consultations between four essential characteristics, and these were the transitional federal government led by President Sheikh Sharif Sheikh Ahmed; the autonomous region of Puntland in northeastern Somalia; the established administration of Gaalmudug in southern Mudug region; and the Sufi Islamist group of Ahlu Sunna Wal Jama'a, whose anti-al-Shabaab, culminating in complicated selection process in which tribe leaders appointed 825 delegates to an assembly representatives, which thusly chose a 225 parliamentarians, which later elected the president of federal republic.

Many have seen this initiative as one of the most legitimate state-building efforts ever done inside Somalia. In May 2010, 810 tribe leaders had gathered and participated in the Somali peace conference 2000 held at Arta, Djibouti. The peace conference brought the appointment of 245 members of parliament that is called Transitional National Assembly. The Transitional National Assembly appointed Abdulqasim Salad Hassan as the nation's president.

President Hassan was born in 1941 in the town of Galdogob, situated in the north-central Mudug region. He hails from the Habar Gidir sub-clan of the Hawiye. When the president and his government returned to the capital city of Somalia, Mogadishu, his government was wide confronted by sectarian violence and various armed resistance groups, who intended to oppose the Somalia peace process held in Djibouti.

Again, in 2002, another Somali National Reconciliation Conference was held in Nairobi, Kenya under the patronage of the Intergovernmental Authority on Development (IGAD), this time the number of the delegation exceeded over 800, but later this number was reduced by almost half as a result of the cost of feeding and sheltering them. Who carefully considered for two years before supporting a new transitional federal constitution and appointing a 275-members of the Somali transitional federal parliament in 2004.

The newly elected transitional federal parliament appointed Abdillahi Yusuf Ahmed as the country's president of the new transitional federal government. Abdillahi Yusuf Ahmed, former President of Puntland State of Somalia, and who were once considered as a precarious warlord.

When the president took office in late 2004, he authorised the entry of almost 20,000 Ethiopian troops who sought to invade the country under the pretext of supporting the transitional federal government led by President Ahmed. The entry of the Ethiopian troops to Somalia has created a wide division and bloodshed, and significantly deteriorated the situation of the country. This eventually resulted in his removal from office.

In 2007, following the worst fighting in a decade inside the capital city, over 2000 delegates from all the regions of the country and all tribe elders including Somali Diasporas, arrived Mogadishu to participate the first national peace and reconciliation conference to be held in Mogadishu under the patronage of the transitional federal government.

This peace conference has managed to receive large sum of millions of dollars as a financial support from the United Nations alongside the international community and was protected by foreign armed force, the peace agreement included the terms for a clan truce, the sharing of all natural resources and the preparation of a presidential election for 2009. The conclusion of the peace accord gained no apparent progress in propelling the cause for peace, however purportedly made dollar millionaires of the individuals who organised the peace conference.

Like the previous peace and reconciliation initiatives in the country, every step of the 'Road Map' was forcefully challenged especially the credibility and sincerity of the tribe leaders and delegates who met in Mogadishu to the national assembly and a new elect federal parliament. There was a wide accusation of vote buying, and attempt to disqualify or disregard former warlords from taking public offices were reversed under pressure from the outgoing president, Sheikh Sharif Sheikh Ahmed.

As the federal parliament was preparing itself to choose the next president of the federal government, many international observers were completely hopeless of any changes in relation to the government attempts to improve the current situation and the fight against corruption and extremism. The instant reversal of the electoral fortunes was so surprising to the extent that it astounded even the nearest observers of the process, including the elected president Hassan Sheikh Mahamoud.

A critical blemish in the road map process came into effect following the election of President Hassan Sheikh Mahmoud. His main partners, the regional state of Puntland, Gaalmudug and the religious faction of Ahlu Sunna Wal Jama'a were some way or another left behind. The newly established federal government had no longer any significance when it comes to the decision-making, hence appeared without power, regional control and political support that these de facto authorities could have given upon it, and ended up rather bound to those boundless urban zones in southern parts of the country protected by the UN-backed African troops (AMISOM).

Additionally, the Somali Federal Government reinterpretation of the federal system elected pictured by the Road Map signatories has put the new government progressively inconsistent with the elements that had established its foundation, with Puntland President Abdirahman Faroole going far to the extent of accusing the central federal government of having altered the provisional constitution.

As a result, the Somali Federal Government primary virtue was simply that Hassan Sheikh had been elected as the country's President. Many observers indicated that if Sheikh Sharif were elected again as president, they would felt oblige to characterise the new government as legitimate, democratic and credible. Indeed, a small number of foreign governments would have to recognise it.

After the election of President Hassan Sheikh Mahmoud, he was quickly influenced by a moderate Islamist movement who were the Somali affiliates of Egypt's Muslim Brotherhood called Damul Jadiid(New Blood), who were also a faction of Al-Islaah. After the collapse of President Siad Barre, and the breakout of the civil war in 1991, Al-Islaah relentlessly shunned violence, but in 2006 some activist denounced the conservatism of the Al-Islaah, affiliated with the Council Islamic Courts and fought against the transitional federal government and the Ethiopian presence in the country.

Among the most influential individuals from this faction were employees of the African Muslims Agency (currently known as Direct Aid International), a charity organisation based in Kuwait, which was invested in restoring the Somalia's social services especially education. One of the most leading beneficiaries of the Africa Muslims Agency's largesse was the Somali Institute for Management and Development, a school directed by Hassan Sheik Mahmoud.

When the president took office, prominent members of the Damul Jadiid have assumed key ministerial position including interior ministry, justice, social affairs and the powerful state minister for the presidency were all believed to be members of the group. Damul Jadiid is an isolated organisation, whose membership and manifesto remained largely rumours and speculations.

Damul Jadiid's plan for the country's ongoing political transition remains noticeable. Few critics' features the Somalia federal government's confidently and moderate approach to governance to damul jadiid ideologues as opposed to the president and prime minister, where both were regarded as political pragmatist before neither took office.

Since the establishment of the Somali Federal Government, all actions taken by the federal government suggested that Damul Jadiid was some way or another responsible for re-orientating the country's foreign policy away from the African Union and the Intergovernmental Authority on Development (IGAD) towards the Arab and Muslim world, especially the similar minded regimes in Egypt, Turkey and Qatar. Although this gave Somalia and its newly established SFG new allies and partners in reconstructing the country, however, resulted in wide disagreements and deteriorated its relations with its two neighbouring states Ethiopia and Kenya.

Despite damul jadiid's influence on the Somali Federal Government policy, its proximity to the levers of power has added to the discernment that SFG decision making is persistent, and to some degree, by an unelected and unaccountable interest group. That is a delineation the federal government must come up with every possible effort to overcome if is to succeed in binding Somalis more closely together as opposed to dividing them.

On the issue of stabilising the country, President Hassan Sheikh Mahamoud has clearly indicated that his first priority is "security, security and security" as his government inherited a country under siege by violence and extremism, and facing continuous insurgency led by al-Qaeda affiliates and with UN involvement in the Somalia political affairs and creating wide division among the people by creating a federal system which would make the central government complete vulnerable to external enemies e.g. Ethiopia and Kenya.

Several cabinet members including the minister for national security have all emphasised the need for the development of the Somali security forces such as the military, police and security services. To this present day, the government has long sought and received a modification of the UN arms embargo, imposed on Somalia in 1992, that allows the Somali federal government to buy arms, equipment, and ammunitions. Since many governments from the international community have promised the federal government for military assistance.

However, the development of the security was highly regarded as a complex proposition in modern Somalia, and various efforts in the past to build the Somali military and security forces have led to instability and violence. This is due to the challenges of stabilisation in Somalia are not military, but not political. Therefore unless the development of the security sector is properly addressed as a necessary part of the greater political process, it could probably become a source of tension rather than a pillar of peace.

The arms embargo was part of the sanctions on Somalia imposed by the United National Security Council in 1992 due to the increasing humanitarian crisis as a result of the civil war and the rising of terrorism in the country. As the years went past, the embargo was widened into a complex sanctions government, banning a broad range of threats to peace and security, funding insurgency groups, preventing the humanitarian aids and violating extremely the international humanitarian law. But, since the newly federal government took in charge of the country's affairs, they've put all their energy and commitment on one aspect, and this is the arms embargo.

The Somali federal government argued that the embargo of weapons has obstructed the Somali government from equipping and arming its armed forces to the required level to crush the extremist al-Shabaab. Some members of the United Nation Security Council remained unconvinced and regarded this argument has a misinterpretation of the sanctions regime. In 2007, under the presidency of Abdillahi Yusuf Ahmed, the arms embargo was modified to allow some foreign governments to supply arms, military equipment's, training including funding for the Somali security and military forces, as a result of the approval given by the Security Council Sanctions Committee.

The approval process was not as difficult as believed to be, no-obligation procedure- and only one offer to help was apparently ever dismissed, despite few offers to help were postponed while the committee looked for more information or clarifications. As opposed to the TFG's claims that its armed force was desperate for arms and ammunitions, bullets and military equipment from government military stores between 2007 and 2012 recommended that the army was getting more help than it could mindfully retain.

Immediately after the establishment of the Somali Federal Government, they've increased efforts to have the arms embargo lifted when the issue of lifting the sanctions of arms embargo was tabled in the United Nation Security Council in early 2013, the Somali delegates received a warm welcome.

The United States was eager for Somali federal government to be recognized as a sovereign government and made every possible effort to help the SFG to achieve its request, but unfortunately majority of the UN Security Council were not convinced enough to lift the sanctions of the arms embargo, as they feared that weapons could end up in the hands of the radicals and extremist who posed significant threat to the country and the entire region.

After a long argument in the UN Security Council as to whether to lift the sanctions on the Somali federal government, eventually, a compromise has been reached in the form of Security Council Resolution 2093, which relaxed the sanctions for one year period. This step of relaxing the embargo imposed on the Somali government has allowed them to get hold of their weapons, and foreign government who were assisting Somalia with military equipment and training had no longer require to obtain permission from the UN sanctions committee.

But heavy weapons and sophisticated military equipment remained restricted, and the Security Council has imposed thoroughly reporting in which the sanctions committee shall be informed in advance all the deliveries of weapons, and the Somali federal government had to inform the committee once every six months on the structure of the security and armed forces including all steps put in place to ensure the registration, maintenance and the supply of weapons. The Council also assigned a team to monitor the situation and to provide an independent report on these issues.

It seems to the Security Council that the modification of the arms embargo will, in reality, result in the development of the strength of the Somali military and security forces, or either give al-Shabaab and its affiliates in the country the chance to access to weapons and military equipment so they could carry their dangerous and radical actions. However primary indications were not promising, only a week after the Security Council's decision, Somali media reported supplies of arms and bullets were stolen from inside the presidential palace, Mogadishu.

In 2013, affiliates of the Federal Government in lower Juba and Bokol region, both declared a strategic alliance with radical extremist al-Shabaab, and this raised concerns that jihadist would receive military assistance from the federal government. Much more essential in the close term is the possible impact of the Security Council's decision on the internal political spectrum of Somalia.

The Security Council's vote of confidence in the Somali Federal Government was not prominent inside Somalia. The leadership of the two biggest autonomous regions in Somalia (Puntland and Somaliland) including self-governed regions in southern parts of Somalia, objected and opposed widely the decision on the ground as it could threaten and undermine their security.

In 2013, several countries including the Republic of Djibouti, Egypt and Turkey vowed to provide the SFG with military assistance and the U.S. administration led the way for future military assistance. Unsurprisingly, Puntland and Somaliland authorities announced that they were both actively pursuing to acquire arms and other military equipment's to counter dangers coming from Mogadishu. A beginning of weapons contest was in progress.

When the new government led by President Hassan Sheikh was established in 2012. The SFG and its foreign allies designed a strategy and politics that could lead to strong and stabilise Somalia. Joint efforts of the UN-backed African forces (AMISOM), Kenya, Ethiopia and Somali federal government forces, reached the conclusion to change the map of southern parts of Somalia. The radical extremist group (al-Shabaab) was removed from their major strongholds; furthermore, the loss of Kismayo the capital of Jubaland region in September 2012 dispossess the al-Shabaab of their single most critical source of income, making sure that al-Shabaab would never set foot again on their previous strongholds.

However, despite significant efforts by the Somali forces and its regional and international allies to eradicate the insurgent group, al-Shabaab persisted their commitments and continued to control some areas in south central Somalia, particularly rural areas. They've also continued their horrific attacks on government officials, forces and foreign diplomats.

Al-Shabaab continuing influence can be categorised by few factors: the group's determination to grip onto power; the absence of rival forces e.g. government and regional forces across most southern parts of the country and finally the group's ability to exploit legitimate local hardship of their purposes. Al-Shabaab's area footprint on the country's map hence closely with territories occupied by unhappy and rebellious tribes.

The Somali federal government plans for countering the terrorist group 'al-Shabaab' were part of strengthening their security services, and this has built a monopoly on the legitimate use of force. However, in a country that is as disintegrated, divided and intensely armed as Somalia, this isn't only a hostile proposition, but also a complete danger.

The strengthening of the SFG to the detriment of other Somali movements is as of now propagating concerns and tensions. Previous transitional governments took initiatives to come up with efforts to stabilise the country through a genuine political process, but often these turned into failures as a result of lack of political disputes between different political elites in the country.

Al-Shabaab had always adjusted itself with local communities, and the federal government's military oppression against the locals have previously served further problems and hostilities, and this gave the al-Shabaab the opportunity they always sought to turn locals against the SFG. Confronting al-Shabaab the jihadist always required a strong strategy which involves to negotiate and engage with these local communities, recognising their legitimate demands, and persuading them future lie in accepting regional and national political governance process.

The same remains constant in territories freed from the insurgent movement 'Al-Shabaab,' where the similar resentment that once cultivated backing for al-Shabaab overflow into intercommunal disputes as tribe leaders contested for positions, personal interests, and representation of their regions in the post al-Shabaab period.

The Federal Government's military involvement might be seen to support some factions to undermine others, intensifying the situation as opposed to calming it. The federal government's attempts to stabilise were politically led and militarily supported.

The previous state building efforts in Somalia during the transitional era have, without exception, planted its failures in the form of state capture and the corruption on a vast scale, in which personal interests succeed in controlling policy development and constructing the emerging rules of the game to their own, exceptionally significant advantage.

The transitional national government of 2000-2004 was broadly seen as being overwhelmed by individuals, who hailed the same clan as President Abdiqasim Salad Hassan's, including some of its prominent businesspeople, together with components of certain Somali Islamist movements, prominently Al-Islah. The TFG of 2004–2008 was firmly characterised to tribe-based political and security machinery connected to President Abdillahi Yusuf, and also corruption business interests related with Prime Minister Ali Mohamed Gedi.

State capture possibly gained its peak under the leadership of President Sheikh Sharif. When President Sharif took office in early 2009, the president brought with him into the government an interest group known as the Aala Sheikh. However, the Aala Sheikh had no characterised membership or association, and during their time in government, they've appeared to be more unified and undivided by its extraordinary ability to appropriate state coffers than by any compelling ideological orientation. To be sure, the scale of their insatiability was so endless about 70 percent and 80 percent of government incomes went unaccounted for, and the remainder was captivated by the offices of the three top officials that it was characterised as not corruption but as cannibalism of the state assets.

The increasing difficulty of state capture was reflected by the increase of another critical component of the Somali war economy. Various interest groups who were responsible for the chaos that was taking place in the country since the fall of Siad Barre in 1991, have identified themselves as part of the solution to the long-term civil war so they could attract different supports and investments.

On the issue of security and stability of Somalia, this involves describing al-Shabaab as a military problem which enabled the government to access to heavy military equipment and to enhance their security machinery.

This has proved appealing to some foreign partners of the Somali Federal Government, who want to legitimise their military support regarding counterterrorism instead of counterinsurgency. But this has significantly damaged the roots of insecurity in southern parts of the country; while empowering the progress of the real industry in training and arming the Somali armed and security forces. Often these forces remained in tribe militias, and most of them were loyal to individual commanders as opposed to the government.

After years of military assistance on both training programs and hundreds of millions of dollars from the international community to assist the Somali forces to bring peace and stability in the country, the security of the capital city and other parts of the country is extremely outrageous, and government officials are unsafe and large parts of the country is dependent on the UN-backed African troops (AMISOM), and this due to the high level of the corruption that government officials by stealing the foreign assistance rather than investing in the Somali armed and security forces, many believes that this could continue for the foreseeable future.

While corruption was part of the greater problem in Somalia, some opportunistic leaders were threats to the security so they could seek additional asset. An example of this was when a militia commander allied with the AMISOM forces sent his army to viciously attack the African Union headquarters in Mogadishu at night and framed it to al-Shabaab, so he could gain more ammunition and other supplies, which AMISOM provided so that the militia could persist its militia activities.

Piracy was a helpful bribe to obtain foreign assistance, inducing negative partnership between government officials and their pirate allies. Officials in Puntland administration embezzle piracy and protected pirate leaders while calling for support from the international community to counter the insurgency.

The President of the regional state of Puntland at that time, Abdirahman Mohamed Faroole has managed to acquire the huge sum of money from the United Arab Emirates to construct a maritime police force that later turned out to be a private armed force that was working under his leadership. The genuine counterpiracy success of Puntland was accomplished through peaceful engagement with the leaders of the beach of coastal communities when external pressure made it unjustified for the authorities to keep playing both sides against the centre.

President Sharif's transitional government played a similar game to Puntland and requested a large sum of money for a small Coast Guard that operated off the Banaadir coast, in the local area of Mogadishu, where there weren't any pirate safe havens for them to attack. At the same time, President Sharif gave a diplomatic passport to one of the most notorious pirates in Somalia, Mohamed Abdi Afweyne, where the president had appointed him as counterpiracy coordinator for central Somalia, and offered immunity to his militia.

The president described his decision to grant Afweyne's militia immunity as a form to prevent them from further piracy activities; they kept on holding a few vessels and their crew's hostage until they received a huge ransom. Afweyne has subsequently built rehabilitation camps for pirates in Mogadishu and Adaado, another form of attracting lure from foreign donors.

In early 2013, Afweyne declared in the southern city of Adado that he had discarded crime and will retire from the piracy activities. He also indicated that he has managed to get his pirate colleagues to follow him to leave the piracy. According to Mohamed Adan Tiiceey, the head of the Adado local administration and several other officials with the Adado administration have succeeded in disarming Afweyne and his pirate associates, as the bosses had come to the realisation that they would not function with impunity and profits had stopped.

After the creation of the new federal government in Somalia, Afweyne began to negotiate with the government for an agreement to grant amnesty and rehabilitation program for pirates. Mohamed Adan Tiiceey arranged several meeting with officials of the Somali federal government and the leader of the Hobyo-Harardhere Piracy Network.

Afweyne then created the Anti-Piracy Agency in the Somali capital of Mogadishu and requested funding the government and international community for an initiative that anticipated the formation of rehabilitation, training skills for ex-pirates.

Furthermore, Afweyne and his older son tried to negotiate a Grand Bargain, wherein all the remaining hostages held by the Hobyo-Harardhere Network would be freed in return for $2 million payment from the Somali government. The agreement fell apart after an internal dispute and fund misuse, which finished in the collapse of a pirate negotiator.

In October 2013, Afweyne was detained in Belgium as he landed on Belgian soil for perpetrating the 2009 hijacking of the Belgian dredge vessel Pompei and also accused of kidnapping the ship's crew and being part of a criminal organisation. Through Mohamed Adan Tiiceey, Afweyne had been invited to act as a consultant on a television documentary about his piracy exploits. After months of talks, Hassan and Tiiceey began their journey to Belgium to participate in what they thought to be was a documentary project.

The television documentary was a sting operation conducted by Belgian undercover agents, which had been set up after prosecutors resolved to prosecute the perpetrators of the 2009 Pompei hijacking. According to the prosecutors, it took several months to persuade Afweyne to come to Belgium as a documentary consultant, although they did not explain or give details on the plan was executed.

The undercover agents were recruited when prosecutors determined that an international arrest warrant would not be necessary to arrest the men. Both Tiiceey and Hassan were prosecuted in Brugge, and sentenced to twenty years in prison in mid-2016. He was the first pirate leader to be prosecuted externally.

On 2012, Somalia marked the end of the perpetual transition. Despite the terrible continuous refrain that Federal Government was the first government since the collapse of President Siad Barre and his government. The 2012 established federal government was, in fact, an interim government formed on a provisional charter, and its mandate supposed to expire in August 2016 but was later delayed due to lack of political compromise.

Before the expiry of their mandate, the federal government completed some of the unfinished transitional tasks it has inherited from the previous administration such as the development of the federal system, reviewing the constitution and referendum, forming a credible and legitimate electoral system and the preparation for presidential and parliamentary in 2016.

Failure to do so on schedule would indeed create not just a political crisis but also constitutional crisis and would give the international community the space it needs to dictate even more the Somali government officials. It is, therefore, distressing that none of these important duties is clearly addressed in government's Six Pillar Policy and that almost one year before the expiry of the Somali federal government term of office, no significant progress has been made to make it happen.

According to the provisional charter of the Somali federal republic, 12 articles were to be modified and 22 laws to be executed during the federal parliament's first mandate. Other transitional objectives, including the formation of federal authorities and the development of a credible electoral system, were to be assigned to an independent commission that was to be formed within sixty days of the creation of the cabinet.

However, at the time of writing, neither the federal government nor the parliament has shown any genuine feeling of desperation in meeting these vital constitutional duties. Rather, they fought themselves on irrelevant issues, and that has threatened to wreck the transitional procedure and bring Somalia once more into the dark and civil conflict era.

THE JUBALAND INITIATIVE

In mid-2012, the transitional federal government initiated efforts to establish the state government of Jubaland in southern Somalia, and the meeting took place in Nairobi, Kenya under the patronage of the Intergovernmental Authority Development (IGAD). A task force consisted of delegates of the IGAD Secretariat, Ethiopia, Kenya and the TFG was assigned to lead the process, which was named the 'Grand Stabilisation Initiative of Southern Somalia.

A Somali committee originally consisted of members of the main armed groups in the Juba Valley Alliance was increasingly widened to include over delegates from all clans. The compromise intended to bring together all three administrative regions of Lower Juba, Middle Juba, and Gedo under one interim regional government that would constitute a new federal state of Somalia.

Kenya and Ethiopia, whose armed forces led the way to confront the insurgents 'Al-Shabaab' in regions strongly dominated by al-Shabaab, and collectively gave the political force behind the talks; both states have recognised the stability of these regions is important to the security of their borders. The Kenyan government, especially, considered the development of a stable Jubaland leadership would be the foundation of a way out strategy for their military force in Somalia.

For the two neighbors to concede on a common stance on the issue of security was itself an accomplishment. Kenya had for a long time provided support and military training to Azania (now Jubaland) security and military forces, a group led by Ex- Defence Minister Mohamed Abdi Gandhi. But Ethiopia had more prominent confidence in the Ras Kamboni Brigade, a largely Ogaden tribe militia led by ex-commander of al-Shabaab, Ahmed Mohamed Islam Madoobe and armed militants from the Ahlu Sunna Wal Jama'a faction.

Ultimately both Kenyan and Ethiopian regimes consented to leave aside their representatives, with the understanding that only a comprehensive and broadly based process would create a stable leadership in Jubaland. However, critics, including President Sharif's government, deduced more vile intentions, including the extension of Somali region endowed with oil reserves, fisheries, and resources.

Despite President Sharif's hostility, other members of the IGAD task force were optimistic that the newly formed Somali federal government would play an effective role in taking ownership of the process and bring it from Kenya into Mogadishu. After the establishment of the Somali federal government in September 2012, the federal government moved rapidly to abandon the Jubaland talks, urging an alternative process in which the federal government would assign district authorities, increasing building upwards to the regional and interregional levels.

Both Ethiopian and Kenyan authorities considered the Federal Government's recommendations as unrealistic as well as obstructive, and a sign that the new Somali government did not in actuality failed to put in place a federal system of governance.

In February 2013, as the IGAD initiative turned into deadlocked, the technical committee from Somalia moved from Nairobi to Kismayo, continued to prepare for a conference without the legitimate support of IGAD's. On February 28, the conference was officially held with more than 800 delegates. Toward the beginning of May 2013 the delegates approved an interim constitution, and on May 15, the conference elected Ahmed Mohamed Islam Madoobe, commander of the Ras Kamboni forces, as the interim leader of Jubaland regional administration.

Since the formation of the provisional constitution of the federal government of Somalia, many officials within the federal government characterised the Jubaland initiative as unconstitutional and therefore refused to accept the announcement of the 'regional state government of Jubaland' led by President Madoobe.

The government was supported in its resistance by the announcement by Barre Aden Shire, a former warlord who came from Mogadishu to Kismayo weeks before the conference. An announcement made by Prime Minister Shirdoon the next day, and Abdikarim Hussein Guled, the SFG interior minister, both called upon the Somali government forces and AMISOM peacekeepers to be "impartial" in the case of brutality in Kismayo. The federal government's position on the Jubaland initiative was completely problematic for some reasons. The interim federal constitution was itself inadequately crafted document with various contradictions and ambiguities

No place are these failures more evident than on the issue of federalism, leaving a plenty space for real differences over the issue. IGAD mission to Jubaland, following Ahmed Madoobe's election, noticed that, while all concerned parties to the disagreement recognised the need to accept and abide by the after the interim constitution. One of the factors that were deteriorating the Jubaland initiative was that there was a distinction interpretation between the Federal Government and different stakeholders in Kismayo.

The provisional constitution discloses the difference in interpretation, but the differences could be inevitable. Above all, the constitution did not clearly give the Somali Federal Government a leadership role in the formation of federal member states. Rather, it accredits the ultimate duty for deciding the number and limits of federal member states to the lower chamber of Parliament, which formed an independent Federation Commission for that reason. This commission, which had to be established within sixty days of the creation of the federal government, did not exist yet.

The federal charter likewise specifies that one or more regions may willingly integrate, while considering the administrative limits that existed before 1991, yet it doesn't indicate who inside every region, regional governments and elders have the ability to conduct a merger. Rather, it affirmed that, before joining a federal member state, individual regions should be directly led by the Federal Government for two years. This provision permits the federal government a key role federal member state creation, that was captured in stabilisation strategy through the nomination of the provisional local authorities which later came together as regions and states.

However, experts consider the stabilisation strategy as a simply hidden proposal by the federal government to exercise centralised control over improvement of the federal system, and perhaps to wreck the architecture of federalism through. Since the federal government rules not many parts of the country, it seems to be unrealistic in much, if not most of the country. Article 142 of the provisional charter of Somalia, indicates that existing federal member states shall be allowed to participate in the decision-making process in relation to the federal system that has raised the issue of Jubaland from a disagreement over regional administration establishment to political deadlock.

At the time of building the regional administration of Jubaland, there was only one regional administration state which was Puntland, and its views on the issue of Jubaland opposed to those of the federal government mainly because Puntland hails from the same tribe as people from Jubaland. Since the formation of Puntland regional state of Somalia in 1998, Puntland was the only force that was fighting of the introduction a federal constitution and their former president, Abdirahman Faroole, was one of the political figures who helped built the Road Map that led to the provisional federal constitution and the Somali federal government.

Moreover, Puntland characterises itself as the land of the Harti subclan of the Darood, a faction that has profound roots in Kismayo since early twentieth century. Influential Harti political figures were involved in the Jubaland initiative; the Puntland regional state has given Jubaland significant political and economic support to Kismayo conference.

Puntland has recognised Ahmed Madoobe as the regional president of Jubaland. In Tribe terms, this has activated a tribal union known as Kablallah, which joins the Absame (of which the Ogaden are a part of it) and the Harti group. By disregarding entirely Puntland's position on Jubaland, the SFG is potentially creating more tension and animosity in the Somali political scene.

The idea of federalism came to Somalia, when the hostility between federalists and unitary centralists was frequent component within the Somali politics even before the creation of an independent Somali Republic in 1960, reflecting longstanding political and social division not only over the issues of power sharing and security, but also over issues such as the nature of citizenship and Somali identity.

Federalism was initially championed by the Somali Digil-Mirifle Party, which was established in 1947; the faction was afraid by the dominance of an independent Somalia by majority nomadic groups. But eventually, their concerns were wiped out by the voice of the majority of Somalis who were calling for Somali unity and independence under one flag and unitary government, represented mainly by the Somali Youth League. Federalism was again quickly raised in the late 1980s by the radical insurgent forces that were fighting to ouster President Siad Barre from power. But these rebel groups agreed on little else, and any pledge to federal state allegedly fell apart with the Somali government in 1991.

The creation of Puntland regional state in 1998, which sees itself as the foundation of a future government Somalia, rehabilitated the longstanding issue overturning Somali into federal, but in a way that gained threatening suggestions of closeness and regional geopolitics. Puntland's self-identification with the population and lands of the Harti subclan is seen by many Somalis as a dangerous variation of Ethiopia's ethnic federalism and increasing the Ethiopian foreign policy designed to balkanize and weaken the Somali state. The strong baking has fortified this inclination that Puntland has had from Ethiopia since its creation.

In 2000, two years after the creation of the regional administration of Puntland, the transitional national government that was formed at Arta, in Djibouti. The Transitional National Government symbolised a unitary with a centrist vision of the Somali government, reaffirming the eighteen administrative regions that existed in 1991 during the period of the central government. It was a dream for many Somalis, particularly the defenders of federalism, especially the Hawiye tribe, and it had the quiet approval of Egypt.

The Ethiopian aggression to the Transitional National Government combined with the incompetence and arrogance of its leadership have ensured that the new government (TNG) remained mobilised made it ready for the establishment of the TFG led by Puntland's ex-president, Abdillahi Yusuf Ahmed, in 2004. The idea of plunging Somalia into federalism was advocated by Darood leaders who received significant support from the number enemy of Somalia (Ethiopia), who for long-time sought for the destruction of greater Somalia and its sovereignty as a nation.

The TNG has benefited from the support that it received from the different Somali Islamist movements, including ex-jihadists, while the TFG depicted itself as mainstream and Western-leaning, with proven anti-jihadist ideology. The polarisation of contending political visions and the geopolitical allies were hardly pronounced, proclaiming a period of the Somali civil war.

The adoption of the federal constitution in 2004 hence failed to solve the long dispute over federalism, which later aggravated the situation. But as the following, the transitional government has struggled for survival against the dangers that was coming from the terrorist group al-Shabaab, the transitional government and their international allies recognised the values in restoring the constitutional debate over the federalism. The outcome, in 2012, was the rise of a devilish political conundrum: A Somali government with clearly antifederal slants. The long debates over federalism in Somalia continued vigorously, and the essential question rapidly got to be whether the matter would be settled through peacefully or in fighting.

In May 2013, tensions broke out sharply between Jubaland's regional president Ahmed Madoobe and officials of the federal government as both sides engaged in lawfare and appealing the provisional charter to delegitimize their rivals while fighting for their positions. However, neither of them achieved great success, the Somali international partners, were aware of the uncertainty of the constitution and keen to prevent the provocation of a conflict but remained impartial on the issue.

In Somalia, there was a wide division between the public over the issue of federalism, and whether to accept Jubaland as a regional state, the majority of Hawiye supported the federal government, while the Darood, with the exception of Marehan, supported Jubaland. Puntland, who was at that time the only federal member state of Somalia, waged its support of Madoobe, with President Faroole flying to Nairobi to join leaders of Jubaland to meet with Kenyan President Uhuru Kenyatta.

On the ground in Kismayo, there was a minimal sign that either party intended to depend on lawfare to gain its objective, as both started to mobilise and arm clan militias. Ahmed Madoobe has relied on the support of most Darood tribe militia except for the Marehan subclan, while the SFG Defence Minister and other senior military officers made their way to Kismayo to gather militia forces loyal government, planned to mobilise support from different Hawiye factions as well as the Marehan. A silent centerpiece of his strategy was the restoration of the Juba Valley Alliance, a coalition of Hawiye, Habar Gidir, and Ayr and Darood and Marehan forces from Gaalgaduud region, which took control of Kismayo in 1999 and held it until 2006. The chief of the alliance was Barre Hiiraale, Ahmed Madoobe's self- declared rival for the post of Jubaland president.

The federal government was not the only group that were in the fight to block Jubaland from accessing to federal state; al-Shabaab also was another faction which was in the fight against the Jubaland initiative, since Ahmed Madoobe was the founder and former leader of the terrorist group 'al-Shabaab.' But

Madoobe left the group in 2008 and launched an offensive campaign against the group from that point onward, ousting them from Kismayo with the help of the Kenyan government in 2012. Just like the federal government, al-Shabaab was heavily relying on discontent local clans to provide them with technical support to defeat Madoobe.

By May 2013, there were indications of a local conspiracy between pro-government forces and Al-Shabaab militants, as Al-Shabaab permitted pro-government forces to move troops and weapons unmolested through their strongholds as they met on Kismayo to challenge Madoobe. Toward the beginning of July, the federal government vital ally in Lower Juba, Barre Hiiraale, told that his forces were co-situated with Al-Shabaab and preparing joint military operations against Madoobe.

The federal government became too close with Al-Shabaab as they were countering common enemy. In June 2013, both parties decided for veritable warfare. Fighting broke out between local armed militia who affiliated with the federal government and Ahmed Madoobe's forces, which left many killed and forced dozens of civilians to leave Kismayo. In June, forces from Ras Kamboni defeated the local militia and took control of Kismayo, Ahmed Madoobe sent delegates from Jubaland and to meet with the Somali federal government in Addis Ababa to compromise and to find a solution to the longstanding conflict between the two sides.

For the federal government, a continuing political resolution to the Jubaland crisis was a necessity. A confrontation over control of Kismayo, Jubaland would have implications beyond Jubaland. Despite the result, the federal government has the acquired the enduring fightings of Jubaland supporters from inside and outside of the country, a majority of them were from different Darood clans. Relations with Puntland deteriorated. The introduction of the federalism in the Somali politics have created wide division among the general public, undermined the prospect of constitutional dialogue and the election in 2016.

On the issue of Somaliland and the unity of Somalia, the federal government's uncompromising nature on the issue of Jubaland contradicts with its clear desires to engage in a political dialogue with the self-proclaimed republic of Somaliland, which declared its separation and independence from greater

Somalia in 1991, following the ouster of President Barre, and since then fought for international recognition as a sovereign state. The preparation of talks in 2012 between delegates from Somaliland and the Somali federal government headed by President Hassan Sheikh met with Somaliland President Ahmed Silanyo in Ankara on April 13, 2013. Both parties during the meeting signed several accords and agreed to meet again in Turkey, after 90 days. Regardless of these promising prelude, as with the Jubaland issue, any progress was overcome deeply by established positions, ideological rigour and the internal weakness of both governments.

Both delegates hoped for peace negotiation to settle the disagreement. The federal government was very fragile and given the threats that it faced in southern parts of the country, it has no reasonable prospect of forcing its will on Somaliland in their term of office. Any attempts from the federal government to dictate Somaliland would only make the situation worse, and may even distance some of Somalia's international allies particularly the United Kingdom, which hosted the talks between Somalia-Somaliland in 2012.

Somaliland's fortunes are likewise at a low ebb. Twenty-two years after its declaration of independence from Somalia, Somaliland was so far recognised by one foreign country (Ethiopia), the sole purpose of recognising Somaliland, is to divide Somalia even further, so they could achieve their strategic interest in Somalia. The widespread international recognition of the federal government of Somalia, regardless of fragility as a state, the likelihood of third-party recognition was considerably out of reach.

Furthermore, international community sympathy for Somaliland bid for independence been firmly tied to the self-proclaimed nation's reputation in democratisation and human rights. But in Somaliland the electoral system and the way in which the interior ministry handles the election are completely seen as chaotic; in 2012 the local elections were less systematic than previous elections and the outcomes violently contested, and lead to the death of dozens and damaged significantly public confidence in the electoral process.

The legislative elections what were meant to be held in 2010, took place three years later and the upper house of parliament, known as the Guurti, have never occurred. There is no electoral for the Guurti due to the stiff resistance from the current members. A sharp internal disagreement over the issue of voting registration have resulted in further delay of the 2015 parliamentary and presidential elections to 2017, and this has damaged the image of Somaliland in the eyes of the international community.

One of the problems that Somaliland is facing politically is the reduction of the credibility of the government of Somaliland, which had long claimed it had represented all of the tribes within the territory. Minority tribes have opposed Somaliland's bid for a separate and independent state, arguing that its main agenda related with the Isaaq tribe dominance. Previous government could negate this claim by indicating the genuine participation of individuals from all tribes at all levels, across the government.

Former president of Somaliland, Dahir Rayale Kahin, was the first president to be hailed from outside Issaq tribe. He was a member of the Gadabursi tribe; who ruled Somaliland from 2002 until 2010. During his time in office; he appointed members of non-Issaq as heads of Supreme Court, National Electoral Commission and armed forces. But as he left office, his successor and the incumbent President Ahmed Silanyo appointed all Isaaq clan members to the most prestigious positions including finance, interior foreign affairs ministries, governor of the central bank, Supreme court and etc. since the arrival of President Silanyo, the dominance of Issaq was once again back to the Somaliland political landscape.

As the political dialogue between the Somali federal government and Somaliland continued, it kept on getting harder and difficult to achieve common agreements that will end the long disputes between both sides, since both governments remained wedded to conflicting positions. The federal government was mandated and required by the interim constitution to defend the unity and territorial integrity of Somalia and would risk political suicide if it were to accept and recognised Somaliland's quest for independence.

On the other hand, the government of Somaliland was subjected by its own particular constitution to safeguard their independence as a sovereign state and would confront internal upheavals if they accepted to come under Mogadishu. Both sides faced internal difficulties and are unwilling to seem frail on such an unstable, existential issue.

Despite commitments from both sides to abstain from using provocative language or other acts which could threaten the continuation of the dialogues of the two sides, the tenor of public exchanges between both parties was becoming more and more heated more than ever before.

The authorities of Somaliland have openly refused to take part of the international conferences on Somalia such as the one that was held in London, hosted by the British Prime Minister at the time (David Cameron) in 2012, simply because the President of Somaliland administration Ahmed Silanyo, clear indicated that Somalia had failed to recognise 'Somaliland' and told that such participation would undermine Somaliland's quest for independence and its long fight for international recognition.

A week later, the United Nations International Civil Aviation Organisation issued a statement in which they intend to hand over the Mogadishu-based government the Somali airspace, Somaliland authorities which had long controlled its airspace independently, under the UN supervision, had furiously responded to the decision of the UN International Civil Aviation Organisation by banning all UN flights from entering Somaliland or leaving its airspace.

On May 18, 2013, on the 22nd anniversary of Somaliland's declaration of independence, the President of the federal government of Somalia, Hassan Sheikh Mahamoud, delivered a speech in which he stressed the importance of the Somali unity and called upon the self-proclaimed state of Somaliland to renounce its bid for independence. Such acting emphasises that neither sides seemed prepared to surrender ground over their political differences. Nor the government was likely to accept to engage in any talks that will result in fulfilling the needs of the other.

Eventually, the main attainable pathway to the harmonious determination of Somaliland's "last status" was likely to be an open-ended dialogue, probably based on African authoritative example, for example, Ethiopia and Eritrea and Sudan and South Sudan, through which either unity or split could be peacefully and enduringly accomplished. But timing and pace are important: neither one of the sides is at present in a sufficiently solid position to commit on such a risky undertaking.

Another round of dialogue took place in July 2013, during these talks the dialogue made an agreement to create a mechanism for join airspace management and vowed to meet again after 90 days. This low-key progress emphasised that even allegedly safe technical matters such as the distribution of foreign assistance, airspace management, and security cooperation were profoundly charged. Therefore, the consequences have rendered the obvious intransigent problem even more.

This is not the first time that Turkish government showed legitimate interest or support for greater Somalia. During the past couple of years, Turkey has begun their technical and humanitarian assistance to the SFG and its predecessor TFG. Many considered that Turkish government has slightly gained a degree of expertise on the course during its provisional membership on the UN Security Council from 2009 to 2010.

In 2011 the visit of Turkish Prime Minister Erdogan to Somalia drew the attention of many countries to Somalia's humanitarian tragedy, many foreign powers and regional member states kept a close eye to Turkey's policies in the Horn of Africa, particularly Somalia. Beyond the shadow of a doubt, Turkey became one of the leading actors in Somalia and expanded their strategic interest in the country. Since then, there were many strategic, political and security challenges that have accompanied turkey with their mission.

The insecurity remains one of the was biggest threats that Somalia is facing. The main concerns of the Somalis and the international community are the futile political efforts that are not resulting genuine progress towards peace and security. After the fall of the central government in Somalia in 1991, warlords appeared on the political spectrum of the country and caused significant atrocities which resulted in the deaths of thousands, then the Islamic Court Union (ICU) took over from the overlords and delivered justice, peace and order until the Ethiopian invasion, which brought Ethiopian and U.S. puppets into power.

During the era of ICU, they've started to negotiations with different armed groups. However, these negotiations were widely rejected by two extreme groups; the Islamic Youth Movement and al-Shabaab, not only these two movements refused negotiations but also refused any other political solutions under the supervision of the UN and the African Union. From that day onward, al-Shabaab was regarded as the biggest security threat in the history of Somalia. Towards the end of 2011, when Kenyan troops allegedly crushed al-Shabaab with the support of the African Union and Somali government forces, the front left the port of Kismayo.

These difficult conditions have exposed Ankara several security problems, the most recent example these security problems were the August 2013 horrific attack on the Turkish embassy in Mogadishu. On April that year, a Turkish aid worker was a target of similar attack. Also in October 2012, a deadly attacked was targeted at a Turkish official from the Turkish Cooperation and Development Organisation, Mustafa Hashim Palot.

Al-Shabaab claimed the attack and indicated that the attack was in response to the military agreement signed between the Turkish and Somali governments in April 2012. The group believed that this agreement between both governments supported the war against them (al-Shabaab). Despite al-Shabaab's explanation in relation to the attack, the Somali ambassador to Turkey Mohamed Sheikh Abdourahman, gave a statement to the Turkish news agency and told them "al-Shabaab's explanation in relation to the attack on the Turkish embassy in Mogadishu are not sufficient". This remark of the ambassador thickened the shadow of the attack. Despite the Turkish security challenges in Somalia, they've remained committed towards the development and well-being of Somalia, and Bilateral trade volume between both countries reached 72,3 million USD in 2015.

On 3rd June 2013, Turkish president arrived in Mogadishu to inaugurate the opening of the largest Turkish embassy in the world in Somalia and other projects including the health facilities. The president and his delegates were widely welcomed by the Somali government officials at the Mogadishu International Airport. Erdogan's visit to Somalia came after his tour to few countries in East Africa such as Uganda and Kenya, where he promised to expand security and economic ties between his country and East Africa, bring peace into the region. Since Erdogan's first visit to Somalia in 2011, turkey's role and involvement in Somalia has increased and drew world's attention. Erdogan was the first Turkish leader to visit Somalia.

Turkey's effort in restoring peace and development in Somalia has made significant changes to the country in several areas from health to infrastructure. During his visit to Somalia, his government has signed bilateral agreements with the Somali authorities. The bilateral agreement consisted of treaties to train the Somali national army, and Turkish Airlines began flights to Mogadishu. The Turkish government's efforts to boost Somalia have increased the relationship between the two countries to the extent that it brought attention to the region and some actors as well as the international community started to question Turkey's interest and involvement in Somalia.

Turkey also has undertaken strong initiatives to sustain Somalia such as providing over $400 million to fight against the country's starvation. They also set to open its first military base in Africa at which Turkish military will train their Somali counterparts and provide with intensive training to help defeat al-Shabaab.

Somalia, despite the significant efforts from countries who are its Muslim brothers, the country is under the occupation of extremism and the trusteeship of neighboring countries and the international community for almost three decades. These three forces (al-Shabaab, neighboring states and the international community) had a different interest in Somalia but appeared to be united on one thing: the perpetuation of destabilising Somalia and disintegrating the state and society.

Al-Shabaab had long been the main cause of the Somali destruction. It continues to sabotage Somali's quest for peace, security, and reconciliation, indiscriminately killed innocent civilians, poses a significant threat to the peace and stability of the region and in doing so creates the instigation for the recolonization of Somalia in this modern era.

Somalia's biggest regional enemy (Ethiopia and Kenya) took advantage of the collapse of the unitary central government and the opportunities given by the extremists and the lack of nationalism and patriotism among Somalis. Ethiopia and Kenya have widely benefited politically and economically from the anarchy in Somalia. The so-called international community fund endless stabilisation projects in Somalia without understanding the main problems that are blocking the reconstruction of Somalia.

Ethiopia and Kenya along with other African nations in the East Africa were assigned by the United Nations to stabilise the country under the banner of AMISOM about one decade ago. At present, there are almost 22,000 AMISOM forces in Somalia. The AMISOM forces have for the past years benefited from the UN logistical support and bilateral donations. The European Union pays significant amount of money and provides other aid packages to the troops within the framework of the African Peace Facility.

The European Union pays each month $1,028 to each AMISOM soldiers, almost three times what they used to earn in their countries, while the poor-equipped Somali soldiers are $100 a month, which is not a paid on a regular basis. Also, AMISOM countries Members gains considerable financial support for participating in the fight against terrorism in the region. Yet, AMISOM forces are not fighting efficiently and failed to make sustainable peace in the country. They are only sitting in their bases and waiting to be attacked. As al-Shabaab gained substantial flexibility from their rival (AMISOM), al-Shabaab makes frequent attacks on AMISOM bases and usually kills innocent bystanders and patriotic lawmakers in Mogadishu.

The EU is financing an endless project with absolutely zero of success. Moreover, neighboring countries like Ethiopia has decisively opposed the establishment of strong and well-equipped Somali army while giving weapons to divided Somali enclaves as well as the AMISOM forces, undermining efforts to rebuild Somalia's sovereignty. Ethiopia's visible interferences in Somali affairs is particularly worth illustrating. No place is Ethiopia's open violation of Somalia's sovereignty more obvious than it is in the previous north western Somalia region, known as Somaliland today.

Somaliland claimed its independence in 1991 but was not recognised by any country since then. The region has no full jurisdiction over all of its territories not the support of all clans in the north. For instance, tribes in Sool, Sanaag and Cayn are against Somaliland's independence. Likewise, the vast majority of Awdal region opposes Somaliland's quest for independence and pledge their support to United Somalia.

The Ethiopian government gave an office that represents Somaliland in Addis Ababa and similarly the Ethiopian government sent some of its representatives to Hargeisa. The Ethiopian regime showed no interest to officially recognise Somaliland as Ethiopia is confronting its rebellion in the Somali Region that is fighting to free itself from Ethiopia. However, its mission to making Somalia weak and divided, Ethiopia's Tigray military leaders and business people use Somaliland as an entry port for commodities and contraband to Ethiopia. Tigray military elites also use Somaliland as a currency exchange market.

It is unlawful to have dollars or exchange US currency in Ethiopia without the Ethiopian commercial bank. Therefore, when Tigray leaders want hard currency for personal use or even to import goods, they only visit the Tog Wajaale town in the border.

As allegiance to Ethiopia, people of Somaliland have celebrated, along with the other Ethiopian regions, the month Tigrayan People's Liberation Front (TPLF) ousted the Derg government in Ethiopia led by Mengistu Hailemariam. Also, Somaliland business people raised a significant amount of money to support the Blue Nile Dam in the north-west of Ethiopia. In return, some officials from the Somaliland administration were granted Ethiopian passports whenever they need to travel abroad, as Somaliland's passport in invalid. This also applies to Somalia.

The Ethiopian government assigned one of its strong military and intelligent elite Colonel Gabre to govern Somalia and to carry out the Ethiopian agenda to Somalia, so Ethiopia could always dominate Somalia. Any Somalia politician who wants to engage in the Somali political life or inspiring to hold a position within the Somali government has to consult and have the protection of the Ethiopian intelligence based in Mogadishu. In doing as such, Gabre has the power to pick and choose the most illiterate, corrupt and unethical leaders for representing Somalia.

Moreover, to strengthen their grip and takeover, Ethiopian regime has mobilised military, political offices and delegates in Puntland regional state of Somalia, armed forces in Galmudug, Jubaland and Baidao. All of these regional administrates celebrates the month of Tigray People's Liberation Front, and their presidents often travel to Addis Ababa more than to Mogadishu.

The difficult relationship between the Somali federal government, regional administrations including Somaliland and Ethiopia is based on fear and intimidations. While Ethiopia has military bases in most Somali autonomous regions, the Somali region of Ethiopia forces known as Liyu police has continuously crossed the border to enter Somalia and kill innocent civilians. On April 2016, liyu police indiscriminately slaughtered innocent Somali civilians who are part of the Ethiopian territory of Somali region along with the border with Hiiran region of Somalia.

The innocent civilians fled to their closest relatives in Somalia for security purposes. The liyu forces who are 98% Somali ethnic are targeting their own ethnic Somalis to satisfy the Ethiopia regime. The liyu police subsequently followed some of the civilians and entered into the Somali territory and clashed with the Galmudug region armed forces.

When the Galmudug regional president Abdikarim Hussein Guled complained the incident to Addis Ababa, the Ethiopian officials forced him to go to Jigjiga, the capital of the Somali region of Ethiopia and negotiate with the president of the Ethiopian Somali region and settle the issue peacefully.

In July 2016, the Liyu police had killed 22 civilians in Jama Dubad village of Gaashaamo district bordering Somaliland. Indeed, Puntland, Galmudug and Somaliland have in the past handed over the ONLF rebel members, but it appeared that handing over ONLF members did not provide them security nor respect.

The Jama Dubad village incident and aftermath responses were the worst political humiliation to Somaliland administration since its breakaway from greater Somalia in 1991. A young Liyu police officer crossed the border to Somaliland and burnt the Somaliland flag in public. Five journalists were kidnapped in a broad daylight from a Wajale (border town) in Somaliland and taken to Jigjiga. Four of the five were quickly released, but the fifth journalist remained under the Ethiopian detention.

The irony is that rather than condemning the appalling behaviour of the Ethiopian government, demanding justice for the death of the civilians in Jama Dubaad and also the release of the fifth journalist that still remains in the Ethiopia jail, political and community leaders in Somaliland made ridiculous statements, including embracing the Liyu police criminals and by extension a tribe that was for long the victim of the liyu forces for blame by cowardly separated the Liyu from the rest of the Ethiopian armed forces who also took major role in the killings. This self-humiliation and fearfulness of the Somali political and community leaders illustrates the state of Somali politics.

The people of the Somalia, regardless of their tribe or the region in which they hail, they need to learn from the past two and half decade of misery and agony. They can only be respected if they are united. In the death of the single unitary government of Somalia, Somalis will for sure be treated as second-class citizens in their country. Somalis will not have a voice oppose against any of the aggression posed by Ethiopia and Kenya or to defend the thousands of Somalis killed in other African countries or the sea towards Europe.

Both Somalia and Somaliland has to realise that it's time to sit together and negotiate for ways which they could share the power. The recent attacks in border areas by the Ethiopian forces illustrates the complete humiliation that Somalis are suffering from.

Political leaders of Somaliland administration must stop believing in the misconception that Ethiopia is their number one ally. Because in reality, Ethiopia was never in the history of Somaliland been an ally nor to Somalia. Because if Ethiopia sees Somaliland as an ally or friend, they would have accepted and recognise the independence of Somaliland years ago. The truth is that Ethiopia's foreign policy towards Somaliland and Somalia is to create animosity and hatred among the Somali tribes to keep them weak and vulnerable.

In the history of Africa, many countries have experienced civil war and political disputes. If Rwanda ended their worst genocide in history, if South Africa ended the worst apartheid era in the history of civilization, If Ivory Coast emerged from the civil war following the ouster of President Laurent Gbagbo, Somalia can emerge from the civil war and the political colonisation of Ethiopia and the UN and can be respected once again. But can achieve the dignity and respect which they deserve as a sovereign state if they are only united.

Ethiopia and its National Security crisis

In the past, Ethiopia has been the center point of either stability or instability in East Africa. Despite the level poverty in the country, Ethiopia always had a long history of statecraft and a sense of patriotism and national identity, which means that it can act in quest of a clearly perceived national interest. Ethiopia has implement force beyond their borders and can act with adequate restraint to avoid their use of military power from transforming into a destabilising adventure. During the periods in which Ethiopia was strong and had some influence within the Horn and beyond the region, the country was able to contain the forces of instability in the Horn of Africa.

During the periods in which Ethiopia has been strong and respected, the country has been able to contain the forces of instability in the region. When Ethiopia was itself in internal conflict or was regarded as weak and political dilemmas in the region, have remained uncontrolled, and even sometimes ran out of control.

Since the end of Second World War, the Ethiopian regime led by Emperor Haile Selassie laid a foreign policy which focused on maintaining and strengthening the country's independence and its territorial integrity. During the times of regime change, successive regimes supported and used to provide arms and ammunition to rebel groups who were fighting against the governments in Sudan and Somalia, but this was a response to similar actions conducted by neighbouring states against Ethiopia, and in all cases the Ethiopian regime was keen to ensure that these rebel groups concerned unified, with a clear political agenda. The Eritrean independence from Ethiopia was a major concern of the Ethiopian national interest, as they have lost access to a free sea.

The Ethiopian government has raised their concerns over their national security interest and produced a political strategy to achieve its national interest. Historically, Ethiopia's main opponent for controlling the entire Horn of Africa has been Egypt. Egypt had long considered the Nile as a matter of life and death. Many Egyptians were afraid that those who were in charge of the Nile headwaters could hold the country ransom.

The Egyptian concerns about the Nile have significantly increased over the years, as the country has been taking more water than it supposed to have according to the Nile Waters Agreement in 1955. This agreement was based on estimates of river flow from a period of rainfall, which is now coming to an end as a result of the climate change, and also due to the peace in Sudan and the economic development in Ethiopia suggest that developing states will be using more water from the Nile.

The water Nile agreement was jointly signed by almost of the concerning nations of the Nile Basin, with the exceptions of Ethiopia. Almost the entire flow of the Nile comes from the Blue Nile, which has its source in Ethiopia. At the moment, Ethiopia uses some of its potential for irrigation and hydroelectric power. If somehow Ethiopia exploited this resource, which could eventually turn into a national issue survival in Ethiopia, given their vulnerability to drought and famine, Egypt will become seriously concerned.

For Ethiopia's search for a secure stream of water, Egypt has long sought to dominate Sudan and Ethiopia. Under the patronage of the World Bank, the Nile Basin Initiative has so far taken crucial steps towards meeting the interest of all concerning states in a common system of water use. This was a step forward that helped Egypt to realise that Nile water is a zero-sum game. Both Egypt and Ethiopia have a much key common interest that would be better be served by a partnership.

Ethiopia has strong concerns over radical extremism in Egypt and the Arabian peninsula. The population of Ethiopia is mostly Christians and Muslims, and the nation contains the city of Harer, which is considered as the holiest Islamic city in the country. Ethiopia's history for the last four hundred years had been set marked by mutual respect and tolerance among religions.

The stance of succeeding regimes was to develop this system of religion tolerance and confront the politicisation of faith. Ethiopia had to keep a close eye on the activities of foreign extremist in the Horn region, who often promotes an extremist and put forward agenda's that would lead to destabilising the region. The so-called radical Islamists took steps to establish an Islamic state in the Horn, more particularly Somalia, and they were full supported financially and militarily by the Gulf states, and this would pose a serious threat to Ethiopia's security interest. However, the current activities of these radicals in the Horn appeared to pose less threat to the region and to Ethiopia itself.

In terms of the peace and security of the region, the biggest security threat to Ethiopia mainly comes from Somalia. During the 1990', the most serious threat was from extreme radical groups that were based in Sudan and Somalia. These threats came to an end following an assassination attempt made by some Ethiopian under cover intelligent against the then-Egyptian President Mohamed Husni Mubarak in the Ethiopian capital, Addis Ababa, in 1995 and the Egyptian minister for transport and communications Abdel Majid Hussein, in 1996.

The Ethiopian regime laid out a strategy to deal with this threat by militarily and diplomatically. For Sudan, the Ethiopian government often uses military pressure, and provide assistance to Sudanese opposition forces, while also acknowledging united and stable Sudan would be the national interest of Ethiopia. The military pressure that often Ethiopian armed force undertakes include crossing the border into Sudan to conduct a joint operation the Sudan People's Liberation Army.

Sudan had later expelled all militants from extreme groups and introduced a political strategy to make peace with southern parts of the country (today South Sudan) mainly due to the Ethiopian military pressure. The Ethiopian government had improved its relation with the Sudanese government immediately after Sudan had abandoned its policy of accommodating al-Qaeda affiliates. Sudan had for long posed a serious threat to the regional stability by fostering and assisting support to terrorist groups in the early 1990's, but became manageable and contained, despite its internal crisis and instability.

In the case of Somalia, the Ethiopian government carried out a direct military action in 2006 against religious groups who defeated the transitional government, but this military intervention by the Ethiopian government armed forces reflected on the Ethiopian government aims to occupy Mogadishu. In 1996 and 1997, attacks by Ethiopian forces on the al-Ittihad al Islami headquarters have successfully erased the threat posed by affiliates of al-Qaeda.

During the Erit-Ethiopian, the presence of the Eritrean-backed extreme group in Somalia has pushed Ethiopia to invade the country to combat the terrorism. Ethiopia has used this opportunity to gain their strategic interest in Somalia and uses their economic and political power to destabilise Somalia politically and by promoting disintegration of state and society within Somalia.

This illustrates that despite changes of governments in Ethiopia, Ethiopia will always retain its desires to weaken Somalia, it also illustrates that although 'EPRDF' government of Ethiopia took control of the country in 1991 with a strong political agenda, they've rapidly transformed into the regional superpower both politically and economically. Ethiopia has shore up legitimate authorities to neighboring countries as a result of their political and economic power, as they've believed that this would serve their best interest as a country.

The threat of the Eritrean military never demobilised since its liberation from Ethiopia in 1991 and forced Ethiopia to deploy large army with the capacity to project force across its borders. While the danger of a frontal attack by Eritrea can't be marked, the likelihood of Eritrean-supported rebels in the south is an ongoing problem.

Despite the ongoing problems by Ethiopia and Eritrea, the Ethiopian government adopted a political strategy to reconquer Eritrea so that they could have access to the free sea. During the three-decade war of liberating Eritrea, Ethiopia was depleted by the efforts of trying to conquer an Eritrean territory and its people. Although the Eritrean historical claims of an independent and sovereign nation only came after the colonial occupation, the experience of fighting long and bloody war produced a spirit of patriotism among the Eritreans, which is a fundamental reality that no historical analysis can deny.

While Eritrea was sore to Ethiopia, its existence did not pose a strategic threat to Ethiopia. Ethiopia hopes to restore its relations with Eritrea when the current regime is removed from power. Economic cooperation between Eritrea and Ethiopia would be inevitable and a major benefit for both countries and especially to Eritrea.

There are major issues across the Ethiopian borders, and if this is mismanaged, then it could result in major conflict. An example of such conflict was the border dispute at Badme, Gash-Barka in the Eritrean border, which escalated from a small clash into a major global war which led to the deaths of tens of thousands civilians in mid-1998. Ethiopia also has other many disputed borders; this includes many disputed territories on the common border with neighbouring Sudan.

After the resolution war in Eritrea, the ministry of foreign affairs of Ethiopia began deliberate attempts to certify that all of their disputed border areas were resolved agreeably with neighbouring states. With no functioning and stable government in neighbouring Somalia, peace and security have not been possible for Ethiopia on the eastern border. Other possible problems may include in the movement of pastoral tribes from one end of the border to the other, smuggling, contraband and grazing rights along borders. In working with the Intergovernmental Authority on Development (IGAD), the Ethiopian regime has thoroughly examined these issues to reduce the risks they may pose in the future.

Considering the historic antagonism with the Republic of Egypt, and the potential rise of the radicalism backed by the Gulf states, the level of the threats from neighbouring states, the amount of potential flashpoints, the Ethiopian government recognised that it was for their best interest to adopt security and defence policy, that included a credible and powerful army with a strong capacity to deal with anything that could pose a threat to the so-called Ethiopia national interest.

The values of the Ethiopian army like this relies on the political analysis that decides when and how it is to be used, and the political methodology that goes with its use. Considering the Eritrean challenge to the region, the two-year border conflict with its neighbors Ethiopia from 1998 to 2000, experts have acknowledged the conflict as a major setback to both states. In mid-2000, the Ethiopian armed force gained the military upper hand. But instead of continuing its dominance battleground, the Ethiopian regime declared that they'd achieved its objective of the war, and agreed to international mediation on the disputed border.

During the time of this decision, it was extremely for the Eritrean President Afeworki to survive politically due to the defeat of his army and the resistance of most of his cabinet ministers. However, not only the Eritrean regime survived in the Ethiopian victory on the battlefield, but also it continued to survive during difficult economic and political crisis. The strategy of the

Eritrean regime has managed to sustain its regional relevance by creating conflict for Ethiopia and Sudan, clearly in the belief that either or both of these countries will disintegrate and Eritrea will need to be taken into account, restore political direction for the Horn.

When Eritrea declared independence in 1991, the official name given to the state was Eritrea. Eritreans have often traced their statehood back to ancient time; Eritrean have for long tried to compete with the Ethiopian political tradition of state-building. Some experts in have argued that Ethiopia and Eritrea owe their identities to the period of the imperial carve-up of Africa in the late 19th century, during which time both countries were created. This was the time in which Italian colonial cut out the Eritrean territory from northern Ethiopian, and the Ethiopian emperor at the time Emperor Menelik II took control of many parts of the southern Ethiopia and engrossing millions of Oromo ethnic into the Ethiopian Empire.

During the struggle against the military government of Lieutenant Colonel Mengistu Hailemariam from 1974 to 1991, the liberation forces that later took over Addis Ababa and Asmara spent their time in discussing the issue of the identity of the countries, agreeing eventually on the Eritrean fight for independence and self-determination, while the Tigrayan fight against the Derk regime was for self-determination for the Tigray ethnicity within the Ethiopian state.

In the case of whether the Oromo struggle against the regime was internal self-determination like the Tigrayan or national like the case of Eritrean was never fully compromised, either between the Eritrean People's Liberation Front (EPLF) and the Ethiopian People's Revolutionary Democratic Front or among the leaders of the Oromo Liberation Front (OLF) themselves. The federal constitution of the Federal Democratic Republic of Ethiopia was adopted in June 1995 and represented a unique effort to solve this longstanding crisis.

The newly adopted constitution granted the Oromo's, as well as other ethnicities, the privilege to self-determination, but this privilege was subjected to some severe preconditions. After the acceptance of the preconditions by Oromo's and other ethnicities, the federal constitution devolved substantial central government powers to the regional governments and created a balance between national and regional identities.

The implementation of the federal constitution has been the major internal political challenge over the past decade and remains to be a challenge until the adoption of an alternative. During the era of the Eritrean People's Liberation Front (EPLF) armed resistance from its formation in the 1970's until its victory in the early 1990's, the leadership of the Eritrean resistance understood that the State of Ethiopia was just an artificial various nationalities came together during the colonial era in Africa.

The EPLF leaders have provided military assistance to some regionally-based Ethiopian rebels. After earning their independence from Ethiopia, the Eritrean authorities have anticipated that Ethiopia would collapse like the USSR and other countries who went through the collapse. Prior to the Ethio-Eritrean war in 1998, some have described Eritrea as an "Zaire." The velocity of the fall of Mobutu Sese Seko's government in 1997 has emboldened Eritrea to believe that Ethiopia will soon or later collapse in the same way if given a well-prepared military trauma.

Eritrea had a similar policy towards neighboring Sudan. In early 1994, President Isaias Afwerki announced that his Sudanese counterpart Omar Hassan Bashir would be removed from office within the year to come, and began accommodating and financing Sudanese opposition and armed groups. The Justification for this act was that Eritrea was the main target for radical extremist in the region, many saw the country as tiny, vulnerable and naturally within the boundary of the Muslim and Arab world.

The anticipations have not been realised. But the Eritrean regime has not changed their policy towards Ethiopia and Sudan but aggravated it. Eritrea has increased their efforts of hosting several opposition armed and civilian groups and sponsored them. Eritrean president considered Ethiopian's weakest point as its south-east, where he believed that the Ethiopian government did nothing to establish a strong and well-functioning government in the Somali region of Ethiopia, inhabited by Ethiopian national of Somali origin.

Therefore, the Eritrean premier launches a political strategy which was to finance Somali militants in the hope of destabilising Ethiopia heavily. This has created a critical situation in Eritrea while persuading the United States that they are an ally in the war on terror and has indeed begged the U.S. on several times that it should build military bases in Eritrea. Thus, this has meant that Sudan based government, which shares a common understanding with Ethiopia to contain Eritrea, has vowed sympathies for the Somali Islamists groups, but politically adverse to them.

Following the defeat of Eritrea in 2000, it appeared domestically and globally that Afeworki days were numbered and that very soon his regime will be toppled. He has survived from the immediate threats that he faced and carefully watched while neighboring Ethiopia has become engrossed and entangled in the difficulties of the democratic transition.

The 2005 Ethiopian general election and its outcome appeared to Afeworki to prove his anticipations that the time of the Ethiopian disintegration of state and society was coming very fast. Much surrenders from the Ethiopian armed force publicised the point. Indeed, even Djibouti, a neighboring state that has deep economic integration with Ethiopia, was becoming less helpful towards the Ethiopian regime. Eritrea was encouraged both in its policy of supporting the Ethiopian opposition forces, the militarily-forceful Sudanese Redemption Opposition and the Union of Islamic Courts in Somalia.

The illusion of the bravery of the Eritrean armed force having been destroyed in 2000, Asmara was betting on the vulnerability of the neighboring states to destabilisation through rebellion. The Union of Islamic Courts military defeat by the Ethiopian government was a major disappointment to the Eritrean expectation that Ethiopia was weak and its government is on the verge of collapsing. It is also a sign that the Eritrean strategy of anticipating influence through non-state actors has exceeded. But the Eritrean regime will consider their reversal in Somalia as a tactical mishap. It is highly unlikely for Eritrea to change its strategy.

The international and regional actors have developed a mechanism for containing Eritrea and its funding to destabilise neighboring states. While the Ethiopian aim for stability and a strong economy is realistic and achievable, the objective of Isaias Afeworki is that he clearly aims to tighten his grip on power for as long as possible. He persuaded the Eritrean population that Ethiopia is once again trying to reconquer the country, and by keeping Eritrea fully prepared for war and keeping the Horn region instability, he succeeded in keeping a permanent state of emergency.

The political issues that the region is currently facing would be difficult to tackle without Afeworki's continuing involvement, but with that involvement, they are unsolvable. A decade ago, many believed that Eritrean administration saw a region-wide political crisis as the instigator of a new regional order based on various new states such as independent Oromia and maybe independent South Sudan. Although, today the remnants of that speculation remain, along with the political issues that encouraged Asmara's destabilisation strategy, the objective of the Eritrean ruler has just survived. Although his options remained very limited, he has managed to succeed on few aspects of his objective.

The political Islamic has been the major factor of the Horn of Africa since the era of Prophet Mohamed. Islam has given a framework for public administration and military organisation for those who had no established state structures. The horn of Africa has witnessed Jihads in countries within the region such as Ethiopia, Sudan and Somalia against state emperors and imperial colonialism. The most fascinating feature of Islam in the Horn of Africa was that it had been pacific nature and the tolerance of different religions.

For the last decades, efforts by extremist to produce a transformative political Islam have slightly succeeded in mobilising the young Muslims, but have failed to gain the support of the of the majority. One of the main reasons for his failure is that majority of the inhabitants had a strong traditional of tolerance to different forms of Islam, especially the Sufi orders that have the adherent of most Muslims, the power of social ties that cross religious boundaries and the fact some radicals have failed to deliver a real solution to the problem facing the people on a daily basis.

The thing that surprised everyone about the Union of Islamic Courts in Somalia is was not that it was established, but the fact it took almost two decades from the fall of the late President Siad Barre for the Islamist to form such an administration. However, since the Fall of the Derg regime, Ethiopia has widely opposed to political Islam. However, after the US government invasion of Iraq in 2003, there were dangerous indications of militants of propagating awareness young Muslims in the Horn.

The way in which the U.S. government war on terror was described in the media, and also the way in which the Ethiopian regime was perceived in some circles as an assurance of the United States in seeking that agenda. Despite the Ethiopian war on al-Qaeda affiliates in the 1990's without the help of the United States, instigates the danger of creating tensions between Muslim-Christian communities, and aggravating these divisions even further. It is now clear that young Muslims will fall towards political Islam, and that Muslims Oromo may engage with the Islamic ideology and agenda.

War has always been the occurrence of a growth in primitive nationalistic and religious radicalism. The Eritrean-Ethiopian war in 1998 made the Ethiopians to adopt an extreme anti-Eritrean positions and announced that the Ethiopian war would only be won when Eritrea was reconquered. But contrarily this wasn't the position of the Ethiopian regime, but such attitudes expanded the mistrust and animosity between the two people of the two countries. Likewise, the war between the Somali Islamists' and the Ethiopian government created anti-Muslim feelings in some circles. Despite there are Muslims, who are holding positions in the Ethiopian government.

The Ethiopian chief of staff of the armed force is one among the Muslims in senior positions, and it was easy for the Ethiopian government to be characterised as Christians fighting the Muslim. Both in historical and contemporary times, Ethiopia has never faced political problems with the fact several of its neighboring countries are Islam. Ethiopia has never had a problem with its neighboring Sudan to implement the Sharia Law, only with aspects that could lead to extremism and destabilisation.

The EPRDF remained absolute secular, and during its war with the previous administration (the Derg), it received tremendous support from Sudan and Somalia. In fact, leaders of the EPRDF have on several occasions expressed their admiration for the people of Somalia, but later changed their position and took advantage of the collapse of the Somali central government and began arming different militias to destabilise Somalia even further. During the 1970's to 1980's, leaders of the EPRDF traveled on Somali passports and received significant support from Somalia.

The strength of the Islamic militants has always been an adversarial ideology that has mobilised young. One of the issues of today is that conflicts generate jihadi logic, attracting both foreign and Somali militants to a struggle that has been described as global Jihad against the U.S. agenda of dominating the Muslim world. The presence of Ethiopian armed force has been seen as Ethiopian occupation and became a target. The Transitional Federal Government's legitimacy was undermined as a result of allowing the Ethiopian invasion.

A similar threat is that the Ethiopian tradition of religious tolerance has been compromised. Ethiopia has a bigger Muslim population than any other state in the Horn of Africa. The question of Islam as a political power in Ethiopia was never brought to the table, apart from attempts to adopt sharia law as the legal code in communal and family affairs. This illustrated that the Ethiopian regime did not genuinely consider how to manage political Islam as a domestic issue. The Ethiopian government has continued to ignore the issue and indicated that all legal equality of all religions in the country was under the secular constitution of the country.

However, as the geopolitical center of gravity of the region, it's vital that Ethiopia was able to verbalise a plan for an administration that assesses the developing common sentiment among the Muslims regions. The main challenges for Ethiopian government's foreign policy are the public relations and presentation. Since the regime had made few statements of policy and plans, it left the field open for others to surmise motives, such as territorial aggrandisement and Christian chauvinism. The Ethiopian government aims on the issue with relation to Islam have dismissed fears.

The Horn of Africa is considered to be located in the dangerous area. Many viewed the region as one of the most complicated and conflicted regions in the world. The current conflicts and crisis have many have various features, such as the collapse of the Somali central government, the rise of extremism in the Horn, the continuous conflict between Eritrea and Ethiopia and the ongoing war in South Sudan.

These crises have emphasised that Ethiopia must be the center of any stabilisation initiative of the Horn. Although Ethiopia has indeed been the cause of this crisis, weakening and interfering in the Somali government to expand its influence in the region, violating the Eritrean territorial integrity and providing assistance and accommodation to South Sudan rebel leader Riek Machar.

Ethiopia had largely benefited from the U.S. weapon and financial assistance in the name of fighting against terrorism and used this support to strength its status in the Horn, but the most worrying thing is how the U.S. administration has turned blind eye to Ethiopia's aggression to neighboring states. However, for the past couple of years, Ethiopia took part in so-called peace initiative to stabilise Sudan and Somalia, and many viewed that strong and stable Ethiopia, the problems in Somalia and Sudan couldn't be tackled effectively. With Eritrea stuck endlessly in survival mode, the weight falls upon Addis Ababa.

However, the weight of regional peace and stability was believed to be too heavy for one country to manage, particularly in a region that has been undermined by so much distrust and conflicts. If Ethiopia truly wanted to be in the lead of stabilising neighboring states, it must take all the necessary steps to find a real solution to the problem with the help of the international community and the countries affected by these problems (Somalia and Sudan).

Ethiopia has sought its multilateral strategy effectively within the multilateral framework, including the IGAD, the UN and the African Union and even with the Arab League in the case of Somalia. The first step was to build a comprehensive political agenda. The overall game plan must be based on a new peace and security program for the Horn of Africa.

In its Constitutive Act, established in 2002, the African Union (AU) preserved key principles. The first was the only legitimate way to change government was through democratic and election process. The second principle was that no state could increase a barrier to ban attentions of others to its human rights. As the African Union is based in the Ethiopian capital Addis Ababa, it appears that the African Union has more relationship with the Ethiopian government.

The African Union has previously backed Ethiopia's right to defend itself from the terrorist threats coming from Somalia, but also called on Ethiopia to retreat its armed force from Somalia. It has now reached the time where the African Union to rise to the challenges of facilitating the Intergovernmental Authority on Development in making and implementing a regional order for peace and security in the region that ensures the democratic processes of all countries within the Horn of Africa.

Ethiopia should commit more effort to stabilise Sudan like they are doing in Somalia. The relationship between Ethiopia and Sudan and even South Sudan determines the stability in the Horn. Sudan has never achieved either internal stability nor becoming the focus for stabilising the region. The Comprehensive Peace deal between the Khartoum-based government and the SPLA that was signed in January 9, 2005, believed to be the framework for Sudan's peace and stability and transition to democracy. Ethiopia has signaled their commitment towards a united and democratic Sudan, and its roles in supporting Sudan's peace and conducting its democratic transition was crucial.

Ethiopia needs stable Horn for its own national and security interest. Unless the Ethiopia is safe and secure from destabilisation and the threat from extremism, the process of democratisation begun by this regime will not progress. Ethiopia is located in the Horn of Africa; Ethiopia has been the second most populous country in Africa after Nigeria with over 100 million. The country is landlocked country and has borders with Republic of Djibouti, Eritrea, Somalia, Sudan and Kenya. Despite with significant natural resources and vast fertile land, the country remained to be among the poorest countries on earth. Ethiopia is very diverse with 80 ethnic groups, and Somalis and Oromo are among the largest ethnic groups.

Despite there are no agro-pastoralists and inactive farmers, pastoralists consist of 12% of the Ethiopian population. The majority of Somalis, Oromo and Afar are known to be Pastoralist. These ethnics groups tend to produce their livelihood by having a huge number of livestock and cattle rearing. Year by year, the inhabitants live in extreme weather, and environmental conditions, extreme poverty and sometimes these areas face one of the worst droughts in the region.

In previously, these areas have witnessed several conflicts a result of competition for natural resources between different local tribes. The main reasons of these conflicts between the Afar, Oromo and Somalis is because of the extreme environmental conditions and the increasing need for basic human necessity. Previously, one of the main reasons for hostilities between these ethnic groups was the intense competition for water resource and grazing land. On the other hand, the intensity and the constituency of clashing groups and the impacts of these conflicts have heightened in the past three hundred years, as a result of the political and regime changes in Ethiopia.

The different ethnic societies in Ethiopia was under one unitary government from the 19th century until the end of 20th century, but it was under the leadership of Emperor Haile Selassie that state institutions were established. In 1974, Emperor Haile Selassie was ousted from power by the centralized communist regime led by Mengistu. During the imperial rule and the Derg regime, Ethiopia was under central unitary government, where the state wealth was strictly controlled by one totalitarian government and was strongly dominated by the Amharic ethnic.

The control of state power by the Amharic ethnic had created major inequality in politically, economically and socially and gave significant hardship to all other ethnic groups in the country. Thus, various ethnic-based opposition groups began a struggle over the country's leadership. The power struggle between the nationalist movement of the different Ethiopian ethnic rebellion groups had increased the ethnic conflict in Ethiopia. Mengistu's administration period came to an end following the EPRDF coalition forces victory over the Derg regime.

After EPRDF seizure to power, they've introduced federalism into the country which devolved power from the central to regional governments in 1991. The main reason for the federalism was to dismantle the previous centralised system and resolve the long ethnic animosity and wars made by the dominance of the Amharic ethnic. The federal system gave the nine largest ethnic-based groups autonomous regions.

Previously disregarded ethnic groups have welcomed the decentralised system. These factions praised the recognition of their local ethnic culture and language in their newly formed zonal administration. They believed that the new decentralised system would create self-rule and will bring to an end the dominance of the state power by the Amharic ethnic. Also unlike the previous centralised government, there was widespread that this federal system would provide better service to allocate necessities to the municipalities and inhabitants of the countryside.

However, in addition to the conflicts in the past over natural resources, the adoption of the ethnic based federal system in Ethiopia has created new tensions among the different ethnics, especially at the local level. For long, the centralised regime in the past ruled Ethiopia in non-ethnic based administrative divisions. The new federal system was completed with the creation and implementation of boundaries to differentiate ethnic based limits. This has significantly aggravated the ethnic tensions; a highly disputed boundary exists between the Oromo and the Somali regional states where both are widely claiming unfair boundaries by the federal government.

The agro-pastoralists of Oromo and Somali share over 1000 km long of not clearly divided border in the eastern and southern parts of the country. The conditions in these areas were known for its horrific environment. The land dispute between the Somali and Oromo regional states has increased with the establishment of the federal system in Ethiopia in 1991. The disputed areas went from Moyale to Ma' eso that had a vast land to some extent. Along with this border between both regional states, Lake Districts are located in the southern part of Moyale district to those in the northern like Ma'eso district.

During the early period of the federal system in Ethiopia, different ethic-based political movements were formed in the various parts of the country, these political movements consist of OLF, IGLF, EPRDF, OPDO, ESDL and DUP, and they all claimed that they represent their ethnic groups. Thus, the local resource conflicts were turned into politics that were more of a complex, and this has dramatically aggravated the enduring local conflicts in the untested districts.

The 1991 newly established political movements have secured the largest and promising areas under their Jurisdiction. In the meantime, these movements had abused the decentralised authority and resources. They began to mobilise the locals along the tribal lines. In some parts, local people began to claim areas they had shared or lived one next to the other in the past. The local conflicts were previously restricted to simply rural areas and have expanded to major urban settlements and revenue centers.

Growing hostility and animosity has ruined the country's decades' peaceful co-existence among various neighboring ethnic communities. Ma'eso and Babile are among the districts affected by the borderline disputes between the Oromo and Somali regional states. During the Derg government, there were major conflicts due to competition for water and land in Ma'eso and Babile districts.

Since the establishment of the federalism in 1991, conflicts subsequent from the unlawful spar over rivalry for resource and power has significantly intensified among the different ethnic-based political parties. The issue is that ethnic groups had a distinct approach to deal and manage these ongoing conflicts. Unlike in Ma'eso district, where disputes have always ended in deadly violence during the era of the Derg and after its collapse, the people of Babile have never engaged in violence to solve the issue with their neighboring ethnic community.

Among others, different ethnic pastoralist and farmers had strongly shared water and land resources. They are situated in extremely difficult environment conditions, with no borders between them. These conditions had always instigated the local conflicts among the different ethnic communities. In fact, the local pastoral and farmers communities in the country had their way of managing the resource use, and traditional ways of solving the conflicts.

But in the recent years, these traditional mechanisms was changed due to many factors. These factors consisted of environmental problems, population growth, and continuous droughts. Also, disputes and conflicts between the local ethnic communities took political measures, as result of different kind of state structures presented in the country. The communities of Afar and Somali (Issa) pastoralists lives in eastern parts of the country and have extended to the neighboring states such as Eritrea and the Republic of Djibouti, but Issa strongly inhabits in Djibouti and eastern parts of Ethiopia where Afars live some parts of Eretria and Djibouti.

Both Issa and Afars had a long history of violent conflicts and disputes over water and land resources. Modest rainfall and severe environmental conditions have forced Afar and Somalis to search for water and green land. This had brought violent competition over the resources which created dreadful conflicts between the two ethnic communities. Likewise, there were traditional conflicts, for example, animal raiding and a culture of remunerating warriors. Forcefully fighting had always been an indication of bravery, and subsequently, famous warriors were remunerating accordingly.

The 1991 Ethiopian political and state structural changes have reformed the non-ethnic based regional administrations that were governed largely by the unitary government for hundreds of years until the establishment of ethnically based regional states. The afar had the privileged to have their regional states, while the Issa was placed under the Somali regional state.

As a result, due to existed local clashes, other local conflicts that were linked to the claims of rural and urban lands have increased significantly between the two ethnic groups. These clashes involved forceful competition over administrative power. The recent year's deadly clashes between the Issa and Afar took place in towns like Gadamytu, Undufo, Anbule and Adaytu and near rural areas. Despite the Afar have long claimed that these areas historically belonged to them, now Issa dominates most of these lands.

After the collapse of the Derg regime in 1991, the succeeded government have established new towns in different localities in the border between the two ethnics. Following the establishment of the federal system, Issa and Afar began to create new towns by building huge houses in formerly disputed areas. Consequently, these territories are still experiencing violent and continuous clashes.

Previous regimes whether it was the monarchy or the communist regime used to solve the conflicts between the two ethnics by military force. They only used to interfere in certain situations, and it was when these confrontations had a tendency to jeopardise the highways to Addis-Ababa, which was the main routes to Djibouti and Asmara ports.

The approaches that these regimes used to adapt to stop these confrontations were the use of excessive military force and harsh punishments for both ethics when violent clashes occur in these areas. Other strategies that these regimes used to adapt consisted of land reform policies and divide grazing reserves.

Villagization and development in rural farmers were also encouraged. These acts were intended to create peace in the region, and also to reduce the local conflicts between the two ethnic communities, but has failed to serve these intensions.

In perspective of containing brutal clashes between the two factions FDRE and regional states of Afar and Somali, conducted different peace conference in various towns. Joint Peace Committees (JPC) from elders, regional and district administrators were established. The Joint Peace Committees has initiated and took a major role in the peace process.

In April and May 1997, the use of tribe elders together with formal administrative structure has reduced the conflicts between the Issa and Afar. Local clan elders backed by JPC and regional and federal administration officials have returned to many of the invaded livestock, and they were forced to accept blood compensation of those who were killed from both groups. This has reduced the local disputes to some extent.

Despite all of these efforts by both the regional and federal officials, there was little improvements to the longstanding disputes. There is still some devastating flare-up of violent conflicts between the two ethnics. Unlike the border disputes between Oromo and Somali regional states, there was no referendum put forward by the federal government for settling the border dispute between the Afar and Somali states.

Both Oromo (Borana) and Somalis in the southern Ethiopia predominantly depend on the livestock and crop production in their living. The areas that these groups live go beyond the border between Ethiopia and Kenya. Borana, Oromo and some Somali tribes live in southern part of Ethiopia and northern parts of Kenya. In the past before the creation of the Ethiopian state and during the Emperorship of Menelik II, the Borana's grazing land contains a massive area of today's southern parts of Ethiopia and northern parts of Kenya. However today many of these areas are occupied by non-Boranas.

The nature of the local disputes between the ethnic groups was due to the large competition over the natural resources and the land. The disputes over the land between the Borana (Oromo) and the Somalis began during the Italian occupation of Ethiopia. However, conflicts in these regions have widely escalated after the departure of the Italians in the country.

The way of life of these pastoralist communities particularly Borana (Oromo) was widely affected by the reforms of Emperor Haile Selassie and Mengistu regime. The 1948 treaty in Nagele city created the formation of the tribal reserves with divided boundaries. The lands were given back to major tribes lives in these regions where each tribe was given a tribal land over. The aim of this was to settle peacefully the longstanding conflicts in the region.

The activities of the authorities of Borana province had negative impacts upon the local disputes between the various factions. The Mengistu regime had favoured the Somalis over the Borana community, the non-Borana officials who had total control over the local government has favoured their tribes by giving them land and other assistance provided by the central government.

Despite, the establishment of tribal land has relatively reduced the violent clashes between these ethnic groups, the resource conflicts and animal raids between both Borana and the Somalis have continued even after the adoption of these policies. Also, not only violent clashes took place in these localities where the ethnic land policy was not adopted but, inter-ethnic local conflicts persisted in localities where these ethnic land policies were implemented. This was to a great extent due to regional states failure to put in place approved laws for the implementation of ethnic land policy.

The Mengistu regime approved various reforms, such as the creation of peasant associations and the Villagization in urban and rural areas. These policies adopted by the Derg regime had widely affected the living of neighboring local communities and aggravated antagonism between these communities. In pastoral areas, these government policies have restricted the free movement of many pastoralists, and also proposed permanent claims of land by one ethnic group over the others.

Under the current EPRDF regime, previous Borana province was divided into two different regional states. Guji, Borana and some other Oromo factions were in the previous Borana province, but now they all under the Borana administration of the state of Oromia, while the Somali clans of Garre, Digodi and Marehan and some others are part of the Somali regional state. Also under this government, the violent conflicts among the locals were mainly as a result of the contention over land and water resources, these disputes emerged along the boundaries between the regional states of Oromo and Somali. In southern Ethiopia, the border disputes have largely affected different localities from Guradhamole to Gorabaqaqsa, Hudat, Moyale districts.

Although the referendum that took place in the country in 2004 in these localities have to, some extent solved the issue of the border disputes between the Somali and Oromo groups, particularly in urban areas. There were independent reports that have suggested that despite the referendum, the local conflicts persisted. On October 2006, violent clashes took place once again in Hargedeb town, which is located in Gorobaqaqsa district of the Somali regional state.

The referendum turned towards Moyale district as major conflicts and disagreement occurred between the Somali and Oromo regions over the electoral registration process and other similar issues. The Afar, Oromo and the Somali ethnic groups are the biggest pastoralist groups in the country. For many decades, there were violent conflicts between these pastoralist groups. Also, there was a long history of confrontations between Digodi, Garre and Marehan which all of them are Somali clans, and Boran, Oromo clan in the south of the country.

These conflicts happened in the past due to the relentless competition over land and water resources, during the dry seasons. However, the government policies were widely affected by these local clashes. The previous centralised regime used to mediate these confrontations between the local communities by using military means.

The Mengistu regime has brought into force land reform policy. The priority for land under this policy was granted to cultivators and state-sponsored wild life areas. During the leadership of Haile Selassie, his government introduced tribal land reform policy. According to locals, the land was accordingly redistributed on clan bases. These land policies had major impacts on the lives of the locals and later shaped the existed local confrontations.

The current EPRDF regime has put in place a federal system to deter the local ethnic-based disputes in Ethiopia, and to enhance the peaceful co-existence of the various ethnic groups. However, this has created aimless consequences. Since then, the government has initiated several peace conferences. In 2004, the federal authorities in the disputed areas between the Somali and Oromo regional states conducted a referendum.

These actions by the government have reduced the hostilities between the competing ethnic group. Despite the significant efforts by the government, there was no credible solution to the problem. Mieso town is located approximately 290 Km to the east of the Ethiopian capital city. The town situates in the lowland areas close to the Hararghe Mountains. The railway from Djibouti to Addis-Ababa passes through Mieso, Asabot, Mullu towns and Bardobe towns.

In rural parts of the country, large ethnics consist of Issa (Somalis) who are mainly pastoralists, Hawiye clan of the Somali ethnic who does mixed livestock and crop production, and some other mixed Somali clans who live with the Oromo faction in the district.

Almost all Issa speak only Somali language, while other Somali clans including the Hawiye speak both Oromo and Somali language. The local Oromo clans consist of Ittu, Oboro, Nolle and Alia. Most of the Oromo clans in the region are agro-pastoralists and farmers and speak Afaan Oromo. Apart from the Somali and Oromo, there are also a small number of Amhara, Gurage and other small minority ethnic groups.

The district inhabitants make their living from the production of livestock with mixed crop production under harsh climate, where there are extremely low rainfall and continuous droughts. During the Mengistu administration, this district was part of the Asaba-Tefari province of east Hararghe region. But after the establishment of the federal system, the EPRDF regime have restructured the district with ethnic lines. Therefore, the inhabitants of the district were put under the jurisdiction of the Oromo and Somali regional state governments with no divided border between them.

Up until recently, Mieso town has served as home for both Somali and Oromo regions' local government offices. Both Somali and Oromo district administrations have opened their administrations, Health, police and justice and education offices in Ma'eso town. Following the 2004 referendum, the Somali district administration was shifted to Mullu town in the district.

The district of Babile is approximately 561 KM to the east of Addis Ababa, and 72 KM to the West of Jig-Jiga (capital of Somali regional state). The total inhabitants of the district are 93,527, the Somali inhabitants are approximately 93,499, while the Oromo are only 11 and the others minority ethnic groups are seventeen.

The major ethnic factions in the district are Hawiye, Ogaden, Maayo Madigan Garri, Akisho, Dooyo, Maaru, Wara-Dooyo and some other communities. The vast majority of the inhabitants of the district are agro-pastoralist and farmers. The majority inhabitants of northern, western and southern areas of the district are mainly farmers, whereas the eastern and southeastern parts are pastoralists.

As the EPRDF regime restructured the district into two different regional states, several ethnic groups were put under administrations they did not belong to. The district of Babile is encircled by Fik district, where the majority of the Fik population are Ogaden (Somali) of the Somali regional administration to the east and southeast; and the Harari regional administration to the west, Gursum district to the northeast and Oromia regional state to the southwest.

The Somali regional administrations control the southern parts of the district, while the north is administered by the Oromia regional state government. The town of Babile is the major town in the district, and this has resulted that both Somali and Oromo administrations opened their district offices in the town of Babile.

Historically, the town of Mieso was known for vicious local clashes between the various ethnic inhabitant groups of Somali, Afar and Oromo. During the era of Mengistu, there were frequent violent confrontations among Issa Pastoralists and local Oromo groups in the Grazing localities from Mieso to Asebot mountains. During this era, one of the biggest vicious clashes between Issa pastoralists and Oromo were in 1984, and there were plenty of water in the Oromo areas even in the dry seasons.

This conflict occurred a time where huge drought has hit the grazing land and water in the Issa inhabited areas. The Issa pastoralists have then gone to Todobashub to access water wells and the near grazing land. This has resulted in deadly tensions which have caused the deaths of 55 Oromo farmers and displaced almost 40 families, on the other side only 5 Issas lost their lives. The Derg regime has intervened militarily and forced Issa pastoralists to leave these areas within days and have relocated the displaced local Oromos.

The southern Issa pastoralists during the droughts and their relations with the Oromos in these areas have brought violent rivalry and disputes over the use of water resources and the grazing land. The Issa pastoralists had the upper hand in militarily as they were getting guns and ammunition from the government of Somalia particularly during and after the Somali-Ethiopian war, and this gave the Somali pastoralists the chance to use force against the local Oromo in accessing water and the grazing land in the district.

The Somali-Ethiopian war in 1977 and the rise of ethnical rebel groups in the area has increased the weapons in the hands of local people. Also, it has increased the casualties caused by the conflicts in the area. During the leadership of Derg, the strategy to counter these local conflicts were the use of military forces. The different forms of interventions used by the Derg consisted of military raids and severe punishment to any groups which the government believed to pose a threat to the peace and order. The main group that was targeted by the Derg government was the Issa pastoralists.

The implementation of agrarian reform policies and land redistribution during the Derg government have intensified the relationship and integration between the local pastoral and farming groups in the area. The 1978 land for tiller proclamation, priority for getting rural land was given to cultivators and state-owned companies. During this era, heretofore communal grazing land, and lands formerly owned by Somali pastoralists was redistributed to Oromo's in the district. These unfair Derg regime policies aggravated the local tensions, particularly between Hawiya and Ittu local groups.

For security purposes, the Derg regime initiated to limit the movement of the pastoralists. The pastoralists disinclination to accept this policy and Derg government plan of enforcing the policy by force have created mass killings. In

1986, the government launched a war against the Issa, after Issa murdered a senior hydrologist whom the regime sent to make a study for developing water sources in that district.

During that conflict, more than fifty Issa and few government forces were killed. Derg regime confiscated a large number of livestock from Issa. Most of these livestock were sold in the local market of the district, and some others where redistributed to local farmers. This has again heightened the hostility between the local ethnics in the area.

The government of Haile Selassie tribal land policy has divided the rural settlement in the area on clan bases. Which means the land was redistributed and thus owned on tribe bases, and this has carried on during Derg government. During the Derg government, there was no report of violent clashes between Somali and Oromo people in the area as such.

During the leadership of Emperor Haile, there were violent clashes between the different Somali tribal groups (Hawiye and Ogaden) in the district. During this time, hundreds of people have been killed, and a large number of livestock were looted from both sides. After almost a decade of continuous fighting, Haile Selassie regime used all the necessary force to stop the fighting between the two Somali clans (Hawiye and Ogaden).

Besides the conflicts, there has been a long history of cultural and linguistic integration between Somalis and Oromo in the Babile district, which resulted in strong and lasting relationships between the two factions and the decades of cultural exchanges between the both sides of Hawiye and other Oromo clans in the district. The long existence of cultural and linguistic have created a cross-cultural fertilisation and acclimatisation whereby affinity of many cultural traits, including bilingualism of the majority of the people from both ethnic people, occurred.

This idea was widely supported by the Hawiye elders in the Babile district. The elders acknowledged that Maya hails from Karanle which is a sub-clan of Hawiye and Dooyo who also both belong to Gugundhabe of Hawiye clan. However, there were some tensions and fighting among the Hawiye clan in the rural parts of Babile. During the Ethio-Somali conflict, Maru, a sub-clan of Hawiye have fled from their areas to Somalia; then the Derg regime has redistributed their farm lands to Ciye, which is also another sub-clan of Hawiye, who lived in the district during that period.

In 1998, following the civil war in Somalia, the Maru clan moved back from Somalia and sought their land from Ciye clan. This has ended in a deadly violent clash between the two Hawiye sub-clan and caused the death of several people from both sides, and some houses were burnt. This conflict has ended following the immediate intervention of the council of elders of the Hawiye clans. As in the case of Mieso town, there was also mass killings and raids by the Derg military in Babile town as well.

In 1987, the Derg regime sent its armed force to invade Burqo kabale which is 80km from Babile district. During this invasion, the government forces have killed almost 30 people and seized more than 270 livestock from the Burqo kabale inhabitants. The inhabitants justified this vicious military invasion that the government believed that these areas were a haven for armed rebel groups. Also, similar government invasions took place in different localities within the district such as Ibro-Muse and Dhandhame rural towns both located on the eastern side of Babile town.

The 1995 newly established constitution, gave the regions the power to adopt their political, social and economic policies. And also, the power to prepare their plans and own revenues and budgets. Although the international borders of Ethiopia are less known, the regional borders of Ethiopia remain ambiguous. The creation of the ethnically-based regional administrations required to make a boundary between formerly non-ethnic based provincial administrations that Derg and the monarchy ruled in the past.

The formation of the new ethnically-based regional states required to draw a border between previously non-ethnic based provincial (Awraja in the Amharic language) administrations that highly centralised governments administered in the past.

However, as the inter-regional boundary remains ambiguous, there were efforts by the government to design such borders between the federal states which brought new struggles, particularly at the district levels. The new political leaders came from these regions have stopped the local conflicts in places where new regional states share border between them.

The local clashes have increased significantly due to the local political leaders competing to gain large area for their jurisdiction. In their fight to gain more revenue at the local level, violent conflicts began in urban localities and revenue sources in the town. Mieso and Babile towns are among the 30 towns where border disputes between the Oromo and Somali regional states have widely affected the livelihood of the local people along the boundary between the two regional administrations.

After the 1991 federal structure, the town of Mieso has developed widely alongside the adoption of district decentralisation system in Ethiopia. During the transition. All levels of government institutions were very fragile. After the adoption of 1995 federal constitution, several ethnically-based political parties have been formed including OPDO (Oromo political party), OLF, DUP, IGLF, IFLO and later on, the Somali region has formed its own party 'ESDL' (Ethiopian Somali Democratic League). All of these political movement have been indirectly involved in the border dispute and consequently the local clashes in the town.

In Mieso, the Hawiye and other Somali tribes and Oromo clans lived differently. But, the request of each of the ethnically-based political parties to add the district of Mieso in their jurisdictions have ruined the peaceful co-existence between the inhabitants of the district and particularly among the Hawiye and Ittu. The dismantle of the Derg military equipment during this violent period have increased the consequences of the vicious clashes in the district. Subsequently, the two factions have separated their grazing land, then later ceaseless conflicts risen between the two ethnic groups.

At the start, violence emerged between Somali clans (Issa and Hawiye), and the Oromo insurgent movement (Oromo Liberation Front) fighters in Mieso and Mullu localities. Only in the district of Mieso, more than 12 people were reportedly killed from both sides of the groups. As a result, OLF fighters undertook acts of retaliation and killed 17 Hawiye elders, and dozens of Hawiye were displaced from Kora district and other parts of Oromia regional state. Likewise, the local Oromos residing in Afdem, Somali region have been displaced during the violent clashes between the Oromo Liberation Front and the Issa fighters. Luckily, these violent clashes have not occurred in other

Somali minority clans in the town; thus they were not displaced from their homes.

These violent clashes between the fighting ethnically-based political movements came to an end after several Somali clan-based political parties joined the ESDM (Ethiopian Somali Democratic Movement) and later ESDL political party. In 1993 when the Oromo Liberation Front (OLF) rejected the newly established transitional constitution and began insurgency against the federal Ethiopian government, local clashes in the Mieso has taken into new level especially after the transitional era and when all regional administrations began to devolve powers to district level in 2000.

The devolution of power of administrative and budget was the second aspect of the decentralisation in the country from the regional state level to district levels. The town councils were formed and devolve funding were transferred to districts. The regional administration authorities have encouraged the districts authorities to generate additional revenues from the locals so that they could get more financial transfers from their regional administrations.

During this time there were new clashes especially in the urban areas and financial resources in Mieso. Both Oromo and Somalis have officially opened offices in the district of Mieso and expanded their area of administration to the urban centers and rural Kabale in the district. The Oromo regional state has opened their offices in the district Mieso way before the Somali regional state, then in retaliation, the Somali regional state have opened a parallel office in the district.

Since that time, the local conflict between the two ethnics (Somali and Oromo) over disputed areas along the borders between the two states has aggravated to the extent that it became an inter-regional state border dispute between the two regional states.

The new political leaders that rose from both states has utilised the ethnic differences of the locals to gain their political interest, as a form of extending areas under their jurisdiction mainly the urban areas and revenue sources in the town of Mieso, local political leaders from both sides have significantly mobilized the people in the town along ethnic lines. This has once again aggravated the situation and instigated more conflicts and territorial disputes.

The major violent clashes during this period were the conflict that happened in the village of Daima. The village of Daima is a small village, situated in the middle of Asabot and Mieso districts. The majority of the inhabitants of this village are the Oromo, and there some Hawiye, Somali in the neighboring areas. The Daima village is well known for its good grazing and Water Rivers for livestock, this village has subsequently attracted the Issa pastoralists, particularly during dry seasons.

The deadly clashes in June 2000 in the Daima Village occurred after Issa pastoralist with large livestock crossed the path that was separating their area from the neighboring Oromo people. The Oromo community in the village have raided and took almost 600 livestock, and killed two Issa who was herding this livestock. This oromo raid has led to the conflict between Issa and Oromo in Mieso district. This occurred after Issa men heavily armed came into the Mieso livestock market and began shooting the Oromos, including an Oromo policeman.

Once again, two Issa men were killed as vengeance, in June 2000, after the death of the two Issa men, an armed civilian Issa men have hit back the village of Daima. During this attack, the Issa men have killed almost 40 Oromo farmers, including children and elderly. As a result of this incident, the highway and the railway that was connecting Addis-Ababa and Dire Dawa then to Djibouti was closed for days.

The deadly clashes in Daima village have increased the tensions between the locals in the Mieso district also between the two regional state authorities. The Issa traditional elders and officials of the Somali state wanted to make the tradition blood compensation payment, whereas locals and Oromo officials demanded the perpetrators to be executed. This was very difficult for Somalis to accept.

The local conflict in the district came to an end after both regional states (Somali and Oromo) have agreed to solve peacefully the border dispute between the states through a referendum in 2003, but the referendum took place in 2004. This referendum has divided the long-standing border dispute between the two regional states.

Amid this local clashes in the districts and their neighborhoods have involved various actors, particularly after the officials of the two states, agreed to end the long border dispute by referendum, in 2004. The dispute over the issue of the ownership of these major districts and the control of Bardode checkpoint had a glimmer.

Amid this time, violent conflicts took place in Bardode town and Bardode check point, and after the referendum, another deadly clashes took place in Mullu, Asabot and nearby bardode areas. Mullu, Asabot, and Bardode are the major towns in the district which is near to Mieso. All four towns are situated in very strategic locations.

These towns' serves as the prime sources of revenue generation for the local authorities, as there are major livestock markets and trading activities in these towns for the locals. Also, there is a customs checkpoint near the town of Bardode, and this customs check point serves a major source of revenue for local authorities from passing by cars and trains to and from Djibouti and Addis Ababa.

The rural localities around these towns, particularly in Asabot and Bardode, is a great place for animal grazing. Various Oromo factions, Hawiye and some other minority from the Somali ethnic reside in these towns; the Issa pastoralist often comes to these areas during the dry season in the quest for water and grazing land. Once again the border disputes between Oromo and Somali in Mieso town was heightened due to the claims and counter claims of the ownership of these strategic towns.

Following the vicious clashes in Daima village, there were major attacks in the district, especially in Mieso, Asabot, Mullu and Bardode towns. Apparently, the local authorities were indirectly involved in these conflicts, as they were distributing arms and ammunition and used different tactics to mobilize the locals along ethnic lines in the name of protecting their district borders.

In 2004, violent clashes flared up in the town of Bardode. The violent clashes began following the assassination attack conducted by 20 Oromo heavily armed men against the elder of the Hawiye clan in Bardode town. In retaliation, some Hawiye men have killed one Oromo policeman at the customs checkpoint. Also, another deadly attack was carried out by Hawiye gunmen in the Bardode town, which killed more than 12 Oromo and several shops were looted. There was also deadly confrontations between the Somalis and Oromo at the customs checkpoint, where dozens of people were killed from both groups.

In 2004, Oromo armed men attacked Haradimtu rural kabale and killed 9 Somalis, and hundred of houses belonged to Somalis have been burned down. As a result of this incident, the local Hawiye were displaced to Awash town (Afar territory), as the Hawiye had a closer relationship with the Afars.

Also after the 2004 referendum in the Mieso district, there had been several violent confrontations between the two factions. One of the confrontations occurred in 2004 after the referendum was the November 2004 Hawiye attack on the Abansaale rural kabale, where they burned 77 houses. The angry Oromo sought vengeance and killed Somali men, who they believed was a Hawiye, during his journey to Addis Ababa. But the most vicious violent clash after the referendum was the one that occurred in January 2005, when Oromo young men were deported from Djibouti had raided Somali minority groups in Jiriqale rural kabale near Asabot town.

This was very surprising attack as it was the first time that Somali minority factions in the town (other than Issa and Hawiye). These Somali minority groups have never been involved in the different clashes in the district neither during the Derg administration nor after EPRDF took power.

This confrontation has created an enormous damage to these small Somali group; their livestock was looted, and their houses were burned, and many of these small group escaped. Some of these groups went to Jigjiga, some others moved to Errer town in the Somali region, while some others went to Haradimtu, and Abesale rural kabales to join their brothers from the Hawiye and Issa clans.

The violent conflicts became frequent in the district after the referendum. Due to the death of many innocent civilians from both groups (Somali and Oromo). Many others were displaced, and their livelihoods deteriorated. These deadly local clashes were instigated the local militia and the indirect involvement of local authorities of both sides. This has increased the number of casualties in the district, and the instant response of the regime to these clashes was just a rush, as they deployed the federal military and the police to counter the continuous killings and looting.

However, the repetitiveness of the violent conflicts between the two neighboring communities forced the Addis federal administration and the two regional states to take the issue even more serious. The Ethiopian prime minister has assigned the Ministry of federal affairs to deal with the issues of disputed boundary areas in partnership with the authorities of both states and local elders have conducted a series of peace conferences.

The federal government arranged a four-day Peace conference in September 2000 in Addis Ababa. During this conference, over 1000 participants have participated the conference from the Oromo and Somali traditional and tribal leaders, chosen not only from the border dispute affected areas but also nearby towns. Also, officials from the regional states of both Oromo and Somali people were present too. The solution that was proposed in the conference included the hold of a referendum to some locations along the border, and until the occurrence of the of the referendum, both Somalis and Oromos remained in their areas and kept peaceful co-existence.

After this four-day conference in Addis Ababa, several other joint conferences took place in the two regional states. There were continuous meetings between the officials of the two administrations at federal and regional levels. There have been several conferences at the local level for local urban and rural communities of the two regions. The main purpose of these meetings was to lower on a big scale the animosity between local elites and communities.

Moreover, in 2001, leaders from the two regional administrations meet in Addis Ababa following the request of the federal government and was mediated by officials from the Ministry of federal affairs. Officials from the central government have designed a compromise resolution for the disputed areas between the Somali and Oromo regional administrations.

The conference proposal stated that authorities from both regional states must stop mobilising the locals in the name of ethnic lines and prevent claims on particular disputed areas. This was an effort to lessen the complexity if the disputed areas. For example, the Somali ethnic group have received the Kabales that was dominated by Somalis.

This proposal was based on the mutual acceptance of both regions in their respective claims. This proposed solution has lessened the number of disputed kabales in the town. However, this did not solve tensions in urban centers particular in places where local leaders were interested in Bardode customs checkpoint.

Both Somali and Oromo have created an office for neighboring regional affairs to solve cross-border issues in their respective regional states in 2001. Both regions have held several joint conferences where both communities have participated to overcome the tensions over the issues in the border. Also, in 2005 both regions have formed a Joint Peace Committee at regional and district levels, both administrations have similarly agreed to establish a joint development and security co-operation programs and law enforcement to counter the illegal practices in the disputed areas.

The referendum occurred in 2004 in all disputed Kabales with the exceptions of several Kabales in the district of Bardode, Goijano, and Abesale. The reason why the referendum did not occur in these localities is due of the major disagreements between the two administrations on how the referendum was managed, and also due to the continuous violence in the district.

Although various efforts by officials from both sides, no credible solution to the border disputes, and cross-border assaults and local clashes persisted. Mieso district is one of the most vicious areas where violent clashes proceeded up to this point.

Apart from local clashes between the Somali tribes in the rural areas, there had never been any ethnic clashes between the locals in Babile district before 1991. But the creation of ethnically-based regional states in 1991, both Oromo and Somali regional states began to claim the ownership of the district.

Both administrations conflicted over the makeup of the different communities in the district of Babile. Local groups in Babile speaks both Somali and Oromo languages, But Hawiye who is the largest group in the district and few others speaks Afan Oromo language predominantly.

Officials from the Oromia regional administration had always believed that the domination of Afan Oromo language by the large tribes such as Hawiye, Akisho, Madigan and others in Babile is clear indication that these groups are part of the Oromo ethnic. Conversely, the Somalis believed that tribes living in Babile are originally ethnic Somalis, and the fact that they speak Afan Oromo does not systemically make them be Oromo. Many Somalis have argued that the dominance of Afan Oromo is because of the close relationship with neighboring Oromo groups and this dominance came during the leadership of Haile Selassie and Derg.

The Hawiye elders in Babile illustrated that majority of local Hawiye people preferred to speak Afan Oromo than the Somali language. But this was a strategy to prevent the livestock looting and disguised attacks they have sustained from their opponent 'Ogaden people' who speak only Somali. The major political change in the district was the creation of ethnic-based political movements in 1991.

The OPDO movement came to the district in that year. Following that year, the OPDO have successfully established both district administration offices and political party in the district in 1993. The OPDO proceeded to expand its administration bit more to sub-district levels. Another two political movements have followed the same path as OPDO and opened their party office in the same district of Babile. The relationship between the leaders from both sides deteriorated and resulted in a struggle over the administrative power of the district, particularly Babile.

Several violent clashes took place following the establishment of ethnically based regional states and changes of political environment in the district. The first horrific incident of killing took place in 1993 following the death of one of the main leaders of the OPDO in Babile town. Then the following violent killings occurred in 1997 between the OPDO local militia and the ESDL in places close to Darera-Arba rural kabale. Some of the local elders illustrated that these local conflicts and the mass killings were widely instigated by political elites in the district. As a result, the conflicts have unprecedentedly weakened the security and peaceful co-existence between the district inhabitants.

In 1999, other violent clashes occurred once again in the Babile town, which left an Oromo police man severely wounded. This came after the Somali regional authorities opened their administration and police stations after the Oromo state did the same. The Oromo police have tried to intervene by preventing the Somalis from opening their offices in Babile. As a result, the police from both sides have engaged in the clash and exchanged fire, and therefore violent clashes have escalated in the Babile district.

Following the decision from the federal government to hold a referendum to solve the repeating border dispute between the two states in 2000, the political elites of both sides (Somali and Oromo) in the town of Babile, have tremendously increased their campaign to mobilize the local communities. Both Somali and Oromo leaders began to force the locals in Babile who have various things in common such as culture to choose to be part of the Somali or Oromo administrations as being Somalis or Oromos.

The local political leaders of both sides have threatened the locals and used all the means to manipulate the mind of the local people. They began to arrest illegal anyone who rejects their campaigns and also influenced the locals by giving them some allowances. Some have even indicated that that use of grain relief from donors for political mobilization of the locals have aggravated the tensions, particularly in the Babile district.

In spite of their actions and approaches to get the heart and minds of the locals, it was amazing that there was no established violent conflicts and tensions on the ground of Babile. There was not even violent clashes between the local communities in the town. The strong cultural affiliation and the traditional means of solving the conflicts and disputes have prevented these communities not to fall into the trap of violent clashes between them. In an effort to make a border between the contending local elites of both sides, the office of the regional affairs of the prime minister office assigned a delegation to Babile in 1994. The delegation was assigned to come up with a real solution on disputed areas between the two regional states.

The delegation has come to a conclusion to give Babile and other 34 disputed rural kabale to the Oromia administration, while only eight rural kabales were given to the Somali administration. But this decision was widely rejected

Somali state officials and district Somali political elites and referred this decision to unlawful and unfair.

Prior to the referendum, the Ministry in charge of the federal affairs has held a meeting to mediate the situation between the two sides. During the meeting, officials from the ministry have requested from the officials of the two states reduce their claims only to the kabales which they sure that they will gain in case a referendum takes place. But unlike, Mieso district, officials from both sides preceded their claims, despite it did not make any major changes regarding the number of the disputed kabales in the town.

Just like other disputed border areas between the two regional states, the last effort to make a sustainable solution to the longstanding local conflicts in Babile was the occurrence of the referendum in 2004. There were blended results from the 2004 referendum. Some former officials in Babile district told that only eleven out of twenty-seven kabales were won by the Somali administration, while the Oromia only gained 15 rural kabales and the town of Babile.

Both states were mainly interested in Babile town as Babile is the only town in the district and became a hub for competition between the local political elites. The Somalis have opposed the referendum outcome, while Oromos have accepted. However, the brutal clash between the contending local political elites was calmed down following the referendum, to the extent that some have perceived it as frozen conflicts. According to the local elders and political elites considered the expected peace and compromise did not emerge in the district, particularly in Babile town even after the referendum.

The possible collapse of the Ethiopian state in the foreseeable future

Since the 9/11, international efforts to encounter terrorism and pressures to implement democratic reforms have worsened the internal situation in Ethiopia. The challenges of the democratic reforms became more evident particularly following Ethiopia's so-called 2005 parliamentarian election and the brutal crackdown by the Ethiopian law enforcement and security forces.

Moreover, many of the Ethiopian diasporas in the United States and Europe have changed in the interest of Ethiopia the dynamics of global engagements, both in the elections and the disputes after the election. Many of the human rights organizations think tanks, oppositions and the diasporas have urged the international donors to end their financial assistance to the brutal regime (EPRDF).

Despite internal and external pressures, the Ethiopian regime has exerted major regional influence by unlawfully invading neighboring Somalia under the pretext of combating terrorism in December 2006, and at the same time furbished its image as an important partner in the United States' war on terrorism. The Ethiopian head of government at that time, Meles Zenawi and his coalition in government have carefully assessed its threats both in domestic and abroad.

The Ethiopian involvement in the region more particularly in Somali and Eritrea gave Ethiopia a perfect distraction from crumbling the internal politics and the breach of human rights by the national security forces. Few years after the 2005 general election in the country and the considerably more combative post-election deadlock between the opposition and the ruling coalition remained significantly important to understand the country's internal political atmosphere and the other conflicts in the region.

Coming to the third round of the elections in April 2005, both Ethiopians and the international community were highly optimistic about the election and believed that this would advance the process of democracy that the current regime has undertaken since its arrival in power. But the election results lacked transparency and was clear that the government had rigged the election, which led to major violence that took to the street, then government began its crackdown on protestors which killed dozens and arrested thousands of Ethiopians.

Since then, the internal situation in Ethiopia, as well as the region have worsened significantly, and the regional conflict has increased at a record high. The divisions between different political leaders and among different ethnic communities have reduced considerably since the fall of the Derg regime. Under the current regime, people across the country have gained significant economic and cultural achievement such as regional autonomy. The improvements in social services and infrastructure have surpassed the development by the previous governments in Ethiopia.

As the federal government devolved the power to regional administrations, officials from the local government became increasingly suppressive, especially in the countryside. Those residing in the urban are widely divided and hostile to government currently in power. While cities and towns in the country have become increasingly impressive, rural had failed to keep up with the anticipations of the politically engaged voting population.

Many of the Ethiopian diasporas have opposed all the policies of the ruling party and accused the government of mismanaging the Ethiopian economy and repressing the population. The overseas-based opposition has abusively criticized the EPRDF government through social media and public rallies in the US and European capitals.

The rural and urban communities, as well as the diasporas, have such conflicting interests that none of the Ethiopian political parties could do to please them. The current regime has done less for these three communities (urban, rural and diasporas), but its primary support after the Tigray, goes to the rural areas, especially those who have been systemically excluded or even less developed.

The ERPDF has consistently used lethal force against the opposition leaders and its partisans to silence dissident. Since the 2005 massive fraud election and the violent government crackdown against the oppositions, the opposition political parties have disintegrated and were unable to retain a coalition that could confront the EPRDF under the electoral structure. Some of the biggest ethnic communities in Ethiopia such as Oromo and Somali have little political representation and were often faced human rights abuses. The insecurity in the Horn and the Ethiopian role in promoting the instability put Ethiopia at the center of a quickly developing regional.

The Political transition of the 1990s

The political transition in Ethiopia started in 1991, following the collapse of the Derg military government. During the period of Haile Selassie and the Derg, both administrations controlled closely the internal politics in spite of the efforts by youth movements to create real economic and social reforms.

Since the arrival of EPRDF, Ethiopia has witnessed a significant change in the country's institutions and political structure, especially after the adoption of the new federal constitution. The most important among the political changes of that period was the creation of the ethnically-based regional states, the formation of the multiparty system and the Eritrean 1993 referendum towards independence.

The TPLF (Tigray People's Liberation Front) formed a coalition that's called EPRDF which serves their best interest; the EPRDF coalition consists of opportunistic political leaders from all Ethiopian ethnic background, which allowed TPLF to convert their military victory against the Derg into a political one. The so-called EPRDF government have controlled all the political process of the country since its arrival in power and began to exclude political elites representing different Ethiopian ethnicities and diasporas from the political scene. These ethnic groups proceeded to oppose the constitutional and institutional accords made during the transitional era.

Despite the creation of the multiparty system, the EPRDF continued to remain the dominant party since the fall of the previous regime. The failure of previous elections to bring about a genuine democratic change is as a result of the lack of transparency in the elections which unable voters to choose its leaders freely and fairly. The oppositions have widely rejected the 1992, 1994 and 1995 elections and accused EPRDF of rigging the elections and using the media to undermine politically the oppositions.

In the 2000 and 2001 elections, some political opposition parties have abandoned their previous stance of boycotting the elections and decided to participate with optimism, but they were extremely weak to even challenge the ruling party effectively.

In the 2000 legislative election, the oppositions have secured only twelve seats in the House of People's Representatives. Many of these parties represented different local constituencies. There were claims of intimidations in each of the elections, and many of the international observers have claimed that these elections lacked transparency. But it was also clear that the ruling coalition

(EPRDF) had the upper hand due to the weakness and ineffectiveness of the opposition parties who could not challenge the government effectively to win the elections. Also, the oppositions had failed to provide alternatives to voters. Therefore, as a result, voters remained pessimistic about the elections and uncertain about the future that lies ahead.

In the election of May 2005, the elections represented major substantial changes. The oppositions had formed a coalition that was based on various policies that would create good governance and nationalist visions. The main contending political parties consisted of EPRDF, the Coalition for Unity and Democracy (CUD), the United Ethiopian Democratic Forces (UEDF) and other small parties like the Oromo Federalist Democratic Movement (OFDM), all of these political parties have campaigned for different promises and policies to make Ethiopia better than it is currently.

The respective success of the opposition forces after a short period illustrates the improvement in the political process that was unusual to Ethiopia's history and the profound public anger towards the ruling party that was increasing for some years.

EPRDF and the oppositions have finally reached a framework agreement to allow oppositions to have access to state-controlled media, including newspapers and TV. Days before the election, large public gatherings were held peacefully which allowed people to attend without any fear.

EPRDF has obstructed the opposition's efforts in alternating the electoral law and changing the voting system from plurality to proportional representation. In effect, the National Electoral Board of Ethiopia (NEBE) organized joint political-party forums to solve the disputes, and these were effective in the pre-election period.

Despite the expulsion of prominent international observers and other high-profile personalities, the presence of the European Union, the African Union, and some other mission observers indicated some legitimacy of the election process. The media, whether it is a state-owned or private press were offering new sources information for people and voters.

For the first time in the Ethiopian history, leaders of the main political parties have participated debates to discuss the important issues that are effecting the Ethiopians, the important issues that were covered in the debates included the economic development, education, land ownership and ethnic self-determination.

Among these issues, the most important ones were provisions of the federal constitutions and Article 39, which allows 'Self-determination' for different ethnic communities in Ethiopia. There was a great need for a national dialogue on these crucial issues, which were introduced by some of the biggest political party's during the 2005 election, but still remains unsolved.

The Ethiopian Civil Society organizations played an active role during the critical moment prior the elections by raising awareness to voters and giving them accurate information about the political parties and the electoral process. Most importantly, a group of thirty-five civil society organizations, united under one coalition which is called Election Observation Coalition and was led by an Ethiopian NGO called, the Organisation for Social Justice Ethiopia (OSJE), have successfully won high court case propagated by EPRDF regime in May 2005.

Their victory in the case court has allowed them to be the local observers at polling stations and the OSJE had served as the coalition secretariat. The leader of OSJE, Netsanet Demissie, was illegally arrested without any sentence, and the reason for his arrest was in relation to his support to some of the political opposition leaders. Daniel Bekele was sentenced along with Netsanet Demissie, while neither of the men was party leaders.

Despite the coalition victory in the Ethiopian Federal High Court, NEBE which was an independent body was assigned to observe the elections, but their case was rejected at first, but later appealed and succeeded in delaying the process until two days before the election. This halt has prevented the coalition from fielding local observers outside major cities close to Addis Ababa.

The impact of this court victory was not underestimated as it gave the Ethiopian civil society groups a crucial role in observing the elections and illustrated the greater independence of the Ethiopian judiciary. However, this judicial independence has not proceeded after the elections, and the regime involvements on the ongoing trials and prosecutions on journalists, oppositions, and the civil society groups were considerably high.

The legal victory in May 2005 showed the voters that this election that it will be different from the previous ones. It was crystal clear that this court case was as important in the pre-election era as other signs of increasing democracy in the country, such as political rallies and media access for oppositions parties. It was reported that the voter turnout was increasingly high, and many foreign observers indicated that there were only minor irregularities, especially in other cities of the country. The election result gave the opposition an increase from 12 seats to 173 seats out of 547 members of parliament.

However, the ruling party kept the parliamentary majority and had used this as an opportunity to pass any legislations that serve their interest. The position parties have contested the results and the investigation on the NEBE. But the fear of the main contenders of the election immediately undermined the gains of the pre-election era and even of the election day.

Both EPRDF and the main opposition party, CDU, claimed the victory prior to the result. The regime has banned any demonstration to take place in the Ethiopian capital on the election, as the government feared violent confrontation in case the government rigged the election by far. Subsequently, mass demonstrations erupted in June and in late October, which turned into violent crackdown which led to the death of 193 civilians and six security officers and arrested almost tens of thousands.

Political, violent and uncertainty

Despite the legal, institutional and decentralization gains after the fall of Derg regime and the participation of the oppositions in the 2005 elections, Ethiopia has witnessed major disintegration in of the Ethiopian society during the post-election period. Growing public anger has led to mass demonstrations and riots. Subsequently, the regime deployed anti-riot police forces to disperse demonstrators and ease the tense. From 2005 and 2006, Ethiopia struggled politically and seen an intensive period of violence and confrontation between the government and the people.

The Ethiopian institution is highly challenged as the democratic transition since the fall of the Derg remained incomplete. The political agenda of the main opposition parties, most importantly the CDU, had confronted few articles of the 1995 federal constitution. Despite the 1991 Peace and Democracy Conference, the constitution of the transitional government, and the constitutional assembly in 1994 were all meant to draft a new political direction to govern a new democratic Ethiopia; the 1995 Federal Constitution mostly represents the EPRDF's vision for the country.

EPRDF have long ignored, and to some extent, marginalised main groups or parties that were opposing these political and institutional changes, the chance for national dialogue on the issue of the Ethiopian citizenship was lost.

The OLF (Oromo Liberation Front), an armed militia representing the Oromo ethnic, relinquished itself from the process after the adoption of the 1995 constitution, and the regime has never allowed them to return to the process. After the ban of the OLF, the Oromo's have few other alternatives to change and have influence on the Ethiopian politics.

The government forces have continued to harass or target the Oromo's over the past sixteen years. Although the Oromo voters remain by far the largest voters in the country, their concerns were repeatedly ignored and underrepresented, especially in the 2005 election.

Although the Oromo political parties; Oromo National Congress (ONC) and Oromo Federalist Democratic Movement (OFDM) fought so hard to cross the Oromo concerns, the Oromo concerns continued to be disregarded. The political crisis in the post-election in 2005 was a result of the political dispute between the ruling party (EPRDF) and the CDU coalition. It appeared that both coalitions failed to comprehend the Oromo concerns.

Furthermore, components of the urban elites and the Ethiopian diaspora who both were committed to fulfilling the unity of the Ethiopian state has failed to reach an agreement with the regime during the 2005 post-election period. The political disputes over the provisional constitution instigated the violence of the post-election in 2005 and illustrated that the absence of strong compromise represented a profound disintegration in the Ethiopian state.

Unresolved disputes reflected in the CUD platform on the privatization of land, amending the constitution and port access.

Wide social divisions have existed for long alongside policy differences. There was growing division among the rural and urban communities and also among ethnic and religious groups. The abject poverty in Ethiopia and its long religious and ethnic divisions have led to the mass division between the rural voters and the social-economic gains of different urban voters. This mass division was a reflect of the 2005 winner take all result and the occurrence of violent clashes.

The urban communities of Ethiopia especially those living in the larger cities like Addis Ababa and Dire Dawa have rarely made a visit to rural communities and were unaware of the policy preferences. Also, various ethnic communities, including those in urban areas, are to some extent segregated, in various forms like socially and the overlap of religion and ethnicity.

Urban inhabitants have failed to comprehend the reasons in which these rural communities have voted for the EPRDF (ruling party) and as a result appropriate to reject the results of the vote as the government rigged it. The lack of dialogue between the Ethiopians has led to opposition leaders and urban voters to reject the effect of the ruling party policies towards the rural communities.

Since the 2005 general election in the country, the civil society's involvement in the politics has increased considerably to the extent that it changed the landscape of participation. The role of the civil society is extremely vital especially during a period of political disputes, and uncertainty as the civil society acts as a mediator between the state and its citizens.

The Ethiopian civil society took an active role in the pre-election and the Election Day activities; their activities consisted of facilitating the election debates between contending political parties and making opportunities for civic and voter education. However, the brutal violence in the post-election and the regime crackdown on Ethiopian citizens have completely undermined the role and liberties of civil societies in participating the process of democratizing the state of Ethiopia.

The conditions for the Ethiopian civil society after the elections became very critical. After mass arrests of oppositions and angry protesters in October and November 2005, the regime began to target and orchestrates false criminal charges against civil society leaders and gave them harsh imprisonment sentences. EPRDF's refusal to differentiate the different actors most importantly the opposition leaders, the private press, human rights and associations reflected on the regime's intolerance of freedom of expression and civil liberty.

The regime's continuous repression shows that any political activity considered to be in favor of democratic openness will be seen as ant-government. It's a clear indication to civil society, unions, associations and political movements that political activity is illegal and intolerable to the government.

In 2007, the Ethiopian House of People's Representatives had passed an NGO law to allow regulations regarding the NGO participation in future election activities. The EPRDF would only allow the NGO to focus more on the social service and developments, rather than civic education and human rights activities. This would not only restrict the civil society but also could have a negative impact on the democratic development and process of Ethiopia.

The country's NGO has played a significant role in citizen and voter education, despite major repression from the local government officials. The Ethiopian regime promise to open up the democratic system to allow the media operate freely during the pre-election period has been completely reversed since 2005 post-election.

Shortly after the elections, EPRDF began to restrict the media to the present day. The only media that was not affected by this restriction was the state-owned media as well as few others that support the regime such as Addis Fortune and The Reporter.

The Ethiopians have always relied on the accurate and reliable news but often highly false rumor mill. Rather than increasing the negotiated access to state media for opposition elites and civil society, the regime has tightened its grip on the private press. Therefore, the regime has prevented transparency and encouraged the rumor network. The regime has also blocked controversial diasporas online network, which has further incited the anger of urban Ethiopians.

The government officials have deteriorated the situation even further by arresting several high-profile newspaper editions and publishers since the post-election crisis. The foreign NGO's and the International Organization of Journalists have listed Ethiopia as the world's worst predator on the press and placed Ethiopia just after Eritrea as the leading jailer of reporters.

In 2005, Ethiopia experienced two major waves of violence that took place in June and November that year. During this violence, almost 193 civilians have lost their lives, and hundreds of others were severely wounded as a result of this violence. It was reported that at least tens of thousands were thrown into prison and many among these detailed people were later released without charges after some time, and some others were charged for political reasons. Independent bodies have reported that approximately 30, 000 people were arrested without any trial.

The regime had also arrested several opposition MP's who boycotted the Parliament when the House of People's Representatives opened in September 2005. Later, the Parliament has stripped them of their parliamentary impunity. Likewise, dozens of journalists and preeminent civil society elites were illegally detained and later was charged with various of politically motivated charges. Delays marked the court proceedings. In April 2007, twenty-eight out of 111 high-level of political prisoners were released, when the court assessed the case, there was no case against them.

After the vast majority of the remaining defendants refused to enter a plea, the Ethiopian Federal High Court has found almost forty senior opposition members guilty of different charges in June 2007. Despite the prosecutor sought charged them with the death penalty, the sentence that was given were life imprisonment for CUD political leaders and up to eighteen years for journalists. However, several Ethiopian elders have intervened in these sentences and formally requested for the release of the convicted high-level prisoners went on for several months from end 2006 to mid-2007.

The detained opposition leaders presented a letter requesting pardon to the Board of Amnesty, which approved their demand. Girma Wolde-Giorgis, the

Ethiopian president at that time, pardoned thirty-eight CUD political leaders on July 2007. On the same day, Prime Minister Meles Zenawi issued a press conference where he explained the terms of the pardon.

During the press conference, the Prime Minister told that these thirty-eight detainees engaged in activities that have severely undermined the government and the constitution. The Ethiopian legislatures had passed a motion, just weeks before the president pardoned the political prisoners, declaring unoccupied parliamentary seats and called for by-elections for those parliamentary seats at the beginning of 2008.

Despite the president's pardon rehabilitates the political rights of the CUD political leaders to run for elections, it forced the CUD to run again for their parliamentary seats and on the capitals city council, which the CUD had won decisively in 2005 elections. Netsanet Demissie and Daniel Bekele were among the thousands who were not released, both the human rights lawyers and campaigners have refused to sign the pardon document claiming wrongdoing as they argued their activities were legal and acceptable by the Constitution.

Unlike opposition leaders and journalists, Netsanet Demissie and Daniel Bekele indicated their intentions to present a defense since the beginning of the court proceedings. Both Netsanet Demissie and Daniel Bekele their defense started in June 2007, was already delayed and was later followed by the international community.

The regime had formed a special parliamentary commission in charge of inquiry in the post-election crisis in December 2005. After months of work and investigation, the members of the commission have concluded that 199 people have died, as well as six security forces. However, pressures from the government on the commission produced a leaked report that blamed the security forces to use wide excessive force.

The chair and his deputy along with one other member of the commission have fled the country and requested asylum to overseas, and indicated that the government has politically intimidated and harassed them. The official report stated that at almost 193 people have lost their life as a result of the security forces crackdown, but have not concluded that government forces have used excessive force and that the activities that security forces conducted were legal and necessary.

The majority of the parliament endorsed the report in March 2007, with only the majority of the EPRDF MP's. However, the opposition MPs have called on the government to apologized and compensate immediately the victims and for those detained illegally to be released without any conditions.

Since the 2005 election, the situation in Ethiopia has become extremely critical and very fragile. Throughout the summer of 2005, CDU political leaders have debating thoroughly as to whether to participate or boycott their parliamentary seats pending the results of electoral fraud investigations by the courts and NEBE. It was clear that the CDU coalition had diverse objectives and tactics.

The division of the CDU coalition had led to the formation of the Coalition for Unity and Democracy Party (CDUP), whose members had taken their parliamentary seats when parliament was opened in September 2005. Since then, CDUP was registered as a party with the National Electoral Board of Ethiopia (NEBE). While other political parties went through an internal crisis and split, the ruling party has managed to keep unity and deal effectively with its internal dissent.

In 2006, the CDU leaders who refused to take their seats in parliament had formed a new political coalition, the Alliance for Freedom and Democracy (AFD). This coalition consisted of different ethnically-based political parties such as Oromo Liberation Front (OLF), Ogaden National Liberation Front (ONLF). This new coalition was very inactive, and the basis for these political parties to work together was very fragile. Among the several demands of the AFD, the coalition has called an inclusive national conference in the country.

The future of electoral politics in the country does not depend on the ongoing participation of the opposition parties now in parliament. In mid-2006, the ruling party has signed an agreement with the two main position parties that took place their seats in parliament, the United Ethiopian Democratic Forces (UEDF) and Oromo Federalist Democratic Movement (OFDM).

On several occasions, most of the opposition parties have disagreed with ERPDF on different issues. The Majority voting rules meant that opposition votes have occasionally resulted in policy changes, but the opposition had little powers or influence within the parliament. Powers that oppositions had in parliament consisted of the appointment of a new administration in Addis Ababa, removal of immunity for parliamentarians who chose to boycott their seats in parliaments, the report commission which investigated the violence after the elections and Ethiopia's invasion of Somalia in 2006.

There were several occasional that Opposition MPs have walked out of the parliament session in protest and refused to vote, while some other opposition MPs have chosen to vote. In the case of the inquiry commission that was investigating the post-election crisis and government crackdown on civilians, the opposition MPs have stated that the final report was far from independent and accurate.

The opposition MPs has increased its disagreements in every occasion with legislative or policy proposals of the ERPDF, and these have often been reported in the press. In November 2006, an interview conducted by The Reporter interviewed the CDUP leader and during the interview, the leader has told that the ruling party majority in the parliament has excessively blocked discussions and impeded minority MP's participation.

The adequacy of the oppositions in parliament, represent an important step in opening up the democratic system, although it's far less of what the real democracy is demanding. However, the foreign donors have increasingly become more involved by providing excellent training to new MPs and leaders of political parties, to increase the potential creation of a third parliament.

Towards mid-2007, the ruling party has various hold conferences with the capital city inhabitants to talk about and assess ways that the interim government and the ERPDF could solve the continuing problems. The success of these efforts will be measured in the next parliamentary election in 2010, but the public was widely discontent in urban cities like Addis Ababa and Dire-Dawa, especially over the additional taxes and limits on personal freedom introduced by an unelected city administration.

On the issue of the peace agreement between the CUD leaders and the EPRDF, The release of the thirty-eight high-profile members of the CDU coalition has removed a huge stumbling hindrance to the pollical progress in Ethiopia and have created a major sense that has continued for over two years. This has the potential to bring the political leaders back to the active political life, resuming the debates over the future of the Ethiopian politics and society.

However, the boycott of the CDU leaders in the national assembly in 2005 and the preconditions of the pardon that compelled them to participate in the 2008 election meant that political uncertainty was imminent. However, the majority of the Ethiopian citizens hoped that both political parties to leave aside their differences and launch a genuine national reconciliation for the general interest to secure stability in the Ethiopian polity and fairer society and not another period of uncertainty and crisis like the one in 2005.

Coming to the human rights situation in Ethiopia, the international community alongside foreign organizations that deals with the human right such as Amnesty International and Human Rights Watch have expressed their growing concerns over the catastrophic human right conditions in Ethiopia since the 2005 post-election.

The EPRDF regime has launched mass detentions and uses excessive of force on the oppositions and its advocates to tighten its grip on power. The Human Right Watch have told that the Ethiopian federal police together with the local officials, had previously used several measures to oppress the dissents and also punished severally those from the rural communities who voted for opposition parties.

The majority of Oromo's clan and political leaders have stopped supporting the regime due to the systematic oppression of their people. The OFDM opposition party has indicated several times that government forces have continuously targeted the Oromos, killing innocent civilians and illegal detentions in West Wellega and other places. Since the 2005 elections, the number of defections of government officials, journalists, including armed forces and some members of the Parliament has increased significantly.

In mid-2007, the Ogaden National Liberation Front (ONLF) has launched an offensive attack on a Chinese-run oil site in eastern Ethiopia which killed sixty-eight Ethiopians and nine Chinese. After this tragic incident, violence began to escalate within the Somali regional state in Ethiopia. The leaders of the ONLF has called for the UN to investigate reports that the Ethiopian regime is blocking UN food aid in vast areas of the Somali region, carrying out excessive use of force, including genocide and mass detentions to families of suspected ONLF supports.

The government was not only concerned about the offensive attacks made by the insurgent groups but also concerned about the increasing ethnic clashes in the country. In 2003, some major ethnic clashes occurred in Gambela that led to the deaths of hundreds of civilians, several security forces and some other highland communities living in the affected areas. There was widespread of human rights abuses being perpetrated against the Anuak in the Gambela region by the Ethiopian Defense Forces.

Many of the Anuak people in Gambella were subjected to arbitrary arrest, torture, imprisonment and more judicial killings in Ethiopia. Over 40, 000 people were displaced as a result of the conflict in Gambella region. In June 2006 growing clashes between Borane and Guji communities following the changes to administrative borders in Oromia and Somali regional states which claimed the death of 100 civilians and displaced almost 35,000 people.

The fundamental causes in these violent clashes, which are land and resource-based, have not been addressed properly by the federal government and the local authorities, the possibility of further ethnic conflicts in the foreseeable future is very high. The federal parliament passed a bill in 2003 to allow the federal government to mediate and interfere any occurrence of human rights abuses in regional states, which could sabotage the powers of the regional administrations.

The developing religious dynamics

In September 2006, a small village outside the city of Jimma in the Oromia region had witnessed major religious tensions, which dramatically increased the possibility of growing religious clashes in Ethiopia, just like the spreading conflict between the Ethiopian regime and Somalia's Union of Islamic Courts (UIC) in December 2006.

The religious violence outside Jimma received mass media coverage both in overseas and inside the country. The incident took place after the bonfire at the Ethiopian Orthodox Christian ceremony of Meskel in one community started a clash with neighboring Muslims worshipping in a local mosque.

The conflict has led to the death of eight people, and several others were injured, and dozens of churches and home were burned. This violent religion confrontation indicates that the much-proclaimed religious and peace pluralism of Ethiopia is at best tenuous, despite it has various and contradictory causes.

It's progressively clear that religious identity had been a more hostile feature of the political transition process in the country since the fall of the Derg in 1991. The success of EPRDF in previously disadvantaged regions of Ethiopia is partly attributable to much more religious tolerance. The Muslim communities in the country were recognized as part of the Ethiopian society by the previous regimes, but they always had to worship in a way that was compatible with the formal Ethiopian state (in other words state interference).

In Ethiopia's modern history, Muslim communities were subjected to different forms of discrimination, and they were systematically excluded from the Ethiopian polity, some were even forced to convert to Orthodox Christianity. The Orthodox Christianity was named as the historic official religion of Ethiopia to the extent that both abroad and inside the country continued to call Ethiopia a Christian country, although national census figures suggest that there are more Muslims than Christians in the country.

The country's constitution guarantees freedom of religion which enabled religious and ethnic communities to develop religious institutions and their symbols to a wider extent than before. This development came with violent conflicts and confrontations.

Despite the majority of Ethiopian citizens defended the historic peace between the two predominant religion communities (Islam and Christianity), they are deeply annoyed with the growing Muslims in the country. Religious tensions were yet considered as another sign of the challenging nature of the political institutions that came after the 1991 transition. The opinion difference over the religious communities reflects on wider issues of Ethiopian national identity. The Ethiopian election in 2005 appeared to cause occasional discussion of religion affairs, despite it echoed in public debates over land policy.

But the increasing religious expression by the UIC authority accompanied the increasing strength of the Islamic Courts Union in Somalia in 2006. This Jihad was not only called a Jihad against the Ethiopian invasion but even for Muslims inside Ethiopia have risen against the Christian regime oppressors. Foreign media's have critically criticized and portrayed the UIC as a radical jihadist and the Ethiopian invasion as a legitimate who were fighting against terrorism in the region, but the Ethiopian government war against the UIC has angered the Muslim communities in Ethiopia as they perceived a religious conflict.

The Ethiopian government along with the majority of the Christians in the country felt comfortable in framing the dispute as a Muslim-Christian war, despite the anti-Ethiopian among the Somalis in Somalia had less to do with the religion, but much to do with Somali nationalism.

The conflict in Jimma had received wide media coverage due to the ongoing conflict with the UIC, as the international community requested further explanation of the clear well-planned intervention by the Ethiopian Defense Force in December 2006. Besides the regional implication, the clashes indicated that there was a furious tension between the religious communities in the country. Political leaders have played a less important role, as some of the Ethiopian civil society and different communities have opposed the nature of Ethiopian citizenship in their interactions with individuals of other religious and ethnic communities.

Christian and Muslim leaders have both took a decisive and brave action to overcome the religious conflict in Jimma. Many local Ethiopians have hoped that major religious communities would enforce peace and harmony among those who follows and that local political leaders would take similar action to ease the tension.

However, it was clearly evident that religious identity continued to be a threat to the success of the democratic process. The international community's concern of ensuring that political and religious leaders use their influence for ending the democratic process had determined how far will the religious communities in the country would work peacefully to overcome further conflicts.

In 2007, the Ethiopian government put forward a resolution of several crucial issues which could affect widely the political spectrum of the country and the entire region. It has been widely argued that both Domestic and regional considerations would threaten the fragile peace that existed in the country since the 2005 elections. Resolution of these critical issues could tighten EPRDF's grip on power.

• The trial of domestic political prisoners and the of those granted a pardon – the pardon and the release of the thirty-eight CDU coalition high-profile political prisoners could push political negotiations in Ethiopia. But, unfortunately, the political situation inside Ethiopia remains uncertain. The continuous prosecution of civil society elites and the increasing political detentions and the excessive abuse of human rights in some parts of the country, more particularly in the Somali and Oromo regions, will keep on shaping the international community's view of the EPRDF commitment to tighten its grip on power.

Many experts have suggested that few scenarios are very likely to occur and none of these could consolidate the democratic process. The 2005 government forces crackdown on demonstrators and the severe jail sentences of prominent opposition leaders, civil society and journalists have destroyed the legitimacy of the regime.

The Addis Ababa's municipal government had particularly suffered, as the entire of its elected officials as well as the mayor-elect, Dr. Berhanu Nega, were among those arrested and prosecuted. The federal government had immediately appointed a temporary government to lead Addis Ababa's city government, but since then Addis Ababa has doubled its anti-EPRDF sentiment, the advocates of the CDU coalition were frustrated and express their anger by the appointment of the caretaker, not elected, city government.

In 2007, the regime began a series of talks with Addis Ababa inhabitants. But for the loyal advocates of the CDU, especially those who viewed the CDUP as betraying the party's mandate by accepting parliamentary seats, the by-election was believed to be a crucial indicator of a return to democratic politics.

• The Ethiopian national statistic – According to the Ethiopian Constitution, the federal government must conduct national census once every ten years. The first national census since the arrival of the EPRDF took place in 1995. Many believed that in 2005, the government would conduct another census before the elections, in light of the logistical problems both events represented.

The government announced in early 2005 that it would postpone the census to one year period to enable the authorities to give all resources to the election. However, the government couldn't keep its promise to hold the census one year later and extended to two years. The census finally started in May 2007, with all teachers in the country assigned to participate the census process. There were months of delays in Somali and Afar regions.

The national census data was not only vital for the bureaucratic and administrative in a decentralized country like Ethiopia, but also important tool for many domestic and international groups such as foreign NGO's working throughout the country.

Some believed that Ethiopia went through major urbanization, including some demographic shifts among religious and ethnic groups. Especially, figures for two different groups, the Oromo and Muslims, was expected to be sensitive and important. It was argued that both factions were often subjected to undercounted in previous censuses, and their numbers remained an issue of significant dispute.

The accurate census date will assist the government as well as international organizations and the civil society in long-term future. The delay in the national census due to the limited resources has had a negative impact on Ethiopia's development and economic planning.

• The Ethiopian Millennium – Ethiopia had marked the start of its new millennium in September 2007, owing to its utilization of the Julian calendar. The government has arranged several projects, including concerts and cultural heritage events. The government hoped that many diasporas and international tourist would visit Ethiopia on New Year's Eve in mid-September 2007. The Ethiopian government clearly wanted to solve the political deadlock before these important events take place, having said that, the government has encouraged positive media coverage and increased the number of foreign visitors.

• The elections in Kebelle and Woreda and the modified electoral law – after the 2005 regional and national parliamentary elections, Woreda district and Kebelle village elections were set to take place but were later postponed due to political reasons. Almost all the leaders of the political parties in the country agreed in August 2005 that the logistical and political difficulties of holding these elections at that moment in time were impossible. Also, the electoral law was under revision. The opposition leaders sought for changes that could force them a greater leverage, also the chance to appoint few members of the election board.

The additional postponing strategy suggested that EPRDF wanted to consolidate its hold on power even at the local level. Also signal voters that oppositions have gained in the regional and national elections have not been repeated. EPRDF's main concern was that the opposition's boycott in future elections if they NEBE and electoral rules would address better adequacy than the 2005 regional and national elections.

The majority ruling party in the House of Parliament agreed to delay the Kebelle and Woreda elections until the end of 2007 and the beginning of 2008, due to the 2007 national census and the pending modification to the electoral law. This was to some degree damaging the development.

After the World Bank and the European Union decisions to suspend direct budgetary assistance, the vast majority of financial transfers to the Ethiopian regime went through Woreda offices. Such financial transfers were likewise in line with the regime's overall decentralisation program. The direct budgetary assistance to the Woreda district was seen as a good economic development, as it has moved budgetary decision making to lower levels of administration.

In November 2006, the Ethiopian Prime Minister, Meles Zenawi, sacked by decree Ethiopia's federal auditor general, who told that federal distribution to regional administrations were not sufficiently accounted. The report by the federal auditor general and his immediate dismissal from his position raised serious questions over the EPRDF involvement in the different auditing government organisations, including the accounting systems in the woreda offices.

But the Kebelle was believed to be the most direct link to government agencies for the vast majority of the Ethiopians. Crucial development tools that most farmers relied on at the Kebelle level also fertiliser and other farming contributions, as well as hospitals, schools, and courts. Many believed that elections at the Kebelle level played a significant role in the democratic structure for majority Ethiopians.

The Ethiopian experience of politics, whether it was democratic or autocratic, was by the Kebelle and Woreda structures. While it gave negotiation advantages to political leaders in Addis Ababa, the regime's continuous postpone of the election at Woreda and Kebelle was a clear indication to rural communities that their concerns were less significant to the government. What's more troubling was that the opposition parties were unable to field as many candidates, due to the party fracture after the government security forces crackdown on oppositions and its supporters.

EPRDF have restricted domestic and foreign observers, considering the dynamic and critical position that was taken in the 2005 elections, which made transparent and non-violent elections very unlikely as long as EPRDF are in power.

The uncertain future

Ethiopia is currently facing an uncertain future as all sides in the domestic conflicts rejected the ideas of negotiating and compromising for the interest of the Ethiopian citizens and sovereignty. All sides continue to blame one another, but the real danger which the country is currently facing is the idea that politics is not about compromise, but rather party interest and holding tight to power.

Many domestic and foreign observers were critically concerned that post-election period would bring back the old habits of violence and political confrontations that had become central to the Ethiopian political culture and were only the beginning to unfold in recent years. Ethiopia's future democratisation relies heavily on how far the government is willing to consolidate the democratic process and giving the population the voice to express their concerns.

If both EPRDF and CUD refuse to put aside their political differences and do not come back to the political dialogue on real issues affecting the daily livelihood of the Ethiopians, including a proposed by-election, then most urban Ethiopian cities will see a return to violence and crackdown. If once again the regime in place use excessive force as it did in the 2005 post-election period, it will then show the international community that Ethiopia government has no intention of putting forward a genuine dialogue but rather punishing the political dissident and its advocates.

The elections of the woreda and kebelle had to some extent given the government legitimacy. Also, a modified electoral law with a compromise to the opposition and a more representative NEBE have sent a positive message to urban voters and the Ethiopian diasporas. The message that government officials send to the oppositions and its supporters often determine the Ethiopian political future.

Many believe that the most damaging impact of the past couple of years was measured in the long-term civic participation of the democratic process. In the 2001 and 2002 elections, many Ethiopian experts have suggested that the planting of democracy had begun and that also people have begun to understand the values and principles of democracy.

The young generations who cast their votes in the 2005 elections were to some extent optimistic about the power of the vote, unlike their parents from the Derg period. It was certainly unclear that these young generations will keep this faith especially after the violence of the post-election and the way in which the ruling party rigged the election through the excessive use of force.

The young generations began to lose the faith when the federal government toppled Addis Ababa's municipal government and appointed an unelected caretaker government and arrested the legitimate municipal officials and the mayor-elect, Dr. Berhanu Nega.

Most Ethiopians hoped that ruling and oppositions parties to halt their political differences and began to negotiate adequately for the national interest. However, it has clear that the ruling party had no interest or intention in compromising with the oppositions and used every approach that was available to them to hold tight to power.

Many Ethiopians sought for a national dialogue on the conflicting issues of the 2005 regional and national elections and requested from the government to hold these national dialogues appropriately.

The Ethiopians have predicted in 2007 and 2008 that unless the government takes broad steps to compromise with the oppositions, the oppositions will then be forced to boycott the 2010 elections, which will be a total disaster for the country's political progress.

The main concern for the ruling party was the increasing defection of high-profile civil servants e.g. diplomats, teachers, doctors and journalists towards the opposition and that fact majority of citizens were in favor of the oppositions. Therefore, the question that was in front of EPRDF was "Should we attract the voters through democratic persuasion or repression and authoritarianism?".

In 2010, it was clear that Prime Minister Meles Zenawi would not step down from office even if the party nominates another leader to replace him, and the regime's promise of ethnic federalism as a constitutional and institutional structure to address the country's divided polity would not be possible to accomplish without a transparent election.

Ethiopia's economic transformation and growth plan

Ethiopia has witnessed a very fast economic growth since the last two decades, the country is also the fastest-growing non-oil economy in the continent and was placed among the top ten fastest developing economies in the globe.

Since 2000, the country's gross domestic product (GDP) has been growing with an annual of 11.2% and much faster than the annual growth in Africa which was 6%. As a result of this significant economic development, the country's per capita income has also doubled during the same period.

In 2010, Ethiopia's economy was predicted to be the third-fastest growing economy in the world over the next couple of years. In 2010, the Ethiopian government introduced a five-year growth and transformation plan to shape the country's economy. Also in that same year, the World Bank has ranked Ethiopia higher in doing business than three countries in the BRICS countries with only China higher.

Ethiopia's impressive economic growth was attributed to several policy successes, as well as the favorable external conditions. Ethiopia has managed to reduce significantly its fiscal deficit from 4.2% in 2010 of GDP to 1.3% in 2015. Strong institutional and regulatory frameworks like improved business registration procedures have consolidated investors' confidence.

Major investments in the country's infrastructure, which reached just over $6 billion (20% of Ethiopia's GDP, have increased dramatically the domestic demand and improved the economy's productive potential. Remittances from the diasporas is another factor which contributes to the country's economy. Furthermore, growing international commodity prices have enabled the export to grow at an annual rate of 10.5% between 2004 and 2009 and led to the major economic boom.

Ethiopia has implemented the Five-Year Growth and Transformation Plan (GTP) from 2010 to 2015 to maintain a rapid economic growth, which will deliver Ethiopia's long-term vision and sustain economic growth. The major development program of the growth and transformation plan is to achieve a rapid growing economy. The GTP predicted an annual economic growth of 11 to 14.9% over these years.

In the second year of the five-year Growth and Transformation Plan (GTP), the program was completely on track. Just over two years of the GTP implementation, the country has seen a major socio-economic development that was never seen before in the history of modern Ethiopia.

Also, the two-year GTP period has created a wider enthusiasm of citizens and encouraged them to participate in the overall implementation of the plan. The successful implementation of the GTP increased significantly the country's annual GDP rate in 2015. This has clearly elevated Ethiopia's 2010 GDP rate of $86.123 billion, from the 10th largest and fastest to the 5th largest economy in Africa.

In 2011, the economic growth of Ethiopia was at 11.4%, surpassing the GTP target of 11%. Especially, the industrial and agriculture sector have gained a major growth rate higher than its targets set for the year. It was very clear that more effective implementation of macroeconomic policies has led to this strong and fast growing economy. Moreover, the fast-economic growth and the growing social development have led to the remarkable improvement of the living standard and the creation of employment.

The Ethiopian government has succeeded in creating job opportunities in major cities and reducing poverty to a minimum rate. Therefore, the unemployment rate in urban cities has reduced to 18% from the level of 19% in 2009 and the beginning of 2010. The per capita income of Ethiopia has increased to 392 USD from 377 USD in 2009. The poor rural parts of Ethiopia were systematically supported by the productive safety net programs which helped to gain better food security.

Due to the development in the economic and social sectors and the implementation of better welfare programs, the abject poverty rate was reduced 38% in 2005 to 29% in 2011 and the food poverty rate reduced from 38 to 33%. While inequality in income was also reduced in urban areas, it increased widely in the countryside, which left the overall inequality unchanged.

This economic growth rate indicates the prudent macroeconomic conditions and sectoral policies and suggests that Ethiopia will soon achieve the Millennium Development Goals targets. The rapid economic growth that has been seen in the country during the growth and transformation era from 2010 to 2015 has continued to broad-based and therefore impartially beneficial to the society.

But later, the increasing level of inflation had posed a major challenge to the GTP implementation which began from the second quarter of year one. In an attempt to limit the inflation and the growing cost of living, the federal government has taken important and decisive steps including tight cash controls on federal government expenditure and have introduced price caps on some goods. But the major policies that the government has implemented to control the level of unemployment and the inflation were maintaining sustainable economic growth, developing the agricultural productivity and increasing the growth of the manufacturing sector.

The Ethiopian federal government has placed the development of infrastructure as one of their main priorities of its economic development program. To this present moment, the Ethiopian government has been massively investing in the development of IT and telecom sector, water supply; roads; social services; and housing by collecting resources from both its own budget and its foreign partners. Therefore, as the country aims to become a middle-income country by 2025, the country began to increase its export revenue to $16 billion, from the current $3 billion, in the next of couple year. In 2015, the Prime Minister of Ethiopia Hailemariam Desalegn had made few changes in his government.

The Prime Minister appointed Yacob Yala as Trade Minister who replaced the outgoing Minister Kebede Chane and replaced Finance Minister Sufian Ahmed with Abdulaziz Mohamed. The former Trade Minister Kebede Chane was reportedly dismissed for failing to achieve export targets that were outlined in Ethiopia's initial growth and transformation plan, which enabled the country to gain $3 billion of the targeted $5 billion export revenue.

The new growth agenda will open up key areas of the national economy as Ethiopia moves from its reliance in the agricultural sector. The government has managed to reduce the agricultural sector contribution to the GDP by 4% during the period of the growth and transformation plan, to increase the manufacturing industry contribution to the GDP.

The newly established growth plan had proposed the privatisation of some public services to attract foreign investors. This privatisation plan was designed to assist sectors that have been widely dominated by unfair competition by the public sector and government-owned enterprises. For example, in the banking sector, bond purchasing programs and the lack of environment which is hindering the private banks from lending.

Since the implementation of the GTP, Ethiopia was enjoying a major economic transformation wave that raised significant funds through a $1 billion Eurobond, after they realised that they achieved a better rate than forecasted.

The government has also increased heavily its export revenue by 150% during the GTP period; it also predicted that the economy would generate $16 billion in export revenue, with the manufacturing sector that 25% of the total exports. The government has also introduced Industrial Park program which was aimed to attract foreign direct investment through its export-led manufacturing sector.

In 2010, the Ethiopian Communication Minister Redwan Hussein emphasized that the economic transformation plan will be achieved with a strong manufacturing sector during the GTP period. He also indicated that the government is taking every step of the way to improve the transformation of the internal private sector so it could become a strong development force in the country's GDP.

The government has given greater importance to the internal private sector, particularly those who would invest in the manufacturing sector. This initiative was widely improved through incentives packages and produced a better environment for doing business.

The Ethiopian central bank indicated that the government had doubled the country's export revenues from the manufacturing sector. The board of directors of the central bank told that they intend to make the export earnings from this sector to contribute to 25% percent of the USD inflows in the economy, from the current rate of 10%. The central bank has also suggested that they anticipate an increase of 40% of the total export earnings.

The World Bank has published an annual report on Ethiopia's economy, and on the report, the World Bank has indicated that Ethiopia has enjoyed a decade growth of 10.8% from 2003 to 2013, in comparison to East Africa average growth of 4.8%. This remarkable growth was driven by the increasing services such as the agricultural sector which contributed mostly to this growth while manufacturing performance was to some extent modest.

During the period of growth and transformation plan, the Government has succeeded in increasing the country's manufacturing and industrial sectors by 24%. The government also expect that by 2020, the industrial sector will produce $4 billion only from the manufacturing exports. Since the implementation of GTP, the country is working solidly to attract foreign investors to invest in Ethiopia's infrastructure.

In 2011, China and Ethiopia signed a deal of $1.32 billion to construct a 756-kilometre railway network connecting Addis Ababa to Djibouti. The Ethiopian have also signed another deal to construct a railway to the Port of Tadjourah in Djibouti.

Coming to the energy sector, Ethiopia has raised its electricity generation fivefold to 17,000 Mega-Watts and has increased its access to the Ethiopian to 90%. In 2011, the government started to build mega-dams along the Nile river that would generate 2,000 Mega-Watts. The Grand Renaissance Dam deal of $4.1 billion will produce up to 10,000 MW when completed. The director of the state-owned Ethiopian Electric Power Agency, Azeb Asnake, indicated that the cost of this project is $25 billion and that the government will fund 50% of the project, and also indicated that the other 50% would come from International development agencies as a loan.

Ethiopia has also increased its maritime cargo export capacity by 2020 and is currently working to reduce cargo storage days from 40 days to four days. Since the border dispute between Ethiopia and Eritrea, Ethiopian depends on Djibouti for its exports through the sea Port. Before the construction of the railway link line, Ethiopia used trucks to shift its commodities. Therefore, with the contrition of railway, it's expected that delays will be reduced down by 60 percent.

Made in the USA
San Bernardino, CA
20 June 2019